The Philosophy Student Writer's Manual and Reader's Guide

Fourth Edition

Anthony J. Graybosch
California State University, Chico

Gregory M. Scott
University of Central Oklahoma Emeritus

Stephen M. Garrison
University of Central Oklahoma

ROWMAN & LITTLEFIELD

Lanham • Boulder • New York • London

Executive Editor: *Nancy Roberts*
Associate Editor: *Molly White*
Senior Marketing Manager: *Deborah Hudson*
Interior Designer: *Ilze Lemesis*
Cover Designer: *Sally Rinehart*

Credits and acknowledgments for material borrowed from other sources, and reproduced with permission, appear on the appropriate page within the text.

Published by Rowman & Littlefield
A wholly owned subsidiary of The Rowman & Littlefield Publishing Group, Inc.
4501 Forbes Boulevard, Suite 200, Lanham, Maryland 20706
www.rowman.com

Unit A, Whitacre Mews, 26-34 Stannary Street, London SE11 4AB, United Kingdom

British Library Cataloguing in Publication Information Available

Library of Congress Cataloging-in-Publication Data
Names: Graybosch, Anthony, author. | Scott, Gregory M., author. | Garrison, Stephen M., author.
Title: The philosophy student writer's manual and reader's guide / Anthony J. Graybosch, California State University,
    Chico, Gregory M. Scott, University of Central Oklahoma Emeritus, Stephen M. Garrison, University of Central
    Oklahoma.
Other titles: Philosophy student writer's manual
Description: Fourth edition. | Lanham : Rowman & Littlefield, 2017. | Rev. ed. of: The philosophy student writer's
    manual. Third edition. 2014. | Includes bibliographical references and index.
Identifiers: LCCN 2017011417 (print) | LCCN 2017016684 (ebook) | ISBN 9781538100936 (electronic) | ISBN
    9781538100912 (cloth : alk. paper) | ISBN 9781538100929 (pbk. : alk. paper)
Subjects: LCSH: Philosophy—Authorship. | Philosophy—Study and teaching.
Classification: LCC B52.7 (ebook) | LCC B52.7 .G73 2017 (print) | DDC 808.06/61—dc23
LC record available at https://lccn.loc.gov/2017011417

BRIEF CONTENTS

CONTENTS

TO THE STUDENT

WELCOME TO A COMMUNITY OF SKILLED THINKERS

Philosophy occasionally breaks into history with seismic force. Via Lenin and Mao, for example. Marx and Engels spawned communism, the zeitgeist that challenged Locke's, Smith's, and Madison's free-market democratic capitalism for most of the twentieth century. While the holy grail of theology is permanence, order, and stability, philosophy's end is its means: passionate, relentless cognitive instability. It propels social science through provocative inquiry, channels history's topography by guiding its tidal movements, and provides transcendent depth to literature by linking individuals to their common humanity. When the pen is mightier than the sword, its ink is philosophy.

And so the vocation of philosophy, though not normally as lucrative as investment banking, continues making invaluable contributions to the task of engaging life's challenges and opportunities. Western philosophy is now more than 2,600 years old. At least as far back as Pythagoras and Thales, philosophy fully bloomed into systematic observation and analysis with Plato (428–348 BCE) and Aristotle (384–322 BCE).

Philosophy as the academic discipline we know today was launched with the founding of the American Philosophical Society (APS) in 1743 through the efforts of Benjamin Franklin. It has long been noted that the study of philosophy provides students with analytical skills valued in a wide array of professions, and that philosophy majors on average outperform all other disciplines in LSAT scores. Practical values aside, *reading* philosophy provides a rich trove of thoughts to stimulate your thirst for truth and your active imagination. But there is more. Having purchased this book, you have already accepted what may in the end be among your greatest existential challenges: *doing* philosophy.

Underlying philosophy, most fundamentally, is the skill of writing. Your personal intellect may challenge that of Socrates, Jesus, or the Buddha, and you may therefore depend on a Plato, a Matthew, or an anonymous disciple to carry your epiphanies into eternity. Otherwise, to *do* philosophy is to *write*. Much in the way a funnel directs liquid to its intended container, writing channels and refines your thoughts into clear, capable, professional literary "vessels" through which you communicate with a community of scholars and the world at large. And so this book invites and empowers you to join the particular community of skilled-thinking authors known as philosophers.

We wish you all the best.

Tony Graybosch
Greg Scott
Steve Garrison

TO THE TEACHER

WHAT'S NEW IN THE FOURTH EDITION?

Although much of its content is entirely new, this book's primary value to you, the teacher, has remained the same for more than two decades. This book continues to help you deal with three problems commonly faced by teachers of philosophy:

1. Students increasingly need *specific directions* to produce a good paper.
2. Philosophers, as always, want to *teach philosophy, not English*.
3. Students do not yet understand how and why to avoid plagiarism.

How many times have you assigned papers in your philosophy classes and found yourself teaching the basics of writing—not only in terms of content but form and grammar as well? This text, which may either accompany the primary text you assign in any class or stand on its own, allows you to assign any of the types of papers it explores with the knowledge that virtually everything the student needs to know, from grammar to sources of information to reference style, is in this volume.

What's new in *The Philosophy Student Writer's Manual and Reader's Guide, Fourth Edition*? Every chapter and chapter section has been updated and revised, many substantially.

Twelve new chapter sections have been added to the fourth edition:

1.1 Reading Philosophy Analytically
1.2 Reading Is Power
1.3 Read News as a Philosopher
5.1 Welcome to the APA and the APS
5.2 Mining Dissertations and Think Tanks
5.3 Welcome to the National Archives
5.4 Welcome to the Library of Congress
5.5 Welcome to the *Congressional Record*
8.4 Practice the Philosophy of the Mind
8.5 Practice the Philosophy of Religion
8.6 Practice Political Philosophy
8.7 Practice Legal Argumentation

Twenty-six new reading and writing assignments have been added to the fourth edition:

Read & Write 1.1: Analyze "The American Scholar"
Read & Write 1.2: Compare the Slants of Front Pages
Read & Write 1.3: Respond to an Editorial or Op-Ed Essay
Read & Write 1.4: Write Your Own Statement of Ethics
Read & Write 1.5: Start with TED
Read & Write 2.1: Narrowing Topics
Read & Write 2.3: Write an Outline for a Paper Inspired by a Published Article
Read & Write 2.4: Discover Your Own Identity and Style

Read & Write 3.1: Rephrase to Eliminate a Sentence Fragment
Read & Write 3.2: Proofread for the President
Read & Write 3.3: Explain the Data in This Table
Read & Write 3.4: Create an Actually Usable Bibliography
Read & Write 3.5: Properly Summarize an Article from *The Stone*
Read & Write 5.1: Write an Email to an APA Scholar
Read & Write 5.2: Collect Dissertations and Research Institute Studies
Read & Write 5.3: Examine George Mason's Argument against the US Constitution
Read & Write 5.4: Construct a Bibliography from the LOC Catalog
Read & Write 5.5: Refute a Recent Speech in Congress
Read & Write 7.1: Write a Philosophy Research Proposal
Read & Write 7.2: Locate a Dozen High-Quality Sources
Read & Write 8.2: Compare Consequential and Deontological Arguments
Read & Write 8.3: Construct an Ethics for the Singularity
Read & Write 8.4: Explore Problems and Potentials of Artificial Intelligence
Read & Write 8.5: Encounter *Minds and Gods*
Read & Write 8.6: Behold the Panopticon
Read & Write 8.7: Write an Abridged Amicus Brief for the US Supreme Court

We hope you find *The Philosophy Student Writer's Manual and Reader's Guide, Fourth Edition*, to be helpful to you and your students, and we wish you all success.

Tony Graybosch
Greg Scott
Steve Garrison

1

READ AND WRITE

PHILOSOPHY

Get Started

1.1   READING PHILOSOPHY
ANALYTICALLY

Getting Started

It doesn't matter how good a reader you are right now, how much you enjoy reading, how often you read, what sorts of texts you like and what sorts you avoid, how fast you read, or how effective your level of retention is. The fact is that the remainder of your academic career—the remainder, in fact, of your life—would be made richer if you were better at reading than you are now. This book attempts to make you a better reader, by first offering you tips for improvement, suggestions aimed at enhancing your enjoyment and understanding of any text, and then supplying you with exercises to improve your reading in the specific discipline of philosophy.

But why do we need improvement in writing? It's such a basic skill, something we all learned to do in grade school. Right?

Well, sort of. Our grade school teachers taught us the basics: how to distinguish words in the characters on a page and how to pace ourselves through a sentence or a paragraph to arrive at a coherent meaning. Without these fundamental skills, we couldn't read at all. That's what elementary school focuses on: giving us the basics.

The problem is, there is more to reading than just those first few steps. If there weren't, then we would all be able to read any text pretty much as well as anybody else. It goes without saying, however, that all of us read at different levels of comprehension and different levels of enjoyment, depending on what it is we're reading. We are all different people, each with our own preferences and unique set of experiences that resonate easily to certain stimuli and less easily to others.

Think of all the different worlds you inhabit, your favorite pastimes, hobbies, sports, school subjects. Each is its own world, with its own set of rules and traditions, modes of behavior and thought, and language. Do you remember the first time you watched a professional basketball game on television? The action on the court was no doubt dizzying, but so was the conversation by which the sportscasters and commentators explained each play as it happened. What's a "pick and roll"? A "double

double"? Or, for that matter, a "triple double"? Why do some penalties allow for a free throw or two while others don't? Basketball is a world with its own rules and its own ways of thinking and speaking. How long did it take you to become comfortable in this world—to become an *insider*?

Okay, so what about philosophy? If you are a philosophical insider, you will understand at least most of the following sentence:

> He attempted to characterize Fredrick's axiology as prestidigitation, nothing more than a compendium of egregious ad hominem, a gnostic etiological dialectic parading as a nomological lacuna in the canon.

To read well in virtually any subject, particularly in any school subject or profession, it is essential that you acknowledge to yourself, as you begin to read, that you are entering a new world, one inhabited by insiders and one that can be difficult to understand for people who aren't insiders.

Difficult, but not impossible.

It is possible for us to learn how to tailor our reading skills to texts in different disciplines, including those for which we do not have a natural affinity or a set of closely related personal experiences. It requires energy and imagination and, above all, a shift in attitude.

Whether you are reading a textbook chapter, a newspaper or magazine article, a journal essay, a book, or a blog, here are some tips to help you master the text.

Read with Patience

Different texts require different degrees of patience from the reader. Be sure, when you undertake to read a text written in a discipline with which you have little familiarity, that you are willing to read carefully to allow the material—and the world from which it comes—to sink in. Reading with patience means being willing to perform certain prereading activities that can aid in your mastery of the text. Some of these activities are discussed below.

Reading with patience requires making sure to give yourself plenty of time to read the text. If it's a homework assignment, don't start reading for the first time the night before it's due. The sense of urgency—if not panic—that attends a rushed reading assignment can drive the material right out of your head before you can master it. Reading with patience also means eliminating distractions, such as the television blaring in the next room or a device driving songs through those earbuds you're wearing. Too many people in the apartment? Go find a coffee shop with only a few customers. Hit the library and find a comfortable chair in the reading room. Would a snack help or hurt your ability to immerse yourself in the text?

Reading with patience means arranging your environment to enhance the clarity of your reading experience. The optimal environment is different for different people. What if you actually find that television noise or music is a help to your reading? If so, use it, but be honest with yourself about the effect of any external stimulus on your reading. The point is to do whatever you can do to *reduce your resistance to reading*.

Clarify Your Goals before You Begin to Read

What is it *exactly* that you hope reading this text will do for you? Are you merely looking for a few facts to shore up a point you are making in a paper? Are you cramming for a test? Are you working to establish a general understanding of a particular topic or the contours and details of a many-sided argument? Or are you merely reading to amuse yourself? Whatever the reasons that sent you to the text, remind yourself of them from time to time as you read, comparing what you are finding in the text to whatever it is you are hoping to find. Be ready to revise your goals depending on what you learn from the text. If, for example, you begin reading an article in the *Atlantic* that examines contradictions in libertarian ideology, do you become interested in examining the origins of libertarian philosophy?

Explore the Text's Format

Reconnoiter before Diving In   You need to remember that the writer, whoever it is, wants you to understand his or her writing and has used a variety of devices to help you. If the text has headings and subheadings, read through them first to see if they give you a sense of the author's direction and purpose. Note any distinctions among the headings, some of which may use larger and/or boldface type to underscore their organizational importance. Understanding the relationship among headings can help you determine the shape of the text's argument.

Are there illustrations? Graphs? Charts? Photographs or drawings? If so, a quick study of them will enhance your understanding of the text's goals and their potential usefulness to you.

Keep in Mind the Writer's Goals

Read carefully the first paragraph or first page of the text, looking for the writer's main idea and strategy for presenting it. Even if you don't find a specific thesis statement—a sentence or two explaining the purpose of the text—bear in mind that most writers will find a way to signal to you what it is they hope their text accomplishes. Often the thesis is in the title, as it is in this *New York Times* article by Noam Scheiber and Patricia Cohen: "For the Wealthiest, a Private Tax System That Saves Them Billions." Note how the first few lines of this article neatly answer the question implied in the title—namely, "How do these billionaires shape tax policy to suit them?"

> WASHINGTON—The hedge fund magnates Daniel S. Loeb, Louis Moore Bacon and Steven A. Cohen have much in common. They have managed billions of dollars in capital, earning vast fortunes. They have invested large sums in art—and millions more in political candidates.
>
> Moreover, each has exploited an esoteric tax loophole that saved them millions in taxes. The trick? Route the money to Bermuda and back.[1]

Remember, too, that there is always another goal the writer hopes to achieve with any piece of writing: *to change you*—by inviting you to step a little farther and to look from a slightly different angle into the world of the text, whatever that world might be: philosophy, cuisine, sports, fashion design, music, animal physiology, higher mathematics, film history, or something else. The text is the writer's way of

---

[1]   Noam Scheiber and Patricia Cohen, "For the Wealthiest, a Private Tax System That Saves Them Billions," *New York Times*, December 29, 2015, http://www.nytimes.com/2015/12/30/business /economy/for-the-wealthiest-private-tax-system-saves-them-billions.html.

asking you to pass through a doorway into a possibly unfamiliar environment that, the writer is convinced, offers you a worthwhile experience. As you read and understand the text, you are becoming more of an insider in that particular environment and broadening the way you look at the world.

Take Notes

Jot Down Notes Based on Your Early Explorations of Text Features   Your assessment of critical features—headings, illustrations, the introduction—have no doubt set up expectations in your mind about the direction and content of the text. Quickly writing down those expectations, in a list perhaps, and then comparing those notes to what you find as you read the text can help bring it into sharp relief in your mind.

Note-Taking Strategies   Your goal in taking down notes is to help you remember those elements in the text that your reading tells you will be useful to you. Two strategies for effective note-taking stand out:

1. Restating the material from the text in your own language
2. Phrasing notes in a way that establishes a dialogue with the text's writer

Rephrase noteworthy material in your own words   Any method of note-taking where you rewrite the text in your own words also requires you to engage the text at its most basic level—that of its language. In order to restate the text, you have to understand it. Merely copying the text's words doesn't require the level of engagement that restating does.

Likewise, underlining or highlighting text is usually not a very effective way to "own" the text. It's just too easy. You often find yourself highlighting so many passages that the marking loses its effectiveness. Also, highlighting the text doesn't force you to run the material through your own language-making processes, which means you don't participate in the making of meaning as significantly as you should.

Engage in a give-and-take with the author   In addition to recasting the wording of the text into your own language in your notes, you can enhance your understanding by adopting a note format that actually establishes a dialogue with the author.

Ask questions   Rather than simply finding equivalents for key words or phrases from the text, you might consider phrasing your note in the form of a question or a criticism aimed at the writer's argument. This sort of give-and-take allows you to clarify and control the range of expectations that occur to you as you read. It's a good way to keep your thinking about the text sharp. For example, after reading the *New York Times* article quoted above, you might write:

Why do the wealthiest citizens enjoy special tax privileges that most US citizens don't?

Why can't ordinary citizens do what the wealthy do?

Why does the general public let the wealthy get away with not paying their fair share of taxes?

It takes very little time to formulate useful questions about almost any text. Never forget the six basic questions: *Who? What? When? Where? How? Why?* Practice using these questions in the exploratory stages of your reading until asking them becomes reflexive as you read.

Once you have examined the obvious features of a text and formulated some basic questions, you're ready to read.

Observe How Sentence Structure Aids Understanding

Pay Attention to the Little Words   As we thread our way through the pages of any text, our movement is actually directed by little words, mostly prepositions and conjunctions. These little words don't add facts or narrative information but instead act as traffic signals preparing us for a shift in emphasis or direction. Note how *furthermore, however, on the contrary,* and *nevertheless* reinforce our interpretation of a preceding passage and prepare us to understand how the next passage will fit along with it. Some words or phrases *add* the meaning of the coming passage to the last one: *also, and, furthermore, not only . . . but also, too.* And some *contrast* the preceding passage with the coming one: *but, despite, nevertheless, instead of, rather than, yet.* The phrase *of course* indicates that the next fact follows obviously from the last one, as does the word *obviously.* Words such as *if, provided,* and *unless* indicate that the truth contained in the passage you've just read may be challenged by what the next passage adds to the argument.

You know these little words so well that it's easy to overlook their usefulness as markers. Don't. They are extremely important to your reading, shoring up your confidence line by line and preparing your mind for the next passage.

Pay Attention to the Rhythms of the Sentences   Often writers invite you to anticipate the way a sentence will move, perhaps by repeating a word, a phrase, or a syntactical structure, setting up a rhythmic expectation in your mind that, when satisfied, adds greatly to your grasp of the passage's meaning.

In his brief address commemorating the establishment of a military cemetery at the Gettysburg Battlefield, Abraham Lincoln used the repetition of a syntactical pattern to stop the forward motion of his speech to shift its focus from the audience's participation in the ceremony to the sacrifice that has occasioned the need for the graveyard:

> But in a larger sense we can not dedicate—we can not consecrate—we can not hallow—this ground. The brave men, living and dead, who struggled here, have consecrated it, far above our poor power to add or detract.

As You Read, Be Aware of Other Language Tools

Your writer will employ a range of devices calculated to make you feel comfortable in the world of the text. Look for those devices and allow them to do their work.

- An *analogy* is a comparison of two things that are similar in some important way. Expect to find your writer composing analogies in which some element of the world of the text—an element unfamiliar to a noninsider—is compared with some element more common to everyday life. Here's an example. On a campaign stop during the 2012 presidential election, President Obama said:

> This notion that somehow we [Democrats] caused the [budget] deficits is just wrong. It's
> like somebody goes to a restaurant, orders a big steak dinner, martini, all that that stuff,
> and then, just as you're sitting down, they leave, and accuse you of running up the tab![2]

Analogies can be helpful in clarifying policies and issues. To what extent, for example,
is President Obama's steak dinner analogy a valid characterization of the Republican
Party's role in driving up government deficits?

- *Concrete details*—details that evoke and engage the senses—can often do
  more to communicate meaning and intent than the most elaborate abstract
  description. A powerful example is the campaign ad that President Lyndon
  Johnson ran on television—just once—in his 1964 presidential race against
  Republican senator Barry Goldwater. Instead of offering a spoken appeal for
  voters to reject what Johnson's campaign was painting as Goldwater's danger-
  ously warlike attitude toward the Soviet Union, the ad simply showed a little
  girl standing in a field, pulling petals off a flower, and counting them as they
  fell. Suddenly the girl's soft voice was replaced by the harsh tone of a man
  echoing the countdown to a rocket launch, and the image of the girl's face
  was replaced by that of an exploding nuclear bomb.[3]

Test Your Recollection

It is easy to forget material right after you've learned it, so as you read you'll need to
stop occasionally and say back to yourself the material you have just acquired. Recite
it to yourself *in your own words* to make sure you have truly assimilated the content.
This recollection is an important part of the reading process, but it can be dangerous,
in that if you stop to recollect too often you can lose your sense of forward motion.
So, no matter how often you find yourself stopping to recollect material, and it may
happen frequently in a difficult text, try never to stop for long. Remember that
the very next sentence may unravel the difficulty that has induced you to make a
momentary stop. *Keep going.*

Reread

The single most effective strategy for mastering a text is to reread it. The first time
through you are finding your way, and the text's concepts, facts, and lines of argument
are forming themselves in your mind as you read, which means you have difficulty
anticipating the text's direction. To use an analogy, reading a challenging text for the
first time is like driving down a twisting country road at night, one you have never
traveled before, with only your car's headlights to guide you. But once you've experienced that road, you will be able to navigate it again more confidently, anticipating
its tricky turns. The same thing happens when you reread a text. Having been there
before, you now have a better sense of where the argument is going and can see more
clearly not only what the writer is trying to say but his or her motives for saying it.

---

2   Barack Obama, "Weekly Address: Making America Safer for Our Children," The White House, January
     1, 2016, https://www.whitehouse.gov/the-press-office/2016/01/01/weekly-address-making-america
     -safer-our-children.
3   Drew Babb, "LBJ's 1964 Attack Ad 'Daisy' Leaves a Legacy for Modern Campaigns," *Washington Post*,
     September 5, 2014, https://www.washingtonpost.com/opinions/lbjs-1964-attack-ad-daisy-leaves-a
     -legacy-for-modern-campaigns/2014/09/05/d00e66b0-33b4-11e4-9e92-0899b306bbea_story.html.

Rereading as an aid to understanding a text is most effective once you have gotten through the *entire* text. Only then will you have fully experienced the shape of the writer's argument and be able to commit your attention to clarifying passages that were difficult during your first run-through.

Pacing Is Vital

How can you possibly pay attention to all the reading tips just discussed and get any sense at all out of the text they are trying to help you understand? Practice. Learning how to improve your reading effectiveness takes time. Try one or two of the suggestions often enough to incorporate them into your reading routine, and then move on to others. The more reading you do, the better you'll get at it, and the wider and more interesting your world will become.

Read&Write 1.1   Analyze "The American Scholar"

Here is an excerpt from an address by transcendentalist Ralph Waldo Emerson (1803–1882) titled "An Oration Delivered before the Phi Beta Kappa Society, at Cambridge, August 31, 1837," and more commonly known as "The American Scholar." Write an essay in which you identify some of the techniques described earlier in this chapter that Emerson has employed to engage and influence his audience.

Mr. President, and Gentlemen,

. . . I accept the topic which not only usage, but the nature of our association, seem to prescribe to this day,—the AMERICAN SCHOLAR. Year by year, we come up hither to read one more chapter of his biography. Let us inquire what light new days and events have thrown on his character, his duties and his hopes.

It is one of those fables, which out of an unknown antiquity, convey an unlooked-for wisdom, that the gods, in the beginning, divided Man into men, that he might be more helpful to himself; just as the hand was divided into fingers, the better to answer its end.

The old fable covers a doctrine ever new and sublime; that there is One Man,—present to all particular men only partially, or through one faculty; and that you must take the whole society to find the whole man. Man is not a farmer, or a professor, or an engineer, but he is all. Man is priest, and scholar, and statesman, and producer, and soldier. In the *divided* or social state, these functions are parcelled out to individuals, each of whom aims to do his stint of the joint work, whilst each other performs his. The fable implies, that the individual, to possess himself, must sometimes return from his own labor to embrace all the other laborers. But unfortunately, this original unit, this fountain of power, has been so distributed to multitudes, has been so minutely subdivided and peddled out, that it is spilled into drops, and cannot be gathered. The state of society is one in which the members have suffered amputation from the trunk, and strut about so many walking mon-sters,—a good finger, a neck, a stomach, an elbow, but never a man.

Man is thus metamorphosed into a thing, into many things. The planter, who is Man sent out into the field to gather food, is seldom cheered by any idea of the true dig-nity of his ministry. He sees his bushel and his cart, and nothing beyond, and sinks into the farmer, instead of Man on the farm. The tradesman scarcely ever gives an ideal worth to his work, but is ridden by the routine of his craft, and the soul is subject to dollars. The priest becomes a form; the attorney, a statute-book; the mechanic, a machine; the sailor, a rope of a ship.

In this distribution of functions, the scholar is the delegated intellect. In the right state, he is, *Man Thinking*. In the degenerate state, when the victim of society, he tends to become a mere thinker, or, still worse, the parrot of other men's thinking.[4]

1.2   READING IS POWER

Philosophy: Helping You Perceive and Consciously Respond to Power

A critical service of philosophy is the identification of the mechanisms of power: political, economic, cultural, and social. One of most important mechanisms of power on the planet is what we commonly call the news. Without a free-flowing supply of news in a country, freedom, democracy, and security are unavailable, and personal vitality and fulfillment for most people are severely impaired. Even with a free flow of news, those who control that flow have enormous influence.

Power Is Deciding Who Shows Up on Radar and the Size of Their Blip   Control of the news means controlling what people know and what they don't know. It means controlling who "makes the local, national, and international radar screen" and who does not. A local news story about a child dying of cancer can produce an immediate inflow of assistance that many other families in similar situations must go without. In some areas of the world, "making the radar screen" is a matter of life and death for millions of people. At any particular time, tens of thousands of people worldwide face war, disease, famine, and natural disasters. Some get a lot of help, some get moderate assistance, and some virtually none at all. What determines who gets what?

Politics always plays a role, but publicity can be equally important. "The pen is mightier than the sword," wrote Edward Bulwer-Lytton in his play *Richelieu: or, The Conspiracy* in 1839.[5] Here are three historical examples of the power of the press.

---

4   Ralph Waldo Emerson, "The American Scholar," in *The Annotated Emerson*, ed. David Mikics (Cambridge, MA: Belknap Press of Harvard University Press, 2012), 73–74.

5   Edward Bulwer-Lytton, *Richelieu: or, The Conspiracy, a Play in Five Acts* (New York: Samuel French, [186-?]), 39, in *Making of America*, accessed February 23, 2016, http://name.umdl.umich.edu/AAX3994.0001.001.

... to save lives: One of the most notable and successful efforts to save lives by exploiting the media radar screen was conducted by Mohandas Gandhi (1869–1948). Having developed techniques of nonviolent resistance to racial oppression in South Africa in the 1890s, Gandhi went to India during World War I and began organizing peaceful demonstrations against the British occupation there. His first task was to liberate India from the British without a violent civil war. Through several prison terms, large-scale protest marches, and well-orchestrated trips to London to see top officials, Gandhi attracted press attention wherever he went. When civil war between Hindus and Muslims began to threaten India after World War II, Gandhi walked hundreds of miles through villages of both religions. In so doing Gandhi not only succeeded in averting a war of independence, saving hundreds of thousands of lives, he averted a civil war, saving hundreds of thousands more. His deep commitment to justice and nonviolence, and his superior management of publicity, helped him save more lives than anyone else in history.

... to defeat racism: Sometimes lives are saved when the words and actions of certain people are denied an appearance on the media radar screen. Atop Magnetic Mountain, overlooking the rolling, verdant hills of Eureka Springs, Arkansas, stands a 65.5-feet-tall statue of Jesus, beckoning visitors to *The Great Passion Play*, a dramatic depiction of the last week of Jesus's life. The play and statue are monuments to the energies of evangelist and philosophical organizer Gerald L. K. Smith (1898–1976). A powerful speaker who attracted sizeable crowds, Smith was a Christian nationalist and white supremacist. Virulently anti-Semitic, Smith founded the America First Party in 1946. A firm believer that the Jews killed Jesus and that they have served as a primary source of evil ever since, after World War II Smith preached against Jews while defending Nazis at every opportunity. The Holocaust, in which several million Jews were killed in Nazi death camps, was a fresh memory in the late 1940s and early 1950s. The world over, Jews knew they had to energetically combat anti-Semitism wherever they encountered it, so Smith naturally became a prime concern for the Anti-Defamation League (ADL) and the American Jewish Committee (AJC). Jewish leaders adopted a tactic of "dynamic silence." They first asked newspaper editors to consider the extent to which their coverage was helping Smith draw so much attention. Then they asked the editors to consider whether or not Smith's hatred-filled rants deserved the free publicity they were getting. They proposed that if the papers stopped covering Smith's rallies, his movement would dry up along with his publicity. The editors agreed and stopped coverage, and Smith's momentum declined. Although Smith continued work on his statue and passion play, his movement never recovered.

... to make policy, not always for the better: Finally, sometimes the radar screen is purposefully distorted in the interest of particular news media. By the late 1880s, Cuba was a prosperous Spanish colony whose sugar plantations sweetened American muffins, piña coladas, and Coca-Cola. But American-owned Hawaiian plantations became sufficiently powerful to gain from Congress import-tax advantages. Its main market for its primary product gone, Cuba's economy collapsed. Penniless and hungry, the plantation workers revolted. Spain responded by sending troops, who rounded up thousands of protestors, referred to as *concentrados*, and herded them into camps. (The word *concentrados* would be borrowed by the Nazis for use in the Holocaust.) The decade of unrest that ensued unfortunately became useful

to newspaper czar William Randolph Hearst, who wanted to create news to outsell his competition, and to Assistant Secretary of the Navy (later President) Theodore Roosevelt, who wanted to increase America's image as a world power. Through what became known as *yellow journalism*, false charges of cruelty were pumped up against Spain, and the country was also blamed for the sinking of the American battleship USS *Maine* in Havana Harbor. America declared war on Spain in 1898 and wrested control of Spanish territories in the Caribbean and the Pacific.

Read&Write 1.2   Compare the Slants of Front Pages

A *slant* is a repeated emphasis of one viewpoint as opposed to another, or of one type of content as opposed to another. This writing exercise is relatively simple. Start by visiting the home pages of the online versions of the *New York Times* (nytimes.com) and the *Wall Street Journal* (wsj.com). The online versions of major newspapers contain much more content than printed versions because web pages provide more space for links to many more articles than appear on printed front pages.

Note that on each home page, there is a link to "Today's Paper" immediately under the paper's name. Select that link on both of them. Here you will find the most recent news that is featured in their print editions. Copy into a Word file the titles of the half dozen or so boldface articles you find on each site. In a page or two, describe what you infer about the character and aims of each paper from the article titles in each newspaper. How do the priorities of the two papers differ? What are the philosophical implications of that difference? Is there an obvious philosophical slant to the articles selected? To what do you attribute the slant(s) that you find, if any?

1.3   READ NEWS AS A PHILOSOPHER

Because philosophers spend a lot of their time reading newspapers, it is vital for them to know how to read skillfully—how to understand and evaluate newspaper material accurately and quickly. Learning how to do so requires the mastery of certain reading techniques that people may not typically apply to the reading of their local paper. Here are some tips that can help you read a newspaper like a philosopher.

Understand the Task

In addition to entertainment and advertising, the content of any newspaper includes news and opinions, and because these two categories can be easily and even intentionally confused, and because accurately differentiating them is essential, let's take a quick look at them.

News is composed of two types of data: information and analysis.

- *Information* is composed of facts, specifically, accounts of events and background. The title of an account of an event could be "Conservative Christians Hold 'City on a Hill' Conference." A background statement could be "This is the third time this year that Conservative Christians have met in Washington, DC."

- *Analysis* is composed of interpretations of the information rendered in the news story. Having observed the goings-on at the "City on a Hill" conference, the reporter now interprets what he or she has witnessed there: "A primary purpose of the conference seems to have been to encourage Conservative Christians to develop a new strategy to restrict abortions."

Opinions are evaluations of the information reported in newspapers and are composed of editorials, op-ed pieces (opinion pieces written by named authors who are not on the newspaper's staff), opinion columns, blogs, and other contributions such as transcripts of interviews. An opinion concerning the "City on a Hill" conference, published in one of the newspaper's editorials, might read, "Once again conservatives seek to consolidate their weakening power by angering a variety of social constituencies." Clearly, the line between analysis and opinion is a thin one.

A Conundrum   On a daily basis, high-quality newspapers like the *New York Times* and the *Wall Street Journal* attempt to clearly identify and separate news from opinion. Their integrity and their credibility depend on their success. Their articles are clearly identifiable as news or opinion, and most of the time their news articles have a high degree of objectivity. Opinion is opinion and is persuasive to the extent it seems reasonable or appeals to a certain prejudice. Intelligent readers rarely confuse opinion with news.

But "news" suffers from a congenital defect. No matter how objective a reporter tries to be, perfection is intrinsically beyond reach. Philosopher Karl Popper (1902–1994) was fond of starting courses with a simple command to his students: "Observe." He would stand quietly and wait until a student would break the tension with the question "Observe what?" "Precisely," Popper would respond. His point was that no observation is purely objective and value-free. The moment we try to observe we necessarily choose what to observe, and that choice is always full of values.

When editors assign stories, their selections are affected not only by their experienced sense of importance but also by their perceptions of the prospective author and by their estimate of what sells well. Therefore, although "objective reporting" is the hallmark of a good newspaper, good reporters understand and exploit the tension between "news" and "opinion," allowing, at least to some extent, their quest for relevance to temper their thirst for facts.

Read the Front Page

Daily newspapers are much like highway maps, providing thousands of bits of information, which together form a coherent web that can be imagined as a compact image of life on this planet, or on part of it, on any particular day. The newspaper's front page is the symbol key to that map. Start your newspaper reading by noting both what is included on the front page and what is not. Here is your front-page analytical checklist:

Content   What gets premium front-page coverage tells you what the newspaper's priorities and biases are. Here are the front-page stories and featured articles of the *New York Times* on September 27, 2016:

- Hillary Clinton and Donald Trump Press Pointed Attacks in Debate
- How Hillary Clinton Went from Hesitant to Scorching
- U.S. Murders Surged in 2015, F.B.I. Finds

- Inside France's 'Jungle': Desperate Migrants Keep Coming to Calais
- Kerr Putney, Charlotte Chief, Had Cause in His Life to Distrust Police
- For Tenants Facing Eviction, New York May Guarantee a Lawyer
- Lester Holt, Given a Choice Assignment, Opted for Restraint
- Clinton Could Have Corrected Trump, but He Blared 'Wrong!'
- To the Moon, North Korea? Or Does a Rocket Have a Darker Aim?
- Iran's Supreme Leader Advises Ahmadinejad Not to Run for President
- Wells Fargo Workers Claim Retaliation for Playing by the Rules
- Scenes from New England's Drought: Dry Wells, Dead Fish and Ailing Farms
- Arnold Palmer, the Magnetic Face of Golf in the '60s, Dies at 87
- Witness Details Origins of Bridge Plot and Links Scheme to Christie Aides
- Building Blocks: The Resurrection of Greenwich Street
- Pride and Pain on Opening Day at a Museum of African-American History
- How Small Forests Can Help Save the Planet

By contrast, here are the articles on the cover of the *New York Post* for September 27, 2016:

- Arrest made in conjunction with blast that killed FDNY chief
- Man shot by cops in Charlotte bought gun from burglar: report
- Tiger Woods awkwardly kicked out of Ryder Cup pic (twice)
- Online polls showing Trump won the debate were rigged: report
- China swears that their terrifying glass bridge is totally safe
- 'Don't go out': Teammate's advice for distraught Jose Fernandez
- Trump mask sends child into a frenzy

What assumptions about each paper's character can you make by comparing the contents of these front pages?

Layout   Position on the front page reflects the editor's estimate of the importance of the article. A banner headline is big time news. Newspapers traditionally place the lead article in the upper right corner of the front page because, when they are displayed on old style newsstands, the papers are folded in the middle and arrayed so that the upper right part of the paper appears. The second most important story appears on the upper left. The bigger the title font, the more important the article.

Everything about the front page is done on purpose. Did you ever notice that when you enter Walgreen's to pick up a prescription, the pharmacy is in the rear of the store? Try getting to the pharmacy without being distracted, if ever so slightly, by candy, cosmetics, cuticle clippers, coffee cups, crayons, and birthday cards. The front page of a typical newspaper is organized a bit like the aisles in a Walgreen's, offering something for everyone.

The Structure of an Article   Every article in a newspaper has three jobs to do:

1. Get your attention.
2. Tell you the story's bottom line.
3. Tell a convincing story in a very short time.

To meet these goals, news articles must follow a standard format known as the *inverted pyramid*. While literary stories start with small details and build to a climax at the end, news articles do the opposite. The article title is the "bottom line." It tells you the punchline of the story right up front. Details follow in descending order, the most important ones first. Background and incidentals come last.

Reading News Reports   To accurately read a newspaper article, you have a lot of work to do. Happily, as time goes on, you become familiar with the publications, the journalists, their sources and other matters, but it takes practice. Here is a news article appraisal checklist:

- *Reputation*. What does the reading public think of the newspaper? What does the quality of the front page tell you? Earlier in this chapter you were invited to compare front pages from the *New York Times* and the *New York Post*. Which of these two newspapers would you rather cite as a source for information in your own term paper?

- *Author*. What are the credentials and reputation of the author of the news story? Does the author have the background to accurately report the news? A newspaper's website normally provides the credentials of its reporters.

- *Information Sources*. What sources of information does the author use? Are they credible? Are they recognized individuals or institutions? Is the information source appropriate for the article's topic? Is the topic timely, and is the information it provides up to date? Does the author include multiple sources to support his or her statements?

- *Writing Quality*. Is the article well written? Is it clear and cogent? Does it use a lot of jargon? Can you understand it? Does it employ many adverbs? In general, adjectives and adverbs tend to be "opinion words" rather than "news words." Why, for example, is the adverb in the following sentence questionable? "Morgan *willfully* ran over my bicycle in the driveway."

- *Quantity of Information*. Is the article sufficiently comprehensive to substantiate its thesis? Does it answer the proverbial questions, *who? what? when? where? how?* and *why?*

- *Unsupported Assumptions*. Beware statements like this: "Statistics prove that children in traditional two parent households are happier than children in other households." What statistics? Does the article identify them?

- *Balance*. If you are reading a *news* article about a controversial subject, the article should include information from more than one side of an argument. Also, a well-written *opinion* article will normally identify the contents of opposing views, even if only to discredit them.

Reading Opinion Articles: A Tale of Two Journalists

Conservative author and commentator David Brooks and Liberal economist Paul Krugman have both been Op-Ed columnists for the *New York Times* for more than a decade. In July 2015, each wrote a *Times* column that discussed in part recent proposals to raise the minimum wage.

In his article "The Minimum Wage Muddle," David Brooks, in typical conservative fashion, reveals once again his distrust of government intervention in the economy in general and proposals to raise the minimum wage in particular. Brooks states, "Some economists have reported that there is no longer any evidence that raising wages will cost jobs."[6] Brooks may well have had in mind a *New York Times* article by Paul Krugman, titled "Liberals and Wages," that states, "There's just no evidence that raising the minimum wage costs jobs, at least when the starting point is as low as it is in modern America."[7] Both Brooks and Krugman cite multiple studies as evidence for their arguments opposing (Brooks) and supporting (Krugman) the minimum wage.

If you open the *New York Times* website and read both articles (select the "Columnists" link in the "Opinion Pages" section), you will find that each columnist focuses on different if overlapping features of the effects of raising the minimum wage. Each article provides the reader with an interesting, well-supported education in certain aspects of the issue, one that will inspire many studies before the philosophical debate subsides.

But here we can learn an important lesson. What is the central point, the *thesis* of each article? From Brooks we have a bold and unsupported further assertion: "Raising the minimum wage will produce winners among job holders from all backgrounds, but it will disproportionately punish those with the lowest skills, who are least likely to be able to justify higher employment costs."

We have already quoted Krugman's thesis that there is no evidence to suggest raising the minimum wage will cost jobs, "at least when the starting point is as low as it is in modern America." Krugman also continues his argument with an unsupported conclusion, asserting that the market for labor isn't like the market for, say, wheat, because workers are people. And because they're people, there are important benefits, even to the employer, from paying them more: better morale, lower turnover, increased productivity. These benefits, says Krugman, largely offset the direct effect of higher labor costs, so that raising the minimum wage needn't cost jobs after all.

It is evident at this point that, if you want to adequately examine the arguments of each columnist, you need to read their articles and examine the evidence they provide. But the important lesson here is the relative authority of the authors on the subjects they are discussing. Consider the two columnists' credentials.

According to his biography on the *New York Times* website, David Brooks also appears on *PBS NewsHour*, NPR's *All Things Considered*, and NBC's *Meet the Press*. He has authored three books: *Bobos in Paradise: The New Upper Class and How They Got There* (New York: Simon & Schuster, 2000), *On Paradise Drive: How We Live Now (And Always Have) in the Future Tense* (New York: Simon & Schuster, 2004), and *The Social Animal: The Hidden Sources of Love, Character, and Achievement* (New York: Random House, 2011), a "No. 1 *New York Times* best seller." He also teaches at Yale University.

Paul Krugman is professor of economics and international affairs at Princeton University. He has taught at Yale, Stanford, and MIT, and has authored or edited

---

6   David Brooks, "The Minimum-Wage Muddle," *New York Times*, July 24, 2015, http://www.nytimes.com/2015/07/24/opinion/david-brooks-the-minimum-wage-muddle.html.

7   Paul Krugman, "Liberals and Wages," *New York Times*, July 17, 2015, http://www.nytimes.com/2015/07/17/opinion/paul-krugman-liberals-and-wages.html.

twenty-seven books and two hundred academic and professional papers. A founder of "new trade theory," a substantial revision of international trade theory, he has received the American Economic Association's John Bates Clark Medal (1991) and the Nobel Prize in Economics (2008).

Which author is better qualified to draw general conclusions about effects of the minimum wage from his research? Paul Krugman, the economist, is far better qualified to draw conclusions, and due to the enormous amount of research he has done in economics, he is far more credible *on this topic*. If you read numerous columns by David Brooks, you may well conclude that they are well written, entertaining, and full of well-documented support for his theses. But if you read closely, you will find he often oversteps the bounds of his professional credibility. This does not mean that Krugman is obviously correct on this particular issue. But it strongly suggests that if you want to test Krugman's assertions, you need to find an equivalent authority: a solid conservative economist.

Philosophers are predisposed to be suspicious of journalism, rolling their eyes at factual errors and inaccuracies. A healthy skepticism is part of their job. But they will admit that, while they have the luxury of digging deep over a substantial period of time, a journalist must often get a story and get it straight within a matter of hours. And when all is said and done, the academicians will not hesitate to affirm that nothing is as essential to the vitality of democracy as a vigorous, capable, and dedicated news media.

Read & Write 1.3   Respond to an Editorial or Op-Ed Essay

Perhaps at this point you are ready to launch into the real world of public discussion of national issues. One way to do so is to respond to an editorial. It is probably best to start with the newspaper in your hometown. Most, if not all, newspapers provide detailed information on how to submit such a letter. To write a letter to the editor of the *Washington Post*, for example, go to the *Washington Post* website, click on Help and Contact Info found under the link for Contact Us, then follow the link titled "How to Contact the Newsroom."[8]

Be sure to ask your instructor before submitting your letter. Newspapers can be very selective about the letters they accept for publication, and you may be up against a lot of competition. You instructor will be able to provide some suggestions that will increase your chances of success. Follow the paper's directions exactly.

Good luck!

1.4   DEFINE YOUR PERSONAL ETHICS

Life is ethical because choices with ethical implications are unavoidable. Any particular choice or ethical decision may be bad or good, harmful or beneficial, but each has consequences. You may lend your friend money for lunch. You may drive through an automated tollbooth without paying the fare. You may volunteer at a hospital or steal to

---

8   *Washington Post*, http://help.washingtonpost.com/link/portal/15067/15080/ArticleFolder/80 /How-to-Contact-the-Newsroom.

support a drug habit. Whatever you do, you probably justify it to yourself in one way or another. The justifications that you use for your actions all add up to a code of ethics.

When you write your code of ethics, you have an opportunity to understand more clearly the ethical principles by which you live. You have a chance to examine them, review them, and perhaps even revise them. Before you begin to write your own ethics statement, read some that other people have written. A few examples are provided here, but your library contains hundreds of them, and they can be found under many headings, including philosophy, religion, theology, and politics. The following examples are not comprehensive, systematic statements of ethics. Instead, they are excerpts from longer statements that address a wide variety of ethical considerations. As you read, write down notes about things you agree with, things you disagree with, and other thoughts that occur to you. You will find these notes very helpful when you begin to write your own code.

Here are some examples of famous ethics statements.

Kindergarten Wisdom

All I really wanted to know about how to live and what to do and how to be I learned in kindergarten. Wisdom was not at the top of the graduate-school mountain, but there in the sand pile at Sunday School. These are some of things I learned:

1. Share everything.
2. Play fair.
3. Don't hit people.
4. Put things back where you found them.
5. Clean up your own mess.
6. Don't take things that aren't yours.
7. Say you're sorry when you hurt somebody.
8. Wash your hands before you eat.
9. Live a balanced life—learn some and think some and draw and paint and sing and dance and play and work every day some.
10. Take a nap every afternoon.
11. Be aware of wonder. Remember the little seed in the Styrofoam cup: the roots go down and the plant goes up and nobody really knows how or why, but we are all like that.
12. Goldfish and hamsters and white mice and even the little seed in the Styrofoam cup—they all die. So do we.
13. And then remember the Dick-and-Jane books and the first word you learned—the biggest word of all—LOOK.[9]

Ten Commandments

1 And God spoke all these words:
2 "I am the LORD your God, who brought you out of Egypt, out of the land of slavery.

---

[9]   Robert Fulghum, *All I Really Need to Know I Learned in Kindergarten* (New York: Ivy Books, 1988), 4–6.

3 "You shall have no other gods before me.

4 "You shall not make for yourself an image in the form of anything in heaven above or on the earth beneath or in the waters below.

5 You shall not bow down to them or worship them; for I, the LORD your God, am a jealous God, punishing the children for the sin of the parents to the third and fourth generation of those who hate me,

6 but showing love to a thousand generations of those who love me and keep my commandments.

7 "You shall not misuse the name of the LORD your God, for the LORD will not hold anyone guiltless who misuses his name.

8 "Remember the Sabbath day by keeping it holy.

9 Six days you shall labor and do all your work,

10 but the seventh day is a sabbath to the LORD your God. On it you shall not do any work, neither you, nor your son or daughter, nor your male or female servant, nor your animals, nor any foreigner residing in your towns.

11 For in six days the LORD made the heavens and the earth, the sea, and all that is in them, but he rested on the seventh day. Therefore the LORD blessed the Sabbath day and made it holy.

12 "Honor your father and your mother, so that you may live long in the land the LORD your God is giving you.

13 "You shall not murder.

14 "You shall not commit adultery.

15 "You shall not steal.

16 "You shall not give false testimony against your neighbor.

17 "You shall not covet your neighbor's house. You shall not covet your neighbor's wife, or his male or female servant, his ox or donkey, or anything that belongs to your neighbor."[10]

Man Is Born in Tao

Fishes are born in water
Man is born in Tao.
If fishes, born in water
Seek the deep shadow
Of pond and pool,
All their needs
Are satisfied.
If man, born in Tao,
Sinks into the deep shadow
Of non-action
To forget aggression and concern,
He lacks nothing
His life is secure.[11]

---

[10]   Exodus 20:1–17 (NIV).

[11]   *The Way of Chuang-Tzu*, trans. Thomas Merton (New York: New Directions Press, 1969), 65.

Read&Write 1.4 Write Your Own Statement of Ethics

How do you write a code of ethics? A good way to start is to examine some ethical dilemmas, and in so doing discover some of your own ethical values. Although you will find many sources of ethical dilemmas online and in the library, one easily accessible source is the *New York Times*. (As of September 2016 students can subscribe to digital access to the *Times* for one dollar per week as long as they are students.) On the *Times* website (nytimes .com) type "The Ethicist" in the search engine. There you will find a list of recently added ethical dilemmas. On September 28, 2016, for example, this list included the following topics, each with a link to a discussion published earlier in the newspaper:

- What Should I Do with My Dead Husband's Journals?
- Should I Tell My Friend I Had a Fling with Her Ex?
- Should a Teacher at a Sketchy College Help Recruit Students?
- When a Friend Cheats Often on Her Husband, Should You Keep Quiet?
- Can I Put Down My Aging Pooch?
- Can I Stay Friends with an Abusive Husband?
- Can I Tell a Dying Friend's Secret to His Children?
- Should I Have Talked to My Father about His Cross-Dressing?
- You're Going to Sell Your Home. Should You Mention the Snakes?
- Can You Keep a Woman from Courting Your Elderly Dad?
- Should I Help My Sister End Her Life?
- Is It Selfish for a Gay Couple to Have Kids via Surrogacy?
- Must I Tell My Long-Distance Boyfriend I Met Someone Else?
- Is It O.K. to Get a Dog from a Breeder, Not a Shelter?
- Do We Have to Send Our Kid to a Bad Public School?
- Should a Friend Be Told the Real Reason He Didn't Get the Job?
- Can a Young Woman Vote at Her Swing-State College?
- Should a Nephew Be Told Who His Real Father Is?

First, scan through twenty or thirty titles on the list you find online and select five for close attention. Before reading the Ethicist's response to each dilemma, write a paragraph that states your immediate "gut reaction" to the dilemma. Then read the Ethicist's response and rewrite your paragraph to modify it if any new factor occurs to you. Next, create a list of general principles implied by the ethical values you have expressed in your essays. Now revise your list, adding in new principles that have occurred to you in the writing process. Finally, write an essay in which you describe the general and specific ethical principles you have identified, and in the process, be sure to answer the following two questions:

1. From what or whom do you derive the basis of your ethical principles?
2. What are your most important ethical values and principles?

1.5   CLARIFY A TOPIC IN THE HISTORY OF PHILOSOPHY

Although all good history of philosophy papers will define and defend a thesis, most take one of three approaches. The first is to study one aspect of a writer's philosophy, such as the implications of Kant's categorical imperative or Rawls's veil of ignorance or Plato's conception of the soul. The second approach is to compare two or more philosophers on a selected topic, such as comparing Joachim of Fiore's eras of history to Hegel's dialectic, or comparing Marx's concept of human nature to Nietzsche's. The third is to study a philosophical concept, like aesthetics, happiness, free will, existence, identity, ideology, logic, knowledge, matter, meaning, reason, truth, liberty, or justice, as it appears in several authors.

Often, history-of-philosophy papers are meant to be compare-and-contrast papers. The description of the history of philosophy given above suggests some major themes—such as the nature of God, free will versus determinism, and whether induction can be justified—that have been addressed by historically important philosophers. These are topics around which you could organize a history of philosophy paper. And so your history of philosophy paper will often be a position paper designed to show, perhaps, that Hobbes was more convincing than Locke in explaining how mathematical knowledge could be based on experience.

Even if you are explicitly instructed not to develop an evaluative conclusion about the relative worth of Hobbes's and Descartes's explanations of self-identity through time, it will help you write a compare-and-contrast paper as if you were going to produce an evaluative conclusion. Remember: your history of philosophy paper must make a point and defend it. In other words, your paper must have a clearly defined thesis, and then it must provide the arguments and supporting materials necessary to defend your thesis.

Thousands of interpretations of the works of the great philosophers have been published. You do not need to generate a new interpretation in order to write a good paper. You merely need to evaluate the interpretations that are available and present your reasons for claiming that some are better than others.

Read&Write 1.5   Start with TED

For this writing exercise, we propose that you choose the first of the three approaches above. And since one of the objectives of this manual is to introduce you to new sources of information, we propose you identify a topic for your paper by first consulting TED (ted.com). There you will find a vast array of short, interesting, and informative talks, many by well-known speakers. Once on the site, select Topics and from the topic list select Philosophy. Then, listen to some of the talks you find until you encounter a topic that interests you. Once you have identified the topic, ask your instructor for suggestions about philosophers who may have something interesting to say on that topic. From there, follow the instructions in chapter 2 of this manual that will help you further define the issue you have chosen. In your essay, explain what your chosen philosopher has to say about the issue, and then provide your own reflections on the value of his or her contribution to the subject.

2

WRITE EFFECTIVELY

Writing is a way of ordering your experience. Think about it. No matter what you are writing—it may be a paper for your philosophy class, a short story, a limerick, a grocery list—you are putting pieces of your world together in new ways and making yourself freshly conscious of those pieces. This is one of the reasons why writing is so hard. From the infinite welter of data that your mind continually processes and locks in your memory, you are selecting only certain items significant to the task at hand, relating them to other items, and phrasing them with a new coherence. You are mapping a part of your universe that has hitherto been unknown territory. You are gaining a little more control over the processes by which you interact with the world around you.

This is why the act of writing, no matter what its result, is never insignificant. It is always *communication*—if not with another human being, then with yourself. It is a way of making a fresh connection with your world.

Writing, therefore, is also one of the best ways to learn. This statement may sound odd at first. If you are an unpracticed writer, you may share a common notion that the only purpose of writing is to express what you already know or think. According to this view, any learning that you as a writer might have experienced has already occurred by the time your pen meets the paper; your task is thus to inform and even surprise the reader. But, if you are a practiced writer, you know that at any moment as you write, you are capable of surprising yourself. And it is that surprise that you look for: the shock of seeing what happens in your own mind when you drop an old, established opinion into a batch of new facts or bump into a cherished belief from a different angle. Writing synthesizes new understanding for the writer. E. M. Forster's famous question, "How can I tell what I think till I see what I say?" is one that all of us could ask.[1] We make meaning as we write, jolting ourselves by little, surprising discoveries into a larger and more interesting universe.

A Simultaneous Tangle of Activities

One reason that writing is difficult is that it is not actually a single activity at all but a process consisting of several activities (that will be discussed later in this chapter).

---

[1]   E. M. Forster, *Aspects of the Novel* (New York: Harvest, 1956), 101.

The activities can overlap, with two or more sometimes operating simultaneously as you labor to organize and phrase your thoughts. The writing process, an often frustrating search for both meaning and the best way to articulate that meaning, tends to be sloppy for everyone.

Frustrating though that search may sometimes be, it need not be futile. Remember this: The writing process uses skills that we all have. In other words, the ability to write is not some magical competence bestowed on the rare, fortunate individual. We are all capable of phrasing thoughts clearly and in a well-organized fashion. But learning how to do so takes practice.

The one sure way to improve your writing is to write.

One of the toughest but most important jobs in writing is to maintain enthusiasm for your writing project. Such commitment may sometimes be hard to achieve, given the difficulties that are inherent in the writing process and that worsen when the project is unappealing at first glance. How, for example, can you be enthusiastic about having to write a paper examining negative eschatology when you have never once thought about the topic and can see no use in doing so now?

Sometimes unpracticed student writers fail to assume responsibility for keeping themselves interested in their writing. No matter how hard it may seem at first to drum up interest in your topic, you have to do it—that is, if you want to write a paper you can be proud of, one that contributes useful material and a fresh point of view to the topic. One thing is guaranteed: If you are bored with your writing, your reader will be, too. So what can you do to keep your interest and energy level high?

Challenge yourself. Think of the paper not as an assignment but as a piece of writing that has a point to make. To get this point across persuasively is the real reason you are writing, not because a teacher has assigned you a project. If someone were to ask you why you are writing your paper and your immediate, unthinking response is, "Because I've been given a writing assignment" or "Because I want a good grade" or some other nonanswer along these lines, your paper may be in trouble.

If, on the other hand, your first impulse is to explain the challenge of your main point—"I'm writing to show how campaign finance reform will benefit every taxpayer in America"—then you are thinking usefully about your topic.

Maintain Self-Confidence

Having confidence in your ability to write well about your topic is essential for good writing. This does not mean that you will always know what the result of a particular writing activity will be. In fact, you have to cultivate your ability to tolerate a high degree of uncertainty while weighing evidence, testing hypotheses, and experimenting with organizational strategies and wording. Be ready for temporary confusion and for seeming dead ends, and remember that every writer faces these obstacles. Out of your struggle to combine fact with fact and to buttress conjecture with evidence, order will arise.

Do not be intimidated by the amount and quality of work that others have already done in your field of inquiry. The array of opinion and evidence that confronts you in the literature can be confusing. But remember that no important topic is ever exhausted. There are always gaps, questions that have not been satisfactorily explored in either the published research or the prevailing popular opinion. It is in these gaps that you establish your own authority, your own sense of control.

Remember that the various stages of the writing process reinforce each other. Establishing a solid motivation strengthens your sense of confidence about the project, which in turn influences how successfully you organize and write. If you start out well, use good work habits, and allow ample time for the various activities to coalesce, you should produce a paper that will reflect your best work, one that your audience will find both readable and useful.

2.1   GET INTO THE FLOW OF WRITING

The Nature of the Process

As you engage in the writing process, you are doing many things at once. While planning, you are, no doubt, defining the audience for your paper at the same time that you are thinking about its purpose. As you draft the paper, you may organize your next sentence while revising the one you have just written. Different parts of the writing process overlap, and much of the difficulty of writing occurs because so many things happen at once. Through practice—in other words, through *writing*—it is possible to learn to control those parts of the process that can in fact be controlled and to encourage those mysterious, less controllable activities.

No two people go about writing in exactly the same way. It is important to recognize the routines, modes of thought as well as individual exercises, that help you negotiate the process successfully. It is also important to give yourself as much time as possible to complete the process. Procrastination is one of the writer's greatest enemies. It saps confidence, undermines energy, and destroys concentration. Writing regularly and following a well-planned schedule as closely as possible often make the difference between a successful paper and an embarrassment.

Although the various parts of the writing process are interwoven, there is naturally a general order in the work of writing. You have to start somewhere! What follows is a description of the various stages of the writing process—planning, drafting, revising, editing, and proofreading—along with suggestions on how to approach each most successfully.

Plan   Planning includes all activities that lead to the writing of the first draft of a paper. The particular activities in this stage differ from person to person. Some writers, for instance, prefer to compile a formal outline before writing the draft. Others perform brief writing exercises to jump-start their imaginations. Some draw diagrams; some doodle. Later, we will look at a few starting strategies, and you can determine which may help you.

Now, however, let us discuss certain early choices that all writers must make during the planning stage. These choices concern *topic, purpose,* and *audience,* elements that make up the writing context, or the terms under which we all write. Every time you write, even if you are only writing a diary entry or a note to the mail carrier, these elements are present. You may not give conscious consideration to all of them in each piece of writing that you do, but it is extremely important to think carefully about them when writing a philosophy paper. Some or all of these defining elements may be dictated by your assignment, yet you will always have a degree of control over them.

Select a Topic No matter how restrictive an assignment may seem, there is no reason to feel trapped by it. Within any assigned subject, you can find a range of topics to explore. What you are looking for is a topic that engages your own interest. Let your curiosity be your guide. If, for example, you have been assigned the subject of the development of rational thought in children, then guide yourself to find some issues concerning the topic that interests you. (For example, how does the neurology of the brain affect reasoning? To what extent do toddlers exhibit a grasp of logic?) Any good topic comes with a set of questions; you may well find that your interest increases if you simply begin asking questions. One strong recommendation: Ask your questions *on paper*. Like most mental activities, the process of exploring your way through a topic is transformed when you write down your thoughts as they come, instead of letting them fly through your mind unrecorded. Remember the words of Louis Agassiz: "A pen is often the best of eyes."[2]

Although it is vital to be interested in your topic, you do not have to know much about it at the outset of your investigation. In fact, having too heartfelt a commitment to a topic can be an impediment to writing about it; emotions can get in the way of objectivity. It is often better to choose a topic that has piqued your interest yet remained something of a mystery to you—a topic discussed in one of your classes, perhaps, or mentioned on television or in a conversation with friends.

Narrow the Topic The task of narrowing your topic offers you a tremendous opportunity to establish a measure of control over the writing project. It is up to you to hone your topic to just the right shape and size to suit both your own interests and the requirements of the assignment. Do a good job of it, and you will go a long way toward guaranteeing yourself sufficient motivation and confidence for the tasks ahead. However, if you do not do it well, somewhere along the way you may find yourself directionless and out of energy.

Generally, the first topics that come to your mind will be too large for you to handle in your research paper. For example, the topic of ideal versus nonideal theories of justice has recently generated a lot of attention on the Internet. Yet despite all the attention, there is still plenty of room for you to investigate the topic on a level that has real meaning for you and that does not merely recapitulate the published research. What about an analysis of how the differences between ideal and nonideal theories interact with the concept of political liberalism?

The problem with most topics is not that they are too narrow or have been too completely explored, but rather that they are so rich that it is often difficult to choose the most useful way to address them. Take some time to narrow your topic. Think through the possibilities that occur to you and, as always, jot down your thoughts.

Students in an undergraduate course on philosophical theory were told to write an essay of 2,500 words on one of the following issues. Next to each general topic is an example of how students narrowed it into a manageable paper topic.

Find a Thesis As you plan your writing, be on the lookout for an idea that can serve as your thesis. A *thesis* is not a fact, which can be immediately verified by data, but an assertion worth discussing, an argument with more than one possible conclusion. Your thesis sentence will reveal to your reader not only the argument you

---

[2]   Catherine Owens Pearce, *A Scientist of Two Worlds: Louis Agassiz* (Philadelphia: Lippincott, 1958), 106.

have chosen but also your orientation toward it and the conclusion that your paper will attempt to prove.

General Topic	Narrowed Topic
Pope Francis	Pope Francis's view of the role of philosophy in religion
Freedom	A comparison of Jean-Jacques Rousseau's concept of freedom with that of John Locke
Metaphors	How to test the logic of metaphors
Bart Simpson	Bart Simpson's philosophy

In looking for a thesis, you are doing many jobs at once:

- You are limiting the amount and kind of material that you must cover, thus making them manageable.
- You are increasing your own interest in the narrowing field of study.
- You are working to establish your paper's purpose, the reason you are writing about your topic. (If the only reason you can see for writing is to earn a good grade, then you probably won't!)
- You are establishing your notion of who your audience is and what sort of approach to the subject might best catch its interest.

In short, you are gaining control over your writing context. For this reason, it is a good idea to come up with a thesis early on, a *working thesis,* which will very probably change as your thinking deepens but will allow you to establish a measure of order in the planning stage.

The thesis sentence   The introduction of your paper will contain a sentence that expresses the task that you intend to accomplish. This *thesis sentence* communicates your main idea, the one you are going to prove, defend, or illustrate. It sets up an expectation in the reader's mind that it is your job to satisfy. But, in the planning stage, a thesis sentence is more than just the statement that informs your reader of your goal: It is a valuable tool to help you narrow your focus and confirm in your own mind your paper's purpose.

Developing a thesis   Students in a class on policy analysis were assigned a twenty-page paper on a problem currently being faced by the municipal authorities in their own city. The choice of the problem was left to the students. One, Nora Garrison, decided to investigate the problem posed by the presence of a large number of abandoned buildings in a downtown neighborhood through which she drove on her way to the university. Her first working thesis was as follows:

> Abandoned houses result in negative social effects to the city.

The problem with this thesis, as Nora found out, was that it was not an idea that could be argued, but rather a fact that could be easily corroborated by the sources she began to consult. As she read reports from such groups as the Urban Land

Institute and the City Planning Commission and talked with representatives from the Community Planning Department, she began to get interested in the dilemma her city faced in responding to the problem of abandoned buildings. Nora's second working thesis was as follows:

> Removal of abandoned buildings is a major problem facing the city.

While her second thesis narrowed the topic somewhat and gave Nora an opportunity to use material from her research, there was still no real comment attached to it. It still stated a bare fact, easily proved. At this point, Nora became interested in the even narrower topic of how building removal should best be handled. She found that the major issue was funding and that different civic groups favored different methods of accomplishing this. As Nora explored the arguments for and against the various funding plans, she began to feel that one of them might be best for the city. As a result, Nora developed her third working thesis:

> Assessing a demolition fee on each property offers a viable solution to the city's building-removal problem.

Note how this thesis narrows the focus of Nora's paper even further than the other two had, while also presenting an arguable hypothesis. It tells Nora what she has to do in her paper, just as it tells her readers what to expect.

At some time during your preliminary thinking on a topic, you should consult a library to see how much published work on your issue exists. This search has at least two benefits:

1. It acquaints you with a body of writing that will become very important in the research phase of your paper.
2. It gives you a sense of how your topic is generally addressed by the community of scholars you are joining. Is the topic as important as you think it is? Has there been so much research on the subject as to make your inquiry, in its present formulation, irrelevant?

As you go about determining your topic, remember that one goal of your philosophy writing in college is always to enhance your own understanding of the philosophical process, to build an accurate model of the way philosophy works. Let this goal help you direct your research into those areas that you know are important to your knowledge of the discipline.

Define a Purpose   There are many ways to classify the purposes of writing, but in general most writing is undertaken either to inform or to persuade an audience. The goal of informative, or expository, writing is simply to impart information about a particular subject, whereas the aim of persuasive writing is to convince your reader of your point of view on an issue. The distinction between expository and persuasive writing is not hard and fast, and most writing in philosophy has elements of both types. Most effective writing, however, is clearly focused on either exposition or persuasion. Position papers (arguments for adopting particular policies), for example, are designed to persuade, whereas policy analysis papers (chapter 8) are meant to inform. When you begin writing, consciously select a primary approach of exposition or persuasion, and then set out to achieve that goal.

To Explain or Persuade?   Can you tell from the titles of these two papers, both on the same topic, which is an expository paper and which is a persuasive paper?

1. The Concept of the Future in Nietzsche's Philosophy
2. How Nietzsche's Concept of the Future Influences His Philosophical Anthropology

Taking up the subject of political campaign ethics, let us assume that you must write a paper explaining how ethics influenced the 2016 Republican presidential campaign. If you are writing an expository paper, your task could be to describe as coherently and impartially as possible the methods by which the Republicans made ethical choices. If, however, you are attempting to convince your readers that the 2016 Republican campaign ethics were purely Machiavellian, you are writing to persuade, and your strategy will be radically different. Persuasive writing seeks to influence the opinions of its audience toward its subject.

Stating the thesis clearly   By the time you write your final draft, you must have a very sound notion of the point you wish to argue. If, as you write that final draft, someone were to ask you to state your thesis, you should be able to give a satisfactory answer with a minimum of delay and no prompting. If, on the other hand, you have to hedge your answer because you cannot easily express your thesis, you may not yet be ready to write a final draft. You may have to write a draft or two or engage in various prewriting activities to form a secure understanding of your task.

EXERCISE Knowing What You Want to Say

Two writers have been asked to state the thesis of their papers. Which one better understands the writing task?

Writer 1: "My paper is about ethics reform for the American Psychological Association."

Writer 2: "My paper argues that ethics reform for the American Psychological Association should reflect society's changing views about gender equality, same-sex marriage, and gender discrimination by religious groups providing commercial services."

Watch Out for Bias!   There is no such thing as pure objectivity. You are not a machine. No matter how hard you may try to produce an objective paper, the fact is that every choice you make as you write is influenced to some extent by your personal beliefs and opinions. In other words, what you tell your readers is truth is influenced, sometimes without your knowledge, by a multitude of factors: your environment, upbringing, and education; your attitude toward your audience; your philosophical affiliation; your race and gender; your career goals; and your ambitions for the paper you are writing. The influence of such factors can be very subtle, and it is something you must work to identify in your own writing as well as in the writing of others in order not to mislead or to be misled. Remember that *self-discovery* is one of the reasons for writing. The writing you will do in philosophy classes—as well as the writing you will do for the rest of your life—will give you a chance to discover and confront honestly your own views on your subjects. Responsible writers keep an eye on their own biases and are honest about them with their readers.

Define Your Audience   In any class that requires you to write, you may sometimes find it difficult to remember that the point of your writing is not simply to jump through the technical hoops imposed by the assignment. Rather, the point is *communication*—the transmission of your knowledge and your conclusions to readers in a way that suits you. Your task is to pass on to your readers the spark of your own enthusiasm for your topic. Readers who were indifferent to your topic before reading your paper should look at it in a new way after finishing it. This is the great challenge of writing: to enter into a reader's mind and leave behind both new knowledge and new questions.

It is tempting to think that most writing problems would be solved if the writer could view the writing as if another person had produced it. The discrepancy between the understanding of the writer and that of the audience is the single greatest impediment to accurate communication. To overcome this barrier, you must consider your audience's needs. By the time you begin drafting, most, if not all, of your ideas will have begun to attain coherent shape in your mind, so that virtually any words with which you try to express those ideas will reflect your thought accurately—to you. Your readers, however, do not already hold the conclusions that you have so painstakingly achieved. If you omit from your writing the material that is necessary to complete your readers' understanding of your argument, they may well be unable to supply that information themselves.

The potential for misunderstanding is present for any audience, whether it is made up of general readers, experts in the field, or your professor, who is reading in part to see how well you have mastered the constraints that govern the relationship between writer and reader. Make your presentation as complete as possible, bearing in mind your audience's knowledge of your topic.

Read&Write 2.1   Narrowing Topics

Without doing research, see how you can narrow the following general topics:

Example

General topic	Ontology
Narrowed topics	The role of physics in ontology
	The varieties of being
	The extent to which epistemology must precede ontology

General Topics

postmodernism	ethics	truth
Jacques Lacan	logic	semantics
evolutionary psychology	Scripture	argument
freedom of speech	belief	peace

2.2   THINK CREATIVELY

We have discussed various methods of selecting and narrowing the topic of a paper. As your focus on a specific topic sharpens, you will naturally begin to think about the kinds of information that will go into the paper. In the case of papers that do not require formal research, this material will come largely from your own recollections. Indeed, one of the reasons instructors assign such papers is to convince you of the incredible richness of your memory, the vastness and variety of the "database" that you have accumulated and that, moment by moment, you continue to build.

So vast is your hoard of information that it can sometimes be difficult to find within it the material that would best suit your paper. In other words, finding out what you already know about a topic is not always easy. *Invention,* a term borrowed from classical rhetoric, refers to the task of discovering, or recovering from memory, such information. As we write, we go through some sort of invention procedure that helps us explore our topic. Some writers seem to have little problem coming up with material; others need more help. Over the centuries, writers have devised different exercises that can help locate useful material housed in memory. We will look at a few of these briefly.

Freewriting

Freewriting is an activity that forces you to get something down on paper. There is no waiting around for inspiration. Instead, you set a time limit—perhaps three to five minutes—and write for that length of time without stopping, not even to lift the pen from the paper or your hands from the keyboard. Focus on the topic, and do not let the difficulty of finding relevant material stop you from writing. If necessary, you may begin by writing, over and over, some seemingly useless phrase, such as *I cannot think of anything to write,* or perhaps the name of your topic. Eventually, something else will occur to you. (It is surprising how long a three-minute period of freewriting can seem to last!) At the end of the freewriting, look over what you have produced for anything you might be able to use. Much of the writing will be unusable, but there might be an insight or two that you did not know you had.

In addition to its ability to help you recover usable material from your memory for your paper, freewriting has certain other benefits. First, it takes little time, which means that you may repeat the exercise as often as you like. Second, it breaks down some of the resistance that stands between you and the act of writing. There is no initial struggle to find something to say; you just write.

For his Introduction to Philosophy class, Philo Beddoe had to write a paper on the role of logic in career choices. Philo, who felt his understanding of career choices was slight, began the job of finding a topic that interested him with two minutes of freewriting. Thinking about career choices, Philo wrote steadily for this period without lifting his pen from the paper. Here is the result of his freewriting:

Okay okay career choices. Career, what does that include? Like doctor, lawyer, Indian chief? An engineer—whatever that is? Plumbers? Electricians? What careers should I focus on? I got pneumonia last year, went to the doctor, had to take antibiotics, miss soccer practice, bummer. Maybe trace what happens to a single doctor's career. Interview? Find out the doctors who are most satisfied with their career choice? Logic, logic, logic. Is satisfaction the key to logic in making career choices? Money? Prestige? Point point point. To construct a set of criteria to determine if a medical career is logical for any particular individual? Are we just talking personality here? Family pressures—resist them? Attracting a partner? Joining the country club? Wednesdays off? Is logic confined to self-interest? Is it logical to join Doctors Without Borders? Lots of emails to send. Who? Where to start?

Brainstorming

Brainstorming is simply the process of making a list of ideas about a topic. It can be done quickly and at first without any need to order items in a coherent pattern. The point is to write down everything that occurs to you as quickly and briefly as possible, using individual words or short phrases. Once you have a good-sized list of items, you can then group them according to relationships that you see among them. Brainstorming thus allows you to uncover both ideas stored in your memory and useful associations among those ideas.

A professor in a class on contemporary philosophy asked his students to write a seven-hundred-word paper in the form of a letter to be translated and published in a Warsaw newspaper, describing to Polish readers, from an American point of view, the importance of the contribution of a contemporary major Polish philosopher. One student, Melissa Jessup, had been inspired by the writings of Alfred Tarski (1901–1983). She started thinking about the assignment by brainstorming. First, she simply wrote down the topics of Tarski's writings that occurred to her:

topology
model theory
metamathematics
set theory
Warsaw school of mathematics and philosophy
measure theory
algebraic logic
truth theory
geometry

Thinking through her list, Melissa decided to divide it into two separate lists: one devoted to mathematics, the other to broader aspects of philosophy. As you can see, some of the entries do not fit exclusively into one or the other of the categories.

Mathematics	Other Concepts
Warsaw school of mathematics and philosophy	model theory
metamathematics	topology
algebraic logic	measure theory
geometry	set theory
	truth theory

At this point, Melissa decided that her topic would be about the ways in which mathematics were essential to Tarski's monumental contribution to truth theory. Which items on her lists would be relevant to her paper?

Asking Questions

It is always possible to ask most or all of the following questions about any topic: *Who? What? When? Where? Why? How?* They force you to approach the topic as a journalist does, setting it within different perspectives that can then be compared.

A professor asked her class on the philosophy of human development to write a paper describing the effects of sugar on attention span in preadolescents. One student developed the following questions as he began to think about a thesis:

How does sugar affect the human body?
In what ways does sugar affect preadolescents, in particular?
How does sugar interact with other consumables?
Why does physical activity affect the effects of sugar consumption?
Does gender affect the effects of sugar consumption?
Does sugar consumption in childhood affect one's health later in life?
What is the role of sugar in childhood obesity?

Can you think of other questions that would make for useful inquiry?

Maintaining Flexibility

As you engage in invention strategies, you are also performing other writing tasks. You are still narrowing your topic, for example, as well as making decisions that will affect your choice of tone or audience. You are moving forward on all fronts, with each decision you make affecting the others. This means that you must be flexible enough to allow for slight adjustments in your understanding of the paper's development and of your goal. Never be so determined to prove a particular theory that you fail to notice when your own understanding of it changes. Stay objective.

Read&Write 2.2   Freewriting to Engage Your Creativity

Philosophers are, at heart, prospectors and investigators. The problems and potentials of human existence intrigue them intensely. The foremost agents for understanding human beings are, as Einstein was fond of saying, inspiration and perspiration, and inventor Thomas Alva Edison (1847–1931) famously noted his view that genius was 1 percent the former and 99 percent the latter.

Though this may be the case, let's look at the 1 percent for a moment. This exercise is an opportunity to engage your creativity through freewriting and to have some fun in the process.

Cartoons in newspapers can be fabulous outlets for philosophy. Scan the cartoons in several issues of your favorite newspaper and select a cartoon that touches a topic of interest to philosophy. Then freewrite, as in the exercise above, about whatever intrigues you about the cartoon. Follow up your freewriting by taking the additional steps shown in this chapter for writing a paper, and you will produce a viable philosophy paper topic. As you assemble all the steps that you take in this exercise, you will be creating a paper you can submit to your professor.

2.3 ORGANIZE YOUR WRITING

A paper that contains all the necessary facts but presents them in an ineffective order will confuse rather than inform or persuade. Although there are various methods of grouping ideas, none is potentially more effective than outlining. Unfortunately, no organizing process is more often misunderstood.

The Importance of Outlining

Outline for Yourself Outlining can do two jobs. First, it can force you, the writer, to gain a better understanding of your ideas by arranging them according to their interrelationships. There is one primary rule of outlining: Ideas of equal weight are placed on the same level within the outline. This rule requires you to determine the relative importance of your ideas. You have to decide which ideas are of the same type or order, and into which subtopic each idea best fits.

If, in the planning stage, you carefully arrange your ideas in a coherent outline, your grasp of your topic will be greatly enhanced. You will have linked your ideas logically together and given a basic structure to the body of the paper. This sort of subordinating and coordinating activity is difficult, however, and as a result, inexperienced writers sometimes begin to write their first draft without an effective outline, hoping for the best. This hope is usually unfulfilled, especially in complex papers involving research.

EXERCISE Organizing Thoughts

Rodrigo, a student in a second-year class in government management, researched the impact of a worker-retraining program in his state and came up with the following facts and theories. Number them in logical order:

____ A growing number of workers in the state do not possess the basic skills and education demanded by employers.

____ The number of dislocated workers in the state increased from 21,000 in 2001 to 32,000 in 2011.

___ A public policy to retrain uneducated workers would allow them to move into new and expanding sectors of the state economy.

___ Investment in high technology would allow the state's employers to remain competitive in the production of goods and services in both domestic and foreign markets

___ The state's economy is becoming more global and more competitive.

Outline for Your Reader   The second job an outline can perform is to serve as a reader's blueprint to the paper, summarizing its points and their interrelationships. By consulting your outline, a busy policy maker can quickly get a sense of your paper's goal and the argument you have used to promote it. The clarity and coherence of the outline help determine how much attention your audience will give to your ideas.

As philosophy students, you will be given a great deal of help with the arrangement of your material into an outline to accompany your paper. A look at the formats presented in chapter 3 of this manual will show you how strictly these formal outlines are structured. But, although you must pay close attention to these requirements, do not forget how powerful a tool an outline can be in the early planning stages of your paper.

The Formal Outline Pattern   Following this pattern accurately during the planning stage of your paper helps to guarantee that your ideas are placed logically.

Thesis sentence (precedes the formal outline).

   I. First main idea
     A. First subordinate idea
       1. Reason, example, or illustration
         a. Supporting detail
         b. Supporting detail
         c. Supporting detail
       2. Reason, example, or illustration
         a. Supporting detail
         b. Supporting detail
         c. Supporting detail
     B. Second subordinate idea
   II. Second main idea

Notice that each level of the paper must have more than one entry; for every A there must be at least a B (and, if required, a C, a D, and so on), and for every 1 there must be a 2. This arrangement forces you to *compare ideas,* looking carefully at each one to determine its place among the others. The insistence on assigning relative values to your ideas is what makes an outline an effective organizing tool.

Read&Write 2.3   Write an Outline for a Paper Inspired by a Published Article

This is a relatively simple exercise, but it does require some thought. Start by perusing today's newspaper (local or national). When you come to an article that gets under your skin, stop. Suppose the article is one like this, from the *New York Times*:

> HEMPSTEAD, N.Y.—A man accused of firing the bullet that fatally struck a 12-year-old girl as she sat in her Long Island home in October was retaliating after his younger brother's hoverboard was stolen, the police said on Monday.
>
> The man, Jakwan Keller, 20, wearing a bulletproof vest, declined to comment as detectives led him out of Nassau County Police Headquarters. He later pleaded not guilty to murder, weapons possession and other charges in connection with the death of the girl, Dejah Joyner.[3]

Think. What is it about the article that irritates you? Is it the waste of a person's life? Is it the availability of guns? Is it a lack of law enforcement?

Now, following the outline format described in this chapter section, write an outline of a paper you might write because you read this article. Your outline will not *summarize* the article, although a short summary might be included in your paper. Your paper outline might look something like this:

How to Reduce Accidental Gun Deaths

I. The history of accidental deaths is a long one.
  A. Most deaths on nineteenth-century wagon trains were accidental shootings.
    1. Loaded guns were always at hand.
    2. Bumpy trails led to frequent discharges.
  B. Loaded guns at home are a danger to children.
    1. Children play with guns.
    2. Adults are not required to store guns securely.
    3. Adults want loaded guns easily available.
II. The number of accidental gun deaths is alarming.
  A. The number of accidental gun deaths has risen from 1860 to 2016.
    1. There were few early efforts to reduce the death rate.
    2. Gun deaths were accepted as a way of life.
  B. The prevalence of guns is increasing in the twenty-first century.
    1. Gun sales rise with each new mass shooting.
    2. The NRA presses for open carry laws.
    3. Open carry on campus and in bars becomes controversial.
III. The number of options for reducing gun deaths is growing.
  A. There are criminal penalties for negligent parents.
    1. Some parents have received long prison sentences.
    2. Capital punishment is an alternative under discussion.

---

[3]   Associated Press, "Stray Bullet That Killed Long Island Girl Was Fired in Retaliation for Hoverboard Theft, Police Say," *New York Times*, January 11, 2016, http://www.nytimes.com/2016/01/12/nyregion/stray-bullet-that-killed-long-island-girl-was-fired-in-retaliation-for-theft-police-say.html.

B. The outlawing of semiautomatic weapons is a controversial possibility.
  1. Critics complain about financial costs.
  2. Philosophical costs may prevent meaningful legislation.
C. Advocates see public education on gun safety as essential.
  1. Courses in elementary and secondary schools are becoming feasible.
  2. Enrollments in online seminars for adults are on the incline.

The Patterns of Philosophy Papers

The structure of any particular type of philosophy paper is governed by a formal pattern. When rigid external controls are placed on their writing, some writers feel that their creativity is hampered by a kind of "paint-by-numbers" approach to structure. It is vital to the success of your paper that you never allow yourself to be overwhelmed by the pattern rules for any type of paper. Remember that such controls exist not to limit your creativity but to make the paper immediately and easily useful to its intended audience. It is as necessary to write clearly and confidently in a position paper or a policy analysis paper as in a term paper for English literature, a résumé, a short story, or a job application letter.

2.4 DRAFT, REVISE, EDIT, AND PROOFREAD

Write the Rough Draft

After planning comes the writing of the first draft. Using your thesis and outline as direction markers, you must now weave your amalgam of ideas, data, and persuasion strategies into logically ordered sentences and paragraphs. Although adequate prewriting may facilitate drafting, it still will not be easy. All writers establish their own individual methods of encouraging themselves to forge ahead with the draft, but here are some general tips:

- Remember that this is a rough draft, not the final paper. At this stage, it is not necessary that every word be the best possible choice. Do not put that sort of pressure on yourself. You must not allow anything to slow you down now. Writing is not like sculpting in stone, where every chip is permanent; you can always go back to your draft and add, delete, reword, and rearrange. *No matter how much effort you have put into planning, you cannot be sure how much of this first draft you will eventually keep.* It may take several drafts to get one that you find satisfactory.

- Give yourself sufficient time to write. Do not delay the first draft by telling yourself there is still more research to do. You cannot uncover all the material there is to know on a particular subject, so do not fool yourself into trying. Remember that writing is a process of discovery. You may have to begin writing before you can see exactly what sort of research you need to do. Keep in mind that there are other tasks waiting for you after the first draft is finished, so allow for them as you determine your writing schedule.

   More important, give yourself time to write because the more time that passes after you have written a draft, the better your ability to view it with objectivity. It is very difficult to evaluate your writing accurately soon after you complete it. You need to cool down, to recover from the effort of putting all those words together. The "colder" you get on your writing, the better you are able to read it as if it were written by someone else and thus acknowledge the changes you will need to make to strengthen the paper.

- Stay sharp. Keep in mind the plan you created as you narrowed your topic, composed a thesis sentence, and outlined the material. But, if you begin to feel a strong need to change the plan a bit, do not be afraid to do so. Be ready for surprises dealt you by your own growing understanding of your topic. Your goal is to record your best thinking on the subject as accurately as possible.

Paragraph Development   There is no absolute requirement for the structure of any paragraph in your paper except that all its sentences must be clearly related to each other and each must carry *one step further* the job of saying what you want to say about your thesis. In other words, any sentence that simply restates something said in another sentence anywhere else in the paper is a waste of your time and the reader's. It isn't unusual for a paragraph to have, somewhere in it, a *topic* sentence that serves as the key to the paragraph's organization and announces the paragraph's connection to the paper's thesis. But not all paragraphs need topic sentences.

What all paragraphs in the paper *do* need is an organizational strategy. Here are four typical organizational models, any one of which, if you keep it in mind, can help you build a coherent paragraph:

- *Chronological organization:* The sentences of the paragraph describe a series of events or steps or observations as they occur over time. This happens, then that, and then that.
- *Spatial organization:* The sentences of the paragraph record details of its subject in some logical order: top to bottom, up to down, outside to inside.
- *General-to-specific organization:* The paragraph starts with a statement of its main idea and then goes into detail as it discusses that idea.
- *Specific-to-general organization:* The paragraph begins with smaller, nuts-and-bolts details, arranging them into a larger pattern that, by the end of the paragraph, leads to the conclusion that is the paragraph's main idea.

These aren't the only organizational strategies available to you, and, of course, different paragraphs in a paper can use different strategies, though a paragraph that employs more than one organizational plan is risking incoherence. The essential thing to remember is that each sentence in the paragraph must bear a logical relationship to the one before it and the one after it. This notion of *interconnectedness* can prevent you from getting off track and stuffing extraneous material in your paragraphs.

Like all other aspects of the writing process, paragraph development is a challenge. But remember, one of the helpful facts about paragraphs is that they are relatively small, especially compared to the overall scope of your paper. Each paragraph can basically do only one job—handle or help handle a single idea, which is itself only a part of the overall development of the larger thesis idea. That paragraphs are small and aimed at a single task means that it is relatively easy to revise them. By focusing clearly on the single job a paragraph does and filtering out all the paper's other claims for your attention, you should gain enough clarity of vision during the revision process to understand what you need to do to make that paragraph work better.

Authority   To be convincing, your writing has to be authoritative—that is, you have to sound as if you have complete confidence in your ability to convey your ideas in words. Sentences that sound stilted or that suffer from weak phrasing or the use of clichés are not going to win supporters for the positions that you express in your paper. So a major question becomes, *How can I sound confident?*

Here are some points to consider as you work to convey to your reader that necessary sense of authority.

Level of Formality   Tone is one of the primary methods by which you signal to the readers who you are and what your attitude is toward them and toward your topic. Your major decision is which level of language formality is most appropriate to your audience. The informal tone you would use in a letter to a friend might well be out of place in a paper on Daoism written for your philosophy professor. Remember that tone is only part of the overall decision that you make about how to present your information. Formality is, to some extent, a function of individual word choices and phrasing. For example, is it appropriate to use contractions such as *isn't* or *they'll*? Would the strategic use of a sentence fragment for effect be out of place? The use of informal language, the personal *I*, and the second-person *you* are traditionally forbidden—for better or worse—in certain kinds of writing. Often, part of the challenge of writing a formal paper is simply how to give your prose impact while staying within the conventions.

Jargon   One way to lose readers quickly is to overwhelm them with *jargon*—phrases that have a special, usually technical, meaning within your discipline but that are unfamiliar to the average reader. The very occasional use of jargon may add an effective touch of atmosphere, but anything more than that will severely dampen a reader's enthusiasm for the paper. Often the writer uses jargon in an effort to impress the reader by sounding lofty or knowledgeable. Unfortunately, all that jargon usually does is cause confusion. In fact, the use of jargon indicates a writer's lack of connection to the audience.

Philosophy is a haven for jargon. Perhaps writers of conference papers believe their readers are all completely attuned to their terminology. Or some may hope to obscure damaging information or potentially unpopular ideas in confusing language. In other cases, the problem could simply be unclear thinking by the writer. Whatever the reason, the fact is that philosophy papers too often sound like prose made by machines to be read by machines.

Some students may feel that, to be accepted as philosophers, their papers should conform to the practices of their published peers. This is a mistake. Remember that it is never better to write a cluttered or confusing sentence than a clear one, and burying your ideas in jargon defeats the effort that you went through to form them.

EXERCISE   Revising Jargon

What words in the following sentence from an article in a philosophy journal are jargon? Can you rewrite the sentence to clarify its meaning?

Professor Geer insisted that ISIL's attempt to immanentize the eschaton defies deontological deconstruction.

Clichés   In the heat of composition, as you are looking for words to help you form your ideas, it is sometimes easy to plug in a cliché—a phrase that has attained universal recognition by overuse. Our collective vocabulary is brimming with clichés:

It's raining cats and dogs.

That issue is as dead as a doornail.

It's time for the governor to face the music.

Angry voters made a beeline for the ballot box.

> **Note:** Clichés differ from jargon in that clichés are part of the general public's everyday language, whereas jargon is specific to the language of experts in a field.

The problem with clichés is that they are virtually meaningless. Once colorful means of expression, they have lost their color through overuse, and they tend to bleed energy and color from the surrounding words. When revising, replace clichés with fresh wording that more accurately conveys your point.

Descriptive Language   Language that appeals to readers' senses will always engage their interest more fully than language that is abstract. This is especially important for writing in disciplines that tend to deal in abstracts, such as philosophy. The typical philosophy paper, with its discussions of principles, demographics, or points of law, is usually in danger of floating off into abstraction, with each paragraph drifting farther away from the felt life of the readers. Whenever appropriate, appeal to your readers' sense of sight, hearing, taste, touch, or smell.

EXERCISE   Using Descriptive Language

Which of these two sentences is more effective?

1. Professor Gingrich's lecture was inscrutable.
2. Professor Gingrich's lecture was inscrutable; jargon grew like weeds from every sentence, he mumbled with his back to the audience, and he pursued tangents at critical junctures in his argument.

Bias-Free and Gender-Neutral Writing   Language can be a very powerful method of either reinforcing or destroying cultural stereotypes. By treating the sexes in subtly different ways in your language, you may unknowingly be committing an act of discrimination. A common example is the use of the pronoun *he* to refer to a person whose gender has not been identified.

Some writers, faced with this dilemma, alternate the use of male and female personal pronouns; others use the plural to avoid the need to use a pronoun of either gender:

Sexist: A professor should always treat his students with respect.

Corrected: A professor should always treat his or her students with respect.

Or: Professors should always treat their students with respect.

Sexist: Man is a political animal.

Corrected: People are political animals.

Remember that language is more than the mere vehicle of your thoughts. Your words shape perceptions for your readers. How well you say something will profoundly affect your readers' responses to what you say. Sexist language denies to a large number of your readers the basic right to fair and equal treatment. Make sure your writing does not reflect this form of discrimination.

Revise

After all the work you have gone through writing it, you may feel "married" to the first draft of your paper. However, revision is one of the most important steps in ensuring your paper's success. Although unpracticed writers often think of revision as little more than making sure all the *i*'s are dotted and *t*'s are crossed, it is much more than that. Revising is *reseeing* the essay, looking at it from other perspectives, trying always to align your view with the one that will be held by your audience. Research indicates that we are actually revising all the time, in every phase of the writing process, as we reread phrases, rethink the placement of an item in an outline, or test a new topic sentence for a paragraph. Subjecting your entire hard-fought draft to cold, objective scrutiny is one of the toughest activities to master, but it is absolutely necessary. You have to make sure that you have said everything that needs to be said clearly and logically. One confusing passage will deflect the reader's attention from where you want it to be. Suddenly the reader has to become a detective, trying to figure out why you wrote what you did and what you meant by it. You do not want to throw such obstacles into the path of understanding.

Here are some tips to help you with revision:

1. Give yourself adequate time for revision. As discussed above, you need time to become "cold" on your paper in order to analyze it objectively. After you have written your draft, spend some time away from it. Then try to reread it as if someone else had written it.

2. Read the paper carefully. This is tougher than it sounds. One good strategy is to read it aloud yourself or to have a friend read it aloud while you listen. (Note, however, that friends are usually not the best critics. They are rarely trained in revision techniques and are often unwilling to risk disappointing you by giving your paper a really thorough examination.)

3. Have a list of specific items to check. It is important to revise in an orderly fashion, in stages, looking first at large concerns, such as the overall organization, and then at smaller elements, such as paragraph or sentence structure.

4. Check for unity—the clear and logical relation of all parts of the essay to its thesis. Make sure that every paragraph relates well to the whole of the paper and is in the right place.

5. Check for coherence. Make sure there are no gaps between the various parts of the argument. Look to see that you have adequate transitions everywhere they are needed. *Transitional elements* are markers indicating places where the paper's focus or attitude changes. Such elements can take the form of one word—*however, although, unfortunately, luckily*—or an entire sentence or a paragraph: *In order to fully appreciate the importance of deconstruction as a shaping presence in post–Cold War philosophy, it is necessary to examine briefly the volumes of philosophical scholarship it generated.*

   Transitional elements rarely introduce new material. Instead, they are direction pointers, either indicating a shift to new subject matter or signaling how the writer wishes certain material to be interpreted by the reader. Because you, the writer, already know where and why your paper changes direction and how you want particular passages to be received, it can be very difficult for you to catch those places where transition is needed.

6. Avoid unnecessary repetition. Two types of repetition can annoy a reader: repetition of content and repetition of wording.

   Repetition of content occurs when you return to a subject you have already discussed. Ideally, you should deal with a topic once, memorably, and then move on to your next subject. Organizing a paper is a difficult task, however, which usually occurs through a process of enlightenment in terms of purposes and strategies, and repetition of content can happen even if you have used prewriting strategies. What is worse, it can be difficult for you to be aware of the repetition in your own writing. As you write and revise, remember that any unnecessary repetition of content in your final draft is potentially annoying to your readers, who are working to make sense of the argument they are reading and do not want to be distracted by a passage repeating material they have already encountered. You must train yourself, through practice, to look for material that you have repeated unnecessarily.

   Repetition of wording occurs when you overuse certain phrases or words. This can make your prose sound choppy and uninspired, as the following examples demonstrate:

   > The subcommittee's report on education reform will surprise a number of people. A number of people will want copies of the report.

   > The chairman said at a press conference that he is happy with the report. He will circulate it to the local news agencies in the morning. He will also make sure that the city council has copies.

   > I became upset when I heard how the committee had voted. I called the chairman and expressed my reservations about the committee's decision. I told him I felt that he had let the teachers and students of the state down. I also issued a press statement.

   The last passage illustrates a condition known by composition teachers as the *I-syndrome*. Can you hear how such duplicated phrasing can hurt a paper? Your language should sound fresh and energetic. Before you submit your final draft, make sure to read through your paper carefully, looking for such repetition.

Still, not all repetition is bad. You may wish to repeat a phrase for rhetorical effect or special emphasis: *I came. I saw. I conquered.* Just make sure that any repetition in your paper is intentional, placed there to produce a specific effect.

Edit

Editing is sometimes confused with the more involved process of revising. But editing is done later in the writing process, after you have wrestled through your first draft—and maybe your second and third—and arrived at the final draft. Even though your draft now contains all the information you want to impart and has the information arranged to your satisfaction, there are still many factors to check, such as sentence structure, spelling, and punctuation.

It is at this point that an unpracticed writer might be less than vigilant. After all, most of the work on the paper is finished, as the "big jobs" of discovering, organizing, and drafting information have been completed. But watch out! Editing is as important as any other part of the writing process. Any error that you allow in the final draft will count against you in the mind of the reader. This may not seem fair, but even a minor error—a misspelling or the confusing placement of a comma—will make a much greater impression on your reader than perhaps it should. Remember that everything about your paper is your responsibility, including performing even the supposedly little jobs correctly. Careless editing undermines the effectiveness of your paper. It would be a shame if all the hard work you put into prewriting, drafting, and revising were to be damaged because you carelessly allowed a comma splice!

Most of the tips given above for revising hold for editing as well. It is best to edit in stages, looking for only one or two kinds of errors each time you reread the paper. Focus especially on errors that you remember committing in the past. If, for instance, you know that you have a tendency to misplace commas, go through your paper looking at each comma carefully. If you have a weakness for writing unintentional sentence fragments, read each sentence aloud to make sure that it is indeed a complete sentence. Have you accidentally shifted verb tenses anywhere, moving from past to present tense for no reason? Do all the subjects in your sentences agree in number with their verbs? *Now is the time to find out.*

Watch out for *miscues*—problems with a sentence that the writer simply does not see. Remember that your search for errors is hampered in two ways:

1. As the writer, you hope not to find any errors in your work. This desire can cause you to miss mistakes when they do occur.
2. Because you know your material so well, it is easy, as you read, to unconsciously supply missing material—a word, a piece of punctuation—as if it were present.

How difficult is it to see that something is missing in the following sentence?

Unfortunately, legislators often have too little regard their constituents.

We can guess that the missing word is probably *for*, which should be inserted after *regard*. It is quite possible, however, that the writer of the sentence would automatically supply the missing *for* as if it were on the page. This is a miscue, which can be hard for writers to spot because they are so close to their material.

One tactic for catching mistakes in sentence structure is to read the sentences aloud, starting with the last one in the paper and then moving to the next-to-last, then to the previous sentence, and thus going backward through the paper (reading each sentence in the normal, left-to-right manner, of course) until you reach the first sentence of the introduction. This backward progression strips each sentence of its rhetorical context and helps you focus on its internal structure.

Editing is the stage in which you finally answer those minor questions that you had put off when you were wrestling with wording and organization. Any ambiguities regarding the use of abbreviations, italics, numerals, capital letters, titles (When do you capitalize the title *president*, for example?), hyphens, dashes (usually created on a typewriter or computer by striking the hyphen key twice), apostrophes, and quotation marks have to be cleared up now. You must also check to see that you have used the required formats for footnotes, endnotes, margins, page numbers, and the like.

Guessing is not allowed. Sometimes unpracticed writers who realize that they do not quite understand a particular rule of grammar, punctuation, or format do nothing to fill that knowledge gap. Instead they rely on guesswork and their own logic—which is not always up to the task of dealing with so contrary a language as English—to get them through problems that they could solve if they referred to a writing manual. Remember that it does not matter to the reader why or how an error shows up in your writing. It only matters that you have dropped your guard. You must not allow a careless error to undo all the good work that you have done.

Proofread

Before you hand in the final version of your paper, it is vital that you check it one more time to make sure there are no errors of any sort. This job is called *proofreading*, or *proofing*. In essence, you are looking for many of the same things you had checked for during editing, but now you are doing it on the last draft, which is about to be submitted to your audience. Proofreading is as important as editing; you may have missed an error that you still have time to find, or an error may have been introduced when the draft was recopied or typed for the last time. Like every other stage of the writing process, proofreading is your responsibility.

At this point, you must check for typing mistakes: transposed or deleted letters, words, phrases, or punctuation. If you have had the paper professionally typed, you still must check it carefully. Do not rely solely on the typist's proofreading. If you are creating your paper on a computer or a word processor, it is possible for you to unintentionally insert a command that alters your document drastically by slicing out a word, line, or sentence at the touch of a key. Make sure such accidental deletions have not occurred.

Above all else, remember that your paper represents you. It is a product of your best thinking, your most energetic and imaginative response to a writing challenge. If you have maintained your enthusiasm for the project and worked through the stages of the writing process honestly and carefully, you should produce a paper you can be proud of, one that will serve its readers well.

Read&Write 2.4   Discover Your Own Identity and Style

Here is another opportunity to do some freewriting. The wisdom of the Oracle of Delphi was noted by Socrates, who affirmed the Oracle's belief that the key to wisdom itself was "Know Yourself." Fulfilling this admonition can become a lifelong occupation. As philosophers may tell you, helping others know themselves offers a potentially fulfilling career. Let's start our writing project by accepting, though with apologies for an ancient philosopher's gender bias, Aristotle's observation that "Man is by nature a political animal."[4] If you are a political animal, what does this mean about you personally? In this case, think about politics in the broadest sense, which refers not just to running for office, but as a mode of conduct in which you exert influence on other people, most specifically to get your needs and desires met. Have fun! When you are done freewriting, write one solid paper in which you describe who you are as a "political animal."

---

[4]   Aristotle, *Politics*, 1.1253a, http://www.perseus.tufts.edu/hopper/text?doc=Perseus:text:1999.01.0058.

3

PRACTICE THE CRAFT

OF SCHOLARSHIP

3.1   THE COMPETENT WRITER

Good writing places your thoughts in your readers' minds in exactly the way you want them to be there. Good writing tells your readers just what you want them to know without telling them anything you do not want them to know. This may sound odd, but the fact is that writers have to be careful not to let unwanted messages slip into their writing. Look, for example, at the passage below, taken from a paper exploring violence in religious sects. Hidden within the prose is an element that jeopardizes the paper's success. Can you detect the element?

> Recent articles written on the subject of violent religious movements have had little to say about the particular problems dealt with in this paper. Because few of these articles focus on the problem at the international level.

Chances are, when you reached the end of the second "sentence," you felt that something was missing and perceived a gap in logic or coherence, so you went back through both sentences to find the place where things had gone wrong. The text following the first sentence is actually not a sentence at all. It does have certain features of a sentence—for example, a subject (*few*) and a verb (*focus*)—but its first word (*Because*) subordinates the entire clause that follows, taking away its ability to stand on its own as a complete idea. The second "sentence," which is properly called a *subordinate clause*, merely fills in some information about the first sentence, telling us why recent articles about violent religious movements fail to deal with problems discussed in the present paper.

The sort of error represented by the second "sentence" is commonly called a *sentence fragment*, and it conveys to the reader a message that no writer wants to send: that the writer either is careless or, worse, has not mastered the language. Language errors such as fragments, misplaced commas, or shifts in verb tense send out warnings in readers' minds. As a result, readers lose some of their concentration on the issue being discussed; they become distracted and begin to wonder about the language competency of the writer. The writing loses effectiveness.

Note: Whatever goal you set for your paper—whether to persuade, describe, analyze, or speculate—you must also set a goal for yourself: to display language competence. If your paper does not meet this goal, it will not completely achieve its other aims. Language errors spread doubt like a virus; they jeopardize all the hard work you have done on your paper.

Language competence is especially important in philosophy, for credibility in philosophy depends on such skill. Anyone who doubts this should remember the beating that Vice President Dan Quayle took in the press for misspelling the word *potato* at a 1992 spelling bee. His error caused a storm of humiliating publicity for the hapless Quayle, adding to an impression of his general incompetence.

Correctness Is Relative

Although they may seem minor, the sort of language errors we are discussing—often called *surface errors*—can be extremely damaging in certain kinds of writing. Surface errors come in a variety of types, including misspellings, punctuation problems, grammar errors, and the inconsistent use of abbreviations, capitalization, and numerals. These errors are an affront to your readers' notion of correctness, and therein lies one of the biggest problems with surface errors. Different audiences tolerate different levels of correctness. You know that you can get away with surface errors in, say, a letter to a friend, who will probably not judge you harshly for them, whereas those same errors in a job application letter might eliminate you from consideration for the position. Correctness depends to an extent on context.

Another problem is that the rules governing correctness shift over time. What would have been an error to your grandmother's generation—for example, the splitting of an infinitive or the ending of a sentence with a preposition—is taken in stride by most readers today.

So, how do you write correctly when the rules shift from person to person and over time? Here are some tips.

Consider Your Audience   One of the great risks of writing is that even the simplest of choices regarding wording or punctuation can sometimes prejudice your audience against you in ways that may seem unfair. For example, look again at the old grammar rule forbidding the splitting of infinitives. After decades of telling students to never split an infinitive (something just done in this sentence), most composition experts now concede that a split infinitive is *not* a grammar crime. But suppose you have written a position paper trying to convince your city council of the need to hire security personnel for the library, and half of the council members—the people you wish to convince—remember their eighth-grade grammar teacher's warning about splitting infinitives. How will they respond when you tell them, in your introduction, that librarians are compelled "to always accompany" visitors to the rare-book room because of the threat of vandalism? How much of their attention have you suddenly lost because of their automatic recollection of what is now a nonrule? It is possible, in other words, to write correctly and still offend your readers' notions of language competence.

Make sure that you tailor the surface features and the degree of formality of your writing to the level of competency that your readers require. When in doubt, take a conservative approach. Your audience might be just as distracted by a contraction as by a split infinitive.

Aim for Consistency When dealing with a language question for which there are different answers—such as whether to use a comma before the conjunction in a series of three (*The professor's speech addressed ethics, economics, and the job situation.*)—always use the same strategy throughout your paper. If, for example, you avoid splitting one infinitive, avoid splitting *all* infinitives.

Have Confidence in What You Know about Writing!

It is easy for unpracticed writers to allow their occasional mistakes to shake their confidence in their writing ability. The fact is, however, that most of what we know about writing is correct.

Read&Write 3.1 Rephrase to Eliminate a Sentence Fragment

See how many ways you can rewrite the following two-"sentence" passage to eliminate the fragment and make the passage syntactically correct.

A person's personality type predicts the complexity of his moral philosophy only about 10 percent of the time. Except when the person is extremely introverted.

3.2 AVOID ERRORS IN GRAMMAR AND PUNCTUATION

As various composition theorists have pointed out, the word *grammar* has several definitions. One meaning is "the formal patterns in which words must be arranged in order to convey meaning." We learn these patterns very early in life and use them spontaneously, without thinking. Our understanding of grammatical patterns is extremely sophisticated, despite the fact that few of us can actually cite the rules by which the patterns work. Patrick Hartwell tested grammar learning by asking native English speakers of different ages and levels of education, including high school teachers, to arrange these words in natural order:

French the young girls four

Everyone could produce the natural order for this phrase: *the four young French girls*. Yet none of Hartwell's respondents was able to cite the rules that govern the order of the words.[1] We are all capable of writing grammatically sound phrases, even if we cannot list the rules by which we achieve coherence. Most writers who worry about their chronic errors make fewer mistakes than they think. Becoming distressed about errors makes writing even more difficult.

---

[1] Patrick Hartwell, "Grammar, Grammars, and the Teaching of Grammar," *College English* 47 (February 1985): 105–27.

Eliminate Chronic Errors But if just thinking about our errors has a negative effect on our writing, how do we learn to write more correctly? Perhaps the best answer is simply to write as often as possible. Give yourself lots of practice in putting your thoughts into written shape—and then in revising and proofing your work. As you write and revise, be honest—and patient—with yourself. Chronic errors are like bad habits; getting rid of them takes time.

You probably know of one or two problem areas in your writing that you could have eliminated but have not yet done so. Instead, you may have fudged your writing at critical points, relying on half-remembered formulas from past English classes or trying to come up with logical solutions to your writing problems. (*Reminder:* The English language does not always work in a way that seems logical.) You may have simply decided that comma rules are unlearnable or that you will never understand the difference between the verbs *lay* and *lie*. And so you guess, and you come up with the wrong answer a good part of the time. What a shame, when just a little extra work would give you mastery over those few gaps in your understanding and boost your confidence as well.

Instead of continuing with this sort of guesswork and living with the holes in your knowledge, why not face the problem areas now and learn the rules that have heretofore escaped you? What follows is a discussion of those surface features of writing in which errors most commonly occur. You will probably be familiar with most if not all of the rules discussed, but there may well be a few you have not yet mastered. Now is the time to do so.

Apostrophes

An apostrophe is used to show possession. When you wish to say that something belongs to someone or something, you add either an apostrophe and an *s* or an apostrophe alone to the word that represents the owner(s).

- When the owner is singular (a single person or thing), the apostrophe precedes an added *s*:

  According to Professor Anderson's secretary, the ethics class has been canceled.

  The deontologist's challenge to a debate was accepted by a teleologist.

  Somebody's briefcase was left in the auditorium.

- The same rule applies if the word showing possession is a plural that does not end in *s*:

  The women's club sponsored several debates during the last presidential campaign.

  Dean Smith has proven himself a tireless worker for children's rights.

- When the word expressing ownership is a plural ending in *s*, the apostrophe follows the *s*:

  The new philosophy seminar was discussed at the secretaries' conference.

There are two ways to form the possessive for two or more nouns:

1. To show joint possession (both nouns owning the same thing or things), only the last noun in the series is possessive:

   The president and first lady's invitations were sent out yesterday.

2. To indicate that each noun owns an item or items individually, each noun must show possession:

   Professor Scott's and Professor MacKay's speeches took different approaches to the same problem.

The importance of the apostrophe is obvious when you consider the difference in meaning between the following two sentences:

Be sure to pick up the professor's bags on your way to the airport.
Be sure to pick up the professors' bags on your way to the airport.

In the first sentence, you have only one professor to worry about, whereas in the second, you have at least two!

Capitalization

Here is a brief summary of three hard-to-remember capitalization rules:

1. You may, if you choose, capitalize the first letter of the first word in a sentence that follows a colon. Just make sure you use one pattern consistently throughout your paper:

   Our instructions are explicit: Do not allow anyone into the conference without an identification badge.

   Our instructions are explicit: do not allow anyone into the conference without an identification badge.

2. Capitalize *proper nouns* (names of specific people, places, or things) and *proper adjectives* (adjectives made from proper nouns). A common noun following a proper adjective is usually not capitalized, nor is a common adjective preceding a proper adjective (such as *a*, *an*, or *the*):

Proper Nouns	Proper Adjectives
Poland	Polish officials
Iraq	the Iraqi ambassador
Shakespeare	a Shakespearean tragedy

Proper nouns include:

- *Names of monuments and buildings:* the Washington Monument, the Empire State Building, the Library of Congress
- *Historical events, eras, and certain terms concerning calendar dates:* the Civil War, the Dark Ages, Monday, December, Columbus Day

- *Parts of the country:* North, Southwest, Eastern Seaboard, the West Coast, New England.

> **Note:** When words like *north*, *south*, *east*, *west*, and *northwest* are used to designate direction rather than geographical region, they are not capitalized, as in *We drove east to Boston and then made a tour of the East Coast.*

- *Words referring to race, religion, and nationality:* Islam, Muslim, Caucasian, White (or white, depending on context), Asian, Negro, Black (or black, depending on context), Slavic, Arab, Jewish, Hebrew, Buddhism, Buddhists, Southern Baptists, the Bible, the Koran, American
- *Names of languages:* English, Chinese, Latin, Sanskrit
- *Titles of corporations, institutions, universities, and organizations:* Dow Chemical, General Motors, the National Endowment for the Humanities, University of Tennessee, Colby College, Kiwanis Club, American Association of Retired Persons, Oklahoma State Senate.

> **Note:** Some words once considered proper nouns or adjectives have, over time, become common and are no longer capitalized, such as *french fries*, *pasteurized milk*, *arabic numerals*, and *italics*.

3. Titles of individuals may be capitalized if they precede a proper name; otherwise, titles are usually not capitalized:

The committee honored Professor Jones.
The committee honored the professor from Kansas.
We phoned Nurse Brown, who arrived shortly afterward.
We phoned the nurse, who arrived shortly afterward.
A story on Queen Elizabeth's health appeared in yesterday's paper.
A story on the queen's health appeared in yesterday's paper.
Pope Francis's visit to Colorado was a public relations success.
The pope's visit to Colorado was a public relations success.

When Not to Capitalize   In general, you do not capitalize nouns when your reference is nonspecific. For example, you would not capitalize *the professor*, but you would capitalize *Professor Smith*. The second reference is as much a title as it is a term of identification, whereas the first reference is a mere identifier. Likewise, there is a difference in degree of specificity between *the state treasury* and *the Texas State Treasury*.

> **Note:** The meaning of a term may change somewhat depending on its capitalization. What, for example, might be the difference between a *Democrat* and a *democrat?* When capitalized, the word refers to a member of a specific philosophical party; when not capitalized, it refers to someone who believes in the democratic form of government.

Capitalization depends to some extent on the context of your writing. For example, if you are writing a policy analysis for a specific corporation, you may capitalize words and phrases that refer to that corporation—such as *Board of Directors*, *Chairman of the Board*, and *the Institute*—that would not be capitalized in a paper written for a more general audience. Likewise, in some contexts, it is not unusual to see the titles of certain powerful officials capitalized even when not accompanying a proper noun:

The President took few members of his staff to Camp David with him.

Colons

We all know certain uses for the colon. A colon can, for example, separate the parts of a statement of time (*4:25 a.m.*), separate chapter and verse in a biblical quotation (*John 3:16*), and close the salutation of a business letter (*Dear Professor Keaton:*). But the colon has other, less well-known uses that can add extra flexibility to sentence structure.

The colon can introduce into a sentence certain kinds of material, such as a list, a quotation, or a restatement or description of material mentioned earlier:

List

The committee's research proposal promised to do three things: (1) establish the extent of the problem, (2) examine several possible solutions, and (3) estimate the cost of each solution.

Quotation

In his speech, the professor challenged us with these words: "How will your council's work make a difference in the life of our university?"

Restatement or Description

Ahead of us, according to the professor's secretary, lay the biggest job of all: convincing our department of the plan's benefits.

Commas

The comma is perhaps the most troublesome of all marks of punctuation, no doubt because its use is governed by so many variables, such as sentence length, rhetorical emphasis, and changing notions of style. The most common problems are outlined below.

The Comma Splice   A *comma splice* is the joining of two complete sentences with only a comma:

The Vienna Circle were a group of philosophers who came together in 1922, they formed a philosophical association and named it the Ernst Mach Association.

An unemployed worker who has been effectively retrained is no longer an economic problem for the community, he has become an asset.

It might be possible for the clinic to assess fees on the treatment of the indigenous poor, however, such a move would be criticized by the church leaders in the community.

In each of these passages, two complete sentences (also called *independent clauses*) have been spliced together only by a comma, which is an inadequate break between the two sentences.

One foolproof way to check your paper for comma splices is to read the structures on both sides of each comma carefully. If you find a complete sentence on each side, and if the sentence following the comma does not begin with a coordinating conjunction (*and, but, for, nor, or, so, yet*), then you have found a comma splice.

Simply reading the draft to try to "hear" the comma splices may not work because the rhetorical features of your prose—its *movement*—may make it hard to detect this kind of error in sentence completeness. There are five commonly used ways to correct comma splices:

1. Place a period between the two independent clauses.

   INCORRECT   A philosophy job applicant receives many benefits from his or her training in critical thinking, there are liabilities as well.

   CORRECT   A philosophy job applicant receives many benefits from his or her training in critical thinking. There are liabilities as well.

2. Place a comma and a coordinating conjunction (*and, but, for, or, nor, so, yet*) between the independent clauses.

   INCORRECT   The philosopher's lecture described the major differences of opinion over deontology, it also suggested areas of agreement.

   CORRECT   The philosopher's lecture described the major differences of opinion over deontology, and it also suggested areas of agreement.

3. Place a semicolon between the independent clauses.

   INCORRECT   Some people feel that the philosophy department should play a large role in establishing an ethics policy for college admissions, many others disagree.

   CORRECT   Some people feel that the philosophy department should play a large role in establishing an ethics policy for college admissions; many others disagree.

4. Rewrite the two clauses as one independent clause.

   INCORRECT   Television ads played a big part in the philosopher's argument, however, they were not the deciding factor in the argument's popularity.

   CORRECT   Television ads played a large but not decisive role in the popularity of the philosopher's argument.

5. Change one of the independent clauses into a dependent clause by beginning it with a subordinating word (*although, after, as, because, before, if, though, unless,*

when, which, where), which prevents the clause from being able to stand on its own as a complete sentence.

INCORRECT   The election was held last Tuesday, there was a poor voter turnout.

CORRECT   When the election was held last Tuesday, there was a poor voter turnout.

Commas in a Compound Sentence   A *compound sentence* is composed of two or more independent clauses—that is, two complete sentences. When these two clauses are joined by a coordinating conjunction, the conjunction should be preceded by a comma to signal the reader that another independent clause follows. (This is method 2 for fixing a comma splice, described above.) When the comma is missing, the reader is not expecting to find the second half of a compound sentence and may be distracted from the text.

As the following examples indicate, the missing comma is especially a problem in longer sentences or in sentences in which other coordinating conjunctions appear. Notice how the comma sorts out the two main parts of the compound sentence, eliminating confusion.

INCORRECT   The dean promised to visit the department and investigate the problem and then he called the meeting to a close.

CORRECT   The dean promised to visit the department and investigate the problem, and then he called the meeting to a close.

INCORRECT   The ethics committee can neither make policy nor enforce it nor can its members serve on auxiliary policy committees.

CORRECT   The ethics committee can neither make policy nor enforce it, nor can its members serve on auxiliary policy committees.

An exception to this rule arises in shorter sentences, where the comma may not be necessary to make the meaning clear:

The professor phoned and we thanked him for his support.

However, it is never wrong to place a comma after the conjunction between independent clauses. If you are the least bit unsure of your audience's notion of "proper" grammar, it is a good idea to take the conservative approach and use the comma:

The professor phoned, and we thanked him for his support.

Commas with Restrictive and Nonrestrictive Elements   A *nonrestrictive element* is a part of a sentence—a word, phrase, or clause—that adds information about another element in the sentence without restricting or limiting its meaning. Although this information may be useful, the nonrestrictive element is not needed for the sentence to make sense. To signal its inessential nature, the nonrestrictive element is set off from the rest of the sentence with commas.

The failure to use commas to indicate the nonrestrictive nature of a sentence element can cause confusion. See, for example, how the presence or absence of commas affects our understanding of the following sentences:

The philosopher was talking with the policeman, who won the outstanding service award last year.

The philosopher was talking with the policeman who won the outstanding service award last year.

Can you see that the comma changes the meaning of the sentence? In the first version of the sentence, the comma makes the information that follows it incidental: *The philosopher was talking with the policeman, who happened to have won the service award last year.* In the second version of the sentence, the information following the word *policeman* is vital to the sense of the sentence; it tells us specifically *which* policeman—presumably there are more than one—the philosopher was addressing. Here, the lack of a comma has transformed the material following the word *policeman* into a *restrictive element*, which means that it is necessary to our understanding of the sentence.

Be sure that you make a clear distinction in your paper between nonrestrictive and restrictive elements by setting off the nonrestrictive elements with commas.

Commas in a Series   A series is any two or more items of a similar nature that appear consecutively in a sentence. These items may be individual words, phrases, or clauses. In a series of three or more items, the items are separated by commas:

The philosopher, the dean, and the chancellor all attended the ceremony.

Because of the new zoning regulations, all trailer parks must be moved out of the neighborhood, all small businesses must apply for recertification and tax status, and the two local churches must repave their parking lots.

The final comma in the series, the one before *and*, is sometimes left out, especially in newspaper writing. This practice, however, can make for confusion, especially in longer, complicated sentences like the second example above. Here is the way this sentence would read without the final, or serial, comma:

Because of the new zoning regulations, all trailer parks must be moved out of the neighborhood, all small businesses must apply for recertification and tax status and the two local churches must repave their parking lots.

Notice that, without a comma, the division between the second and third items in the series is not clear. This is the sort of ambiguous structure that can cause a reader to backtrack and lose concentration. You can avoid such confusion by always using that final comma. Remember, however, that if you do decide to include it, do so consistently; make sure it appears in every series in your paper.

Misplaced Modifiers

A *modifier* is a word or group of words used to describe—or *modify*—another word in the sentence. A *misplaced modifier*, sometimes called a dangling modifier, appears at either the beginning or the end of a sentence and seems to be describing some word other than the one the writer obviously intended. The modifier therefore "dangles," disconnected from its true antecedent. It is often hard for the writer to spot a dangling modifier, but readers can—and will—find them, and the result can be disastrous for the sentence, as the following examples demonstrate:

INCORRECT   Flying low over Washington, the White House was seen.

CORRECT   Flying low over Washington, we saw the White House.

INCORRECT   Worried at the cost of the program, sections of the budget were trimmed in committee.

CORRECT   Worried at the cost of the program, the committee trimmed sections of the budget.

INCORRECT   To advocate curriculum reform, a lot of effort went into presentation preparation.

CORRECT   Advocates for curriculum reform put a lot of effort into preparing their presentation.

INCORRECT   Stunned, the television broadcast the defeated senator's concession speech.

CORRECT   The television broadcast the stunned senator's concession speech.

Note that in the first two incorrect sentences above, the confusion is largely due to the use of *passive-voice* verbs, as in "the White House *was seen*" and "sections of the bill *were trimmed*." Often, although not always, a dangling modifier results because the actor in the sentence—*we* in the first sentence, *the committee* in the second—is either distanced from the modifier or obliterated by the passive-voice verb. It is a good idea to avoid using the passive voice unless you have a specific reason for doing so.

One way to check for dangling modifiers is to examine all modifiers at the beginning or end of your sentences. Look especially for *to be* phrases or for words ending in *-ing* or *-ed* at the start of the modifier. Then see if the modified word is close enough to the phrase to be properly connected.

Parallelism

Series of two or more words, phrases, or clauses within a sentence should have the same grammatical structure, a situation called *parallelism*. Parallel structures can add power and balance to your writing by creating a strong rhetorical rhythm. Here is a famous example of parallelism from the preamble to the US Constitution. (The capitalization follows that of the original eighteenth-century document. Parallel structures have been italicized.)

> We the People of the United States, in Order to *form a more perfect Union*, *establish Justice*, *insure domestic Tranquility*, *provide for the common defence*, *promote the general Welfare*, and *secure the Blessings of Liberty to ourselves and our Posterity*, do *ordain* and *establish* this Constitution for the United States of America.

There are actually two series in this sentence: the first, composed of six phrases, each of which completes the infinitive phrase beginning with the word *to* (*to form*, [*to*] *establish*, [*to*] *insure*, [*to*] *provide*, [*to*] *promote*, and [*to*] *secure*); the second, consisting of two verbs (*ordain* and *establish*). These parallel series appeal to our love of balance and pattern, and give an authoritative tone to the sentence. The writer, we feel, has thought long and carefully about the matter at hand and has taken firm control of it.

Because we find a special satisfaction in balanced structures, we are more likely to remember ideas phrased in parallelisms than in less highly ordered language. For this reason, as well as for the sense of authority and control that they suggest, parallel structures are common in philosophical utterances:

> *We hold these truths to be self-evident, that all men are created equal, that they are endowed by their Creator with certain unalienable rights, that among these are life, liberty, and the pursuit of happiness.*
>
> —*The Declaration of Independence*, 1776

> *Ask not what your country can do for you, ask what you can do for your country.*
>
> —John F. Kennedy, *Inaugural Address*, 1961

Faulty Parallelism   If the parallelism of a passage is not carefully maintained, the writing can seem sloppy and out of balance. Scan your writing to make sure that all series and lists have parallel structures. The following examples show how to correct faulty parallelisms:

INCORRECT   The chancellor promises not only to reform the humanities department but also the giving of raises to all its employees. (Connective structures such as not only . . . but also and both . . . and introduce elements that should be parallel.)

CORRECT   The chancellor promises not only to reform the humanities department but also to give raises to all its employees.

INCORRECT   The cost of *doing nothing* is greater than the cost to *renovate* the department offices.

CORRECT   The cost of *doing nothing* is greater than the cost of *renovating* the department offices.

INCORRECT   Here are the items on the committee's agenda: (1) to *discuss* the new curriculum; (2) *to revise* the wording of the ethics policy; (3) *a vote* on the chair's request for an assistant.

CORRECT   Here are the items on the committee's agenda: (1) to *discuss* the new curriculum; (2) *to revise* the wording of the ethics policy; (3) *to vote* on the chair's request for an assistant.

Fused (Run-On) Sentences

A *fused sentence* is one in which two or more independent clauses (passages that can stand as complete sentences) have been run together without the aid of any suitable connecting word, phrase, or punctuation. There are several ways to correct a fused sentence:

INCORRECT   The debate team members were exhausted they had debated for two hours.

CORRECT   The debate team members were exhausted. They had debated for two hours. (The clauses have been separated into two sentences.)

CORRECT   The debate team members were exhausted; they had debated for two hours. (The clauses have been separated by a semicolon.)

CORRECT   The debate team members were exhausted, having debated for two hours. (The second clause has been rephrased as a dependent clause.)

INCORRECT   Our policy analysis impressed the independent voters on the committee it also convinced them to reconsider their action.

CORRECT   Our policy analysis impressed the independent voters on the committee and also convinced them to reconsider their action. (The second clause has been rephrased as part of the first clause.)

CORRECT   Our policy analysis impressed the independent voters on the committee, and it also convinced them to reconsider their action. (The clauses have been separated by a comma and a coordinating word.)

Although a fused sentence is easily noticeable to the reader, it can be maddeningly difficult for the writer to catch. Unpracticed writers tend to read through the fused spots, sometimes supplying the break that is usually heard when sentences are spoken. To check for fused sentences, carefully read aloud the independent clauses in your paper, making sure that there are adequate breaks among all of them.

Pronouns

Its **versus** *It's*   Do not make the mistake of trying to form the possessive of *it* in the same way that you form the possessive of most nouns. The pronoun *it* shows possession by simply adding an *s*.

> The philosopher argued the case on its merits.

The word *it's* is a contraction of *it is*:

> It's the most expensive program ever launched by the council.

What makes the *its/it's* rule so confusing is that most nouns form the singular possessive by adding an apostrophe and an *s*:

> The jury's verdict startled the crowd.

When proofreading, any time you come to the word *it's*, substitute the phrase *it is* while you read. If the phrase makes sense, you have used the correct form. For example, if you have written:

> The student paper was misleading in it's analysis of the strength of the argument.

then read it as *it is*:

> The student paper was misleading in it is analysis of the strength of the argument.

If the phrase makes no sense, substitute *its* for *it's:*

> The student paper was misleading in its analysis of the election.

Vague Pronoun References   Pronouns are words that take the place of nouns or other pronouns that have already been mentioned in your writing. The most common pronouns include *he, she, it, they, them, those, which,* and *who.* You must make sure there is no confusion about the word to which each pronoun refers:

> The regent said that he would support our proposal if the dean's council would also back it.

The word that the pronoun replaces is called its *antecedent.* To check the accuracy of your pronoun references, ask yourself, "To what does the pronoun refer?" Then answer the question carefully, making sure that there is not more than one possible antecedent. Consider the following example:

> Several student groups decided to try to defeat the new tuition hike. This became the turning point of the administration's financial reform campaign.

To what does the word *this* refer? The immediate answer seems to be the words *new tuition hike* at the end of the previous sentence. It is more likely, however, that the writer was referring to the attempt of the student groups to defeat the bill, but there is no word in the first sentence that refers specifically to this action. The pronoun reference is thus unclear. One way to clarify the reference is to change the beginning of the second sentence:

> Several student groups decided to try to defeat the new tuition hike. Their attack on the proposal became the turning point of the administration's financial reform campaign.

Here is another example:

> When John F. Kennedy appointed his brother Robert to the position of US attorney general, he had little idea how widespread the corruption in the Teamsters Union was.

To whom does the word *he* refer? It is unclear whether the writer is referring to John or Robert Kennedy. One way to clarify the reference is simply to repeat the antecedent instead of using a pronoun:

> When John F. Kennedy appointed his brother Robert to the position of US attorney general, Robert had little idea how widespread the corruption in the Teamsters Union was.

Pronoun Agreement   A pronoun must agree with its antecedent in both gender and number, as the following examples demonstrate:

> Professor Smith said that he appreciated our club's support in the decision.

> One reporter asked the professor what she would do if the president offered her an administrative post.

> Having listened to our case, the judge decided to rule on it within the week.

Philosophers working on the ethics statement said they were pleased with progress so far.

Certain words, however, can be troublesome antecedents because they may look like plural pronouns but are actually singular:

anyone	each	either	everybody	everyone
nobody	no one	somebody	someone	

A pronoun referring to one of these words in a sentence must be singular too:

INCORRECT   Each of the wives in the philosophy department brought their children.

CORRECT   Each of the wives in the philosophy department brought her children.

INCORRECT   Has everybody received their invitation?

CORRECT   Has everybody received his or her invitation? (The two gender-specific pronouns are used to avoid sexist language.)

CORRECT   Have all the members received their invitations? (The singular antecedent has been changed to a plural one.)

A Shift in Person

It is important to avoid shifting unnecessarily among first person (*I, we*), second person (*you*), and third person (*she, he, it, one, they*) and between singular and plural. Such shifts can cause confusion:

INCORRECT   Most people (third person) who run for office find that if you (second person) tell the truth during your campaign, you will gain the voters' respect.

CORRECT   Most people who run for office find that if they tell the truth during their campaigns, they will gain the voters' respect.

INCORRECT   One (third person singular) cannot tell whether they (third person plural) are suited for public office until they decide to run.

CORRECT   One cannot tell whether one is suited for public office until one decides to run.

Quotation Marks

It can be difficult to remember when to use quotation marks and where they go in relation to other punctuation. When faced with these questions, unpracticed writers often try to rely on logic rather than on a rule book, but the rules do not always seem to rely on logic. The only way to make sure of your use of quotation marks is to memorize the rules. Luckily, there are not many.

Use quotation marks to enclose direct quotations that are no longer than one hundred words or eight typed lines:

In the conclusion of her argument, the speaker made her most important claim very clear when she said, "Nobody should ever take up this side of the argument unless he or she has truly experienced its ramifications."

Quotations of one hundred words or longer, called *block quotations*, are placed in a double-spaced indented block, without quotation marks:

Senator Malorie began her acceptance speech at the evening presentation with a rare moment of autobiographical candor:

> I was born and raised in Central Texas, in a time when nobody ever talked about how tough they were except those who, it turned out, weren't really very tough at all. At a young age I got to equating silence with toughness. My father was a very quiet man, my mother even quieter, and they were the toughest two people I ever knew. Where I got my love of talk I cannot say, but I think it was what led me into politics. I learned pretty fast that you could talk and talk and talk in an election or a debate and yet still be tough as nails.

Use single quotation marks to set off quotations within quotations:

"I intend," said the professor, "to use in my lecture a line from Frost's poem, 'The Road Not Taken.'"

Note: When the quote occurs at the end of the sentence, both the single and double quotation marks are placed outside the period.

Use quotation marks to set off titles of the following:

Short poems (those not printed as a separate volume)
Short stories
Articles or essays
Songs
Episodes of television or radio shows

Use quotation marks to set off words or phrases used in special ways:

- To convey irony:

  The "liberal" administration has done nothing but cater to big business.

- To indicate a technical term:

  To "filibuster" is to delay legislation, usually through prolonged speechmaking. The last notable filibuster occurred just last week in the Senate. (Once the term is defined, it is not placed in quotation marks again.)

Quotation Marks in Relation to Other Punctuation   Place commas and periods *inside* closing quotation marks:

"My fellow Americans," said the president, "there are tough times ahead of us."

Place colons and semicolons *outside* closing quotation marks:

In his speech on voting, the governor warned against "an encroaching indolence"; he was referring to the middle class.

There are several victims of the county's campaign to "Turn Back the Clock": the homeless, the elderly, the mentally impaired.

Use the context to determine whether to place question marks, exclamation points, and dashes inside or outside closing quotation marks. If the punctuation is part of the quotation, place it inside the quotation mark:

"When will the hiring committee make up its mind?" asked the applicant.

The demonstrators shouted, "Free the prisoners!" and "No more slavery!"

If the punctuation is not part of the quotation, place it outside the quotation mark:

Which president said, "We have nothing to fear but fear itself"?

Note that although the quote is a complete sentence, you do not place a period after it. There can only be one piece of *terminal punctuation* (punctuation that ends a sentence).

Semicolons

The semicolon is a little-used punctuation mark that you should learn to incorporate into your writing strategy because of its many potential applications. For example, a semicolon can be used to correct a comma splice:

INCORRECT	The faculty representatives left the meeting in good spirits, their demands were met.
CORRECT	The faculty representatives left the meeting in good spirits; their demands were met.
INCORRECT	Several guests at the fundraiser had lost their invitations, however, we were able to seat them anyway.
CORRECT	Several guests at the fundraiser had lost their invitations; however, we were able to seat them anyway. As an (albeit weaker) alternative to the use of a semicolon: Several guests at the fundraiser had lost their invitations. However, we were able to seat them anyway.

It is important to remember that conjunctive adverbs such as *however, therefore,* and *thus* are not coordinating words (such as *and, but, or, for, so, yet*) and cannot be used with a comma to link independent clauses. If the second independent clause begins with *however*, it must be preceded by either a period—making sure to capitalize the first letter of the next word, which now begins a new sentence—or a semicolon. As you can see from the second example above, connecting two independent clauses with a semicolon instead of a period preserves the suggestion that there is a strong relationship between the clauses.

Semicolons can also separate items in a series when the series items themselves contain commas:

> The newspaper account of the rally stressed the march, which drew the biggest crowd; the professor's speech, which drew tremendous applause; and the party in the park, which lasted for hours.

Avoid misusing semicolons. For example, use a comma, not a semicolon, to separate an independent clause from a dependent clause:

INCORRECT Students from the college volunteered to answer phones during the pledge drive; which was set up to generate money for the new arts center.

CORRECT Students from the college volunteered to answer phones during the pledge drive, which was set up to generate money for the new arts center.

Do not overuse semicolons. Although they are useful, too many semicolons in your writing can distract your readers' attention. Avoid monotony by using semicolons sparingly.

Sentence Fragments

A *fragment* is an incomplete part of a sentence that is punctuated and capitalized as if it were an entire sentence. It is an especially disruptive error because it obscures the connections that the words of a sentence must make in order to complete the reader's understanding.

Students sometimes write fragments because they are concerned, looking back, that a sentence they have composed needs to be shortened. Remember that cutting the length of a sentence merely by adding a period somewhere often creates a fragment. When checking a piece of writing for fragments, it is essential that you read each sentence carefully to determine whether it has (1) a complete subject and a verb; and (2) a subordinating word before the subject and verb, which makes the construction a subordinate clause rather than a complete sentence.

Some fragments lack a verb:

INCORRECT The chairperson of our committee, receiving a letter from the professor. (Watch out for words that look like verbs but are being used in another way—in this example, the word *receiving.*)

CORRECT The chairperson of our committee received a letter from the professor.

Some fragments lack a subject:

INCORRECT Our study shows that there is broad support for improvement in the application review system. And in the unemployment system.

CORRECT Our study shows that there is broad support for improvement in the application review system and in the unemployment system.

Some fragments are subordinate clauses:

INCORRECT After the latest edition of the newspaper came out. (This clause has the two major components of a complete sentence: a subject [*edition*] and a verb [*came*]. Indeed, if the first word [*After*] were deleted, the clause would be a complete sentence. But that first word is a *subordinating word*, which prevents the following clause from standing on its own as a complete sentence. Watch out for this kind of construction. It is called a *subordinate clause*, and it is not a sentence.)

CORRECT   After the latest edition of the newspaper came out, the professor's secretary was overwhelmed with phone calls. (A common method of correcting a subordinate clause that has been punctuated as a complete sentence is to connect it to the complete sentence to which it is closest in meaning.)

INCORRECT   Several representatives asked for copies of the philosopher's position paper. Which, by the way, was his second call for the reform of academic standards.

CORRECT   Several representatives asked for copies of the philosopher's position paper, which, by the way, was his second call for the reform of academic standards.

Spelling

We all have problems spelling certain words that we have not yet committed to memory. But most writers are not as bad at spelling as they believe they are. Usually an individual finds only a handful of words troubling. It is important to be as sensitive as possible to your own particular spelling problems—and to keep a dictionary handy. There is no excuse for failing to check spelling.

What follows are a list of commonly confused words and a list of commonly misspelled words. Read through the lists, looking for those words that tend to give you trouble. If you have any questions, consult your dictionary.

Commonly Confused Words

accept/except	envelop/envelope	principal/principle
advice/advise	every day/everyday	quiet/quite
affect/effect	fair/fare	rain/reign/rein
aisle/isle	formally/formerly	raise/raze
allusion/illusion	forth/fourth	reality/realty
an/and	hear/here	respectfully/respectively
angel/angle	heard/herd	reverend/reverent
ascent/assent	hole/whole	right/rite/write
bare/bear	human/humane	road/rode
brake/break	its/it's	scene/seen
breath/breathe	know/no	sense/since
buy/by	later/latter	stationary/stationery
capital/capitol	lay/lie	straight/strait
choose/chose	lead/led	taught/taut
cite/sight/site	lessen/lesson	than/then
complement/compliment	loose/lose	their/there/they're
conscience/conscious	may be/maybe	threw/through

corps/corpse
council/counsel
dairy/diary
descent/dissent
desert/dessert
device/devise
die/dye
dominant/dominate
elicit/illicit
eminent/immanent/
   imminent

miner/minor
moral/morale
of/off
passed/past
patience/patients
peace/piece
personal/personnel
plain/plane
precede/proceed
presence/presents

too/to/two
track/tract
waist/waste
waive/wave
weak/week
weather/whether
were/where
which/witch
whose/who's
your/you're

Commonly Misspelled Words

acceptable
accessible
accommodate
accompany
accustomed
acquire
against
annihilate
apparent
arguing
argument
authentic
before
begin
beginning
believe
benefited
bulletin
business
cannot
category
committee
condemn
courteous
definitely
dependent
desperate
develop
different
disappear
disappoint
easily
efficient
environment

hurriedly
hypocrite
ideally
immediately
immense
incredible
innocuous
intercede
interrupt
irrelevant
irresistible
irritate
knowledge
license
likelihood
maintenance
manageable
meanness
millennial
mischievous
missile
necessary
nevertheless
no one
noticeable
noticing
nuisance
occasion
occasionally
occurred
occurrences
omission
omit
opinion

realize
receipt
received
recession
recommend
referring
religious
remembrance
reminisce
repetition
representative
rhythm
ridiculous
roommate
satellite
scarcity
scenery
science
secede
secession
secretary
senseless
separate
sergeant
shining
significant
sincerely
skiing
stubbornness
studying
succeed
success
successfully
susceptible

equipped	opponent	suspicious
exceed	parallel	technical
exercise	parole	temporary
existence	peaceable	tendency
experience	performance	therefore
fascinate	pertain	tragedy
finally	practical	truly
foresee	preparation	tyranny
forty	probably	unanimous
fulfill	process	unconscious
gauge	professor	undoubtedly
guaranteed	prominent	until
guard	pronunciation	vacuum
harass	psychology	valuable
hero	publicly	various
heroes	pursue	vegetable
humorous	pursuing	visible
hurried	questionnaire	without
		women

Read & Write 3.2 Proofread for the President

It's January 1941, and you're a staffer for the thirty-second president of the United States. Franklin Roosevelt is about to make one of the most important speeches of his presidency, and it's your job to proofread the text before it can be printed for the world to read. There are fifteen errors embedded in the copy of the speech that appears below this paragraph. As you locate the errors, circle them with a pencil. When you have finished, check the error key on the following page. Below the error key you'll find a copy of this selection from Roosevelt's speech as it was originally published without the embedded errors.

A Selection from "Franklin D. Roosevelts' 'Four Freedoms Speech' Annual Message to Congress on the State of the Union", January 6, 1941.

In the future days, which we seek to make secure, we look forward to a world founded upon four essential human freedoms.

The first is freedom of speach and expression—everywhere in the world.

The second is freedom of every person to worship God in their own way—everywhere in the world.

The third is freedom from want—which translated into world terms, means economic understandings which will secure to every nation a healthy peacetime life for it's inhabitants everywhere in the world.

The fourth is freedom from fear—which, translated into world terms, means a world-wide reduction of armaments to such a point and in such a thorough fashion that no nation will be in a position to commit an act of physical aggression against any neighbor—anywhere in the world.

That is no vision of a distant milennium it is a definite basis for a kind of world attainable in our own time and generation. That kind of world is the very antithesis of the so-called new order of tyranny which the dictator's seek to create with the crash of a bomb.

To that new order we oppose the greater conception—the moral order, a good society is able to face schemes of world domination and foreign revolutions alike without fear.

Since the beginning of our American history; we have been engaged in change—in a perpetual peaceful revolution—a revolution which goes on steady, quietly adjusting itself to changing conditions—without the concentration camp or the quick-lime in the ditch. The world order which we seek is the cooperation of free countries. Working together in a friendly, civilized society.

This nation has placed it's destiny in the hands and heads and hearts of its millions of free men and women; and its faith in freedom under the guidance of God. Freedom means the supremacy of human rights everywhere, our support goes to those who struggle to gain those rights or keep them. Our strength is our unity of purpose. To that high concept there can be no end save victory.

Key to "Find the Errors"

The letters, words, and punctuation in **bold font** and underlined below indicate locations of grammar, spelling, and other errors. You can also check the original, error-free copy to find the correct forms of grammar and usage.

A Selection from "Franklin D. Roosevelt**s**' 'Four Freedoms Speech' Annual Message to Congress on the State of the Union**",** January 6, 1941.

In the future days, which we seek to make secure, we look forward to a world founded upon four essential human freedoms.

The first is freedom of spe**a**ch and expression—everywhere in the world.

The second is freedom of every person to worship God in **their** own way—everywhere in the world.

> **Note:** Nowadays, it is becoming acceptable, in certain types of writing, to allow the plural *their* to stand in place of *his*, which is considered sexist. Another acceptable alternative is *his or her*. Think about what pronoun to use when you come to such a circumstance.

The third is freedom from want—whic**h** translated into world terms, means economic understandings which will secure to every nation a healthy peacetime life for **it's** inhabitants everywhere in the world.

The fourth is freedom from fear—which, translated into world terms, means a worldwide reduction of armaments to such a point and in such a thorough fashion that no nation will be in a position to commit an act of physical aggression against any neighbor—anywhere in the world.

That is no vision of a distant mil**e**nnium**, it** is a definite basis for a kind of world attainable in our own time and generation. That kind of world is the very antithesis of the so-called new order of tyranny which the dictator**'s** seek to create with the crash of a bomb.

To that new order we oppose the greater conception—the moral order**, a** good society is able to face schemes of world domination and foreign revolutions alike without fear.

Since the beginning of our American history**;** we have been engaged in change—in a perpetual peaceful revolution—a revolution which goes on stead**y,** quietly adjusting itself to changing conditions—without the concentration camp or the quick-lime in the ditch. The world order which we seek is the cooperation of free countries**. W**orking together in a friendly, civilized society.

This nation has placed **it's** destiny in the hands and heads and hearts of its millions of free men and women; and its faith in freedom under the guidance of God. Freedom means the supremacy of human rights everywhere**, o**ur support goes to those who struggle to gain those rights or keep them. Our strength is our unity of purpose. To that high concept there can be no end save victory.

Original Four Freedoms Speech

A Selection from "Franklin D. Roosevelt's 'Four Freedoms Speech' Annual Message to Congress on the State of the Union," January 6, 1941.

In the future days, which we seek to make secure, we look forward to a world founded upon four essential human freedoms.

The first is freedom of speech and expression—everywhere in the world.

The second is freedom of every person to worship God in his own way—everywhere in the world.

The third is freedom from want—which, translated into world terms, means economic understandings which will secure to every nation a healthy peacetime life for its inhabitants everywhere in the world.

The fourth is freedom from fear—which, translated into world terms, means a worldwide reduction of armaments to such a point and in such a thorough fashion that no nation will be in a position to commit an act of physical aggression against any neighbor—anywhere in the world.

That is no vision of a distant millennium. It is a definite basis for a kind of world attainable in our own time and generation. That kind of world is the very antithesis of the so-called new order of tyranny which the dictators seek to create with the crash of a bomb.

To that new order we oppose the greater conception—the moral order. A good society is able to face schemes of world domination and foreign revolutions alike without fear.

Since the beginning of our American history, we have been engaged in change—in a perpetual peaceful revolution—a revolution which goes on steadily, quietly adjusting itself to changing conditions—without the concentration camp or the quick-lime in the ditch. The world order which we seek is the cooperation of free countries, working together in a friendly, civilized society.

This nation has placed its destiny in the hands and heads and hearts of its millions of free men and women; and its faith in freedom under the guidance of God. Freedom means the supremacy of human rights everywhere. Our support goes to those who struggle to gain those rights or keep them. Our strength is our unity of purpose. To that high concept there can be no end save victory.[2]

3.3 FORMAT YOUR PAPER AND ITS CONTENTS PROFESSIONALLY

Your format makes your paper's first impression. Justly or not, accurately or not, it announces your professional competence—or lack of competence. A well-executed format implies that your paper is worth reading. More important, however, a proper format brings information to your readers in a familiar form that has the effect of setting their minds at ease. Your paper's format should therefore impress your readers with your academic competence as a philosopher by following accepted professional standards. Like the style and clarity of your writing, your format communicates messages that are often more readily and profoundly received than the content of the document itself.

The formats described in this chapter conform with generally accepted standards in the discipline of philosophy, including instructions for the following elements:

General page formats
Title page
Abstract
Outline page
Table of contents
Text
Chapter headings
Reference page
Tables, Illustrations, Figures, Appendices

Except for special instructions from your instructor, follow the directions in this manual exactly.

General Page Formats

Philosophy assignments should be printed on eight-and-a-half-by-eleven-inch premium white bond paper, twenty pound or heavier. Do not use any other size or color except to comply with special instructions from your instructor, and do not use off-white or poor quality (draft) paper. Philosophy that is worth the time to write and read is worth good paper.

---

[2] Franklin D. Roosevelt, "'Four Freedoms Speech': Annual Message to Congress on the State of the Union," Franklin D. Roosevelt Presidential Library and Museum, https://fdrlibrary.org/four-freedoms.

Always submit to your instructor an original typed or computer-printed manuscript. Do not submit a photocopy! Always make a second paper copy and back up your electronic copy for your own files in case the original is lost.

Margins, except in theses and dissertations, should be one inch on all sides of the paper. Unless otherwise instructed, all papers should be double-spaced in a twelve-point word-processing font or typewriter pica type. Typewriter elite type may be used if another is not available. Select a font that is plain and easy to read, such as Helvetica, Courier, Garamond, or Times Roman. Do not use script, stylized, or elaborate fonts.

Page numbers should appear in the upper right-hand corner of each page, starting immediately after the title page. No page number should appear on the title page or on the first page of the text. Page numbers should appear one inch from the right side and one-half inch from the top of the page. They should proceed consecutively beginning with the title page (although the first number is not actually printed on the title page). You may use lowercase roman numerals (i, ii, iii, iv, v, vi, vii, viii, ix, x, and so on) for the pages, such as the title page, table of contents, and table of figures, that precede the first page of text, but if you use them, the numbers must be placed at the center of the bottom of the page.

Ask your instructor about bindings. In the absence of further directions, do not bind your paper or enclose it within a plastic cover sheet. Place one staple in the upper left-hand corner, or use a paper clip at the top of the paper. Note that a paper to be submitted to a journal for publication should not be clipped, stapled, or bound in any form.

Title Page

The following information will be centered on the title page:

Title of the paper

Name of writer

Course name, section number, and instructor

College or university

Date

The Moral Paradox of Deontology as a Guide to Living

by

Nicole Ashley Linscheid

Introduction to Philosophy

PHIL 101

Dr. Chad Elderberry

Bay of Fundy University

January 1, 2017

As the sample title page above shows, the title should clearly describe the topic addressed in the paper. Note how this title locates the paper's topic within the question of deontology's practical effectiveness as a code of behavior. Titles such as "Deontology" or "Disadvantages of Deontology" are too vague to be effective.

Abstract

An abstract is a brief summary of a paper written primarily to allow potential readers to see if the paper contains information of sufficient interest for them to read. People conducting research want specific kinds of information, and they often read dozens of abstracts looking for papers that contain relevant data. Abstracts have the designation "Abstract" centered near the top of the page. Next is the title, also centered, followed by a paragraph that precisely states the paper's topic, research and analysis methods, and results and conclusions. The abstract should be written in one paragraph of no more than 150 words. Remember, an abstract is not an introduction; instead, it is a summary, as demonstrated in the sample below.

Abstract
Bertrand Russell's View of Mysticism

This paper reviews Bertrand Russell's writings on religion, mysticism, and science, and defines his perspective of the contribution of mysticism to scientific knowledge. Russell drew a sharp distinction between what he considered to be (1) the essence of religion, and (2) dogma or assertions attached to religion by theologians and religious leaders. Although some of his writings, including *Why I Am Not a Christian*, appear hostile to all aspects of religion, Russell actually asserts that religion, freed from doctrinal encumbrances, not only fulfills certain psychological needs but evokes many of the most beneficial human impulses. He believes that religious mysticism generates an intellectual disinterestedness that may be useful to science, but that it is not a source of a special type of knowledge beyond investigation by science.

Outline Page

Chapter 2 discusses two different types of outlines: one that can help the writer of the paper as he or she works to construct a draft, and one that can help the reader of the paper get a secure grasp of the paper's goals and direction once the paper's text is established. The second of these outline types is the one that constitutes the outline page described below.

Most often found in position papers and policy analysis papers, an outline page shows clearly the sections in the paper and the information in each. An outline page is an asset because it allows readers to understand the overall shape of the paper's argument before reading the complete text, or to refer quickly to a specific part for more information. Position papers and policy analysis papers are written for people in positions of authority who normally need to make a variety of decisions in a short period. Outline pages reduce the amount of time these people need to understand a policy problem, the alternative solutions, and the author's preferred solution.

Outline pages sequentially list the complete topic sentences of the major paragraphs of a paper, in outline form. In a position paper, for example, you will be stating a problem, defining possible solutions, and then recommending the best solution. These three steps will be the major headings in your outline. Wait until you have completed the paper before writing the outline page. Take the topic sentences from the leading (most important) paragraph in each section of your paper and place them in the appropriate places in your outline. See the sample outline on page 32 of chapter 2.

Table of Contents

A table of contents does not provide as much information as an outline, but it does include the titles of the major divisions and subdivisions of a paper. Tables of contents are not normally required in student papers or papers presented at professional meetings, but they may be included. They are normally required, however, in books, theses, and dissertations. The table of contents should consist of the chapter or main section titles, and the headings used in the text, with one additional level of titles, along with their page numbers, as the sample below demonstrates.

Contents

Text

Ask your instructor for the number of pages required for the paper you are writing. Use the page formats given in this chapter.

Chapter Headings

Your paper should include no more than three levels of headings:

1. *Primary*, which should be centered, in boldface, and use headline-style capitalization (each word except articles, prepositions, and conjunctions capitalized).

2. *Secondary*, which begins at the left margin, in boldface, and use headline-style capitalization.

3. *Tertiary*, which also begins at the left margin, uses headline-style capitalization, but is underlined instead of boldfaced and followed immediately by a period and then the first line of the succeeding text.

The following illustration shows the proper use of chapter headings:

Immanuel Kant   (Primary Heading)

Kant's Deontology   (Secondary Heading)

<u>Kant's Categorical Imperative</u>. The earliest mention of . . .   (Tertiary Heading)

Reference Page

The format for references is discussed in detail in section 3.4 of this chapter.

Tables, Figures, Illustrations, Appendices

List of Tables, Illustrations, and Figures   If your paper includes tables, illustrations, or figures, include a page after "Contents," and list each of them as they are named in the paper's text. List the items in the order in which they appear in the paper, along with their page numbers. You may list tables, illustrations, and figures together under the title "Figures" (and refer to them all as "figures" in the text), or if you have more than a half page of entries, you may have separate lists for tables, illustrations, and figures (and you would title the objects accordingly in the text). An example of the format for such lists is shown below.

Figures	
1. Population Growth in Five US Cities, 1990–2016	1
2. Welfare Recipients by State, 1980 and 2016	3
3. Economic Indicators, January–June 2015	6
4. Educational Reforms at the Tennessee Convention	11
5. International Trade, 1980–2015	21
6. Gross Domestic Product, Nova Scotia, 1900–2015	22
7. California Domestic Program Expenditures, 1960–2015	35
8. Juvenile Recidivism in Illinois	37
9. Albuquerque Arts and Humanities Expenditures, 2016	39
10. Railroad Retirement Payments after World War II	42

Tables   Tables are used in the text to show relationships among data, to help the reader come to a conclusion or understand a certain point. Tables that show simple results or "raw" data should be placed in an appendix. Tables should not reiterate the content of the text. They should say something new, and they should stand on their own. In other words, the reader should be able to understand the table without reading the text. Clearly label the columns and rows in the table. Each word in the title (except articles, prepositions, and conjunctions) should be capitalized. The source of the information should be shown immediately below the table, not in a footnote or endnote. See table 3.1 for a sample.

TABLE 3.1

Projections of the Total Population of Selected States, 2015–2035 (in thousands)

State	2015	2025	2030	2035
Alabama	4,451	4,631	4,956	5,224
Illinois	12,051	12,266	12,808	13,440
Maine	1,259	1,285	1,362	1,423
New Mexico	1,860	2,016	2,300	2,612
Oklahoma	3,373	3,491	3,789	4,057
Tennessee	5,657	5,966	6,365	6,665
Virginia	6,997	7,324	7,921	8,466

Source: US Census Bureau.

Illustrations and Figures   Illustrations are not normally inserted in the text of a philosophy paper or even in an appendix unless they are necessary to explain the content. If illustrations are necessary, do not paste or tape photocopies of photographs or similar materials to the text or the appendix. Instead, photocopy each one on a separate sheet of paper and center it, along with its typed title, within the normal margins of the paper. The format of illustration titles should be the same as that for tables and figures.

Figures in the form of charts and graphs may be very helpful in presenting certain types of information.

Appendices   Appendices are reference materials provided for the convenience of the reader at the back of the paper, after the text. Providing information that supplements the important facts in the text, they may include maps, charts, tables, and other selected documents. Do not place materials that are merely interesting or decorative in your appendix. Use only items that will answer questions raised by the text or are necessary to explain the text. Follow the guidelines for formats for tables, illustrations, and figures when adding material in an appendix. At the top center of the page, label your first appendix "Appendix A," your second appendix "Appendix B," and so on. Do not append an entire government report, journal article, or other publication, but only the portions of such documents that are necessary to support your paper. The source of the information should always be evident on the appended pages.

Read&Write 3.3 Explain the Data in This Table

Your assignment in this chapter is to

1. Locate, using the sources of information described above, a currently posted chart or table of statistics compiled by a government agency on a topic of your choice.
2. Write a "Data Interpretation Essay" in which you *interpret* what this table tells you, and
3. Find an independent source of information that corroborates your interpretation of the data.

The following sample data and essay will serve as a model to help guide your efforts in completing this exercise.

SAMPLE DATA AND ESSAY

Data Interpretation Essay:

Civilian Casualties in Japan in World War II

Ariana Allen

Sociology 101

Dr. Harry Longabaugh

Sundance University

February 28, 2017

Having enjoyed the opportunity to participate in a study group tour to Japan in the summer of 2016, I decided to explore population growth in Japanese cities from 1900 to the present. I found some interesting trends, especially in the period from 1940 to 1947. From a table that covered a wider time period, I selected the data provided for my chosen time period. The following table, therefore, presents an abridged set of data derived from *Statistics Japan*, published by the Statistics Bureau, Ministry of Internal Affairs and Communications, nation of Japan, through this web portal: http://www.stat.go.jp /english/info/guide/2014guide.htm. The data in the table represent a partial compilation of data from the document *Population of Cities (1920–2015)* (Excel: 37KB), located on this website: http://www.stat.go.jp/english/data/chouki/02.htm.

Population of Selected Japanese Cities, 1940–1947

City	Population		Change, 1940–1947
	1940	1947	
Sendai-shi	223,630	293,816	70,186
Yamaguchi-shi	34,579	97,975	63,396
Akita-shi	61,791	116,300	54,509

Niigata-shi	150,903	204,477	53,574
Sapporo-shi	206,103	259,602	53,499
Kumamoto-shi	194,139	245,841	51,702
Saitama-shi	59,671	106,176	46,505
Kanazawa-shi	186,297	231,441	45,144
Kochi-shi	106,644	147,120	40,476
Fukushima-shi	48,287	86,763	38,476
Matsuyama-shi	117,534	147,967	30,433
Chiba-shi	92,061	122,006	29,945
Yamagata-shi	69,184	98,632	29,448
Morioka-shi	79,478	107,096	27,618
Miyazaki-shi	66,497	92,144	25,647
Nara-shi	57,273	82,399	25,126
Fukuoka-shi	306,763	328,548	21,785
Nagano-shi	76,861	94,993	18,132
Saga-shi	50,406	64,978	14,572
Otsu-shi	67,532	81,426	13,894
Toyama-shi	127,859	137,818	9,959
Oita-shi	76,985	86,570	9,585
Utsunomiya-shi	87,868	97,075	9,207
Tottori-shi	49,261	57,218	7,957
Matsue-shi	55,506	62,136	6,630
Maebashi-shi	86,997	90,432	3,435
Kofu-shi	102,419	104,993	2,574
Tsu-shi	68,625	68,662	37
Mito-shi	66,293	61,416	−4,877
Gifu-shi	172,340	166,995	−5,345
Shizuoka-shi	212,198	205,737	−6,461
Aomori-shi	99,065	90,828	−8,237
Takamatsu-shi	111,207	101,403	−9,804
Tokushima-shi	119,581	103,320	−16,261
Fukui-shi	94,595	77,320	−17,275
Kagoshima-shi	190,257	170,416	−19,841
Okayama-shi	163,552	140,631	−22,921
Wakayama-shi	195,203	171,800	−23,403
Kawasaki-shi	300,777	252,923	−47,854
Nagasaki-shi	252,630	198,642	−53,988
Kyoto-shi	1,089,726	999,660	−90,066
Hiroshima-shi	343,968	224,100	−119,868
Yokohama-shi	968,091	814,379	−153,712
Kobe-shi	967,234	607,079	−360,155
Nagoya-shi	1,328,084	853,085	−474,999
Osaka-shi	3,252,340	1,559,310	−1,693,030
Ku-area	6,778,804	4,177,548	−2,601,256
Total change			−4,925,902

Even without confirmation from other historical or statistical resources, an examination of this chart detailing the population changes in select Japanese cities over a brief but very significant span of time in the middle of the twentieth century leads to one overwhelming conclusion: War is hell—especially a war that features the widespread aerial bombardment of cities. Two salient features of the chart back this interpretation: the specific time period for which the statistics have been taken and the sharp contrast between the group of Japanese cities that lost population during these dates and the group that gained population.

The Second World War began in 1939 and ended in 1945, a time that coincides closely with the time represented by the chart's statistics, 1940 to 1947. It is common knowledge that during the beginning of the war as it was fought in the Pacific, the Japanese, expanding out from their island, enjoyed many victories and added much territory to their empire. It is just as well known that, by the end of the war, their empire had shrunk back almost exclusively to the contours of the main island. In those last days of the war, the Allies dropped hundreds of tons of bombs on Japanese cities either to prepare the island for an Allied invasion or to compel unconditional surrender from the Japanese without the need of an invasion.

The cities in the chart describe a dramatic pattern of population shift, with slightly less than half of them (twenty-two) losing thousands of inhabitants over the time period covered by the chart, and a slightly larger number (twenty-seven) experiencing an intensive population increase. The likeliest reason for this shift is the devastation of Allied bombing, which suggests that the time in which much of the shift actually took place occupies only a fraction of the chart's time frame, say, 1944 to 1945. How harrowing it is to observe that the population increases in those cities that grew in size are not nearly as large as the decreases in population of those cities that lost inhabitants. Sendai-shi, the city that had the highest growth in population, added an amazing total of 70,186 inhabitants, but Ku-area, the city with the biggest decrease, lost a staggering 2,601,256 people. The total change in population density, as reported in the chart, reveals a loss, over these war years, of almost five million people. Since statistical sources estimate that Japan's military casualties in World War II amount to between 2 and 2.5 million, perhaps as many as three million Japanese died in America's conventional-weapon bombing campaign.

Why these specific cities? It is likely to assume that those losing population were industrial centers, prime targets for the Allied strategists working to destroy Japan's ability to wage war. People from the devastated cities must have struggled to reach the safety of cities not directly concerned with the war effort and, therefore, not targeted by the bombers. But two cities famously don't fit the profile: Hiroshima, which according to the chart lost 119,868 of its citizens, and Nagasaki, which lost 53,988. These cities, neither of which contributed significantly to the Japanese war effort, were chosen by the Allies for a special bombardment, namely, the first two—and, so far, the only two—deployments of the atom bomb on civilian populations.

In essence, this population chart serves to underscore the effectiveness of the bombing campaign that ended World War II. But hidden in its numbers is the incalculable cost, in human terms, of that campaign. In order to determine if *our interpretation* of the data in our chart is correct, we need to find an independent source of information that corroborates our conclusion. One source is director Errol Morris's Academy Award–winning documentary *The Fog of War*, in which former secretary of defense Robert McNamara recounts his firsthand participation, as a military intelligence officer in World War II, in planning and executing the conventional fire-bombing campaigns that resulted in the approximately three million civilian casualties indicated as highly likely by the data in our chart.

3.4 CITE YOUR SOURCES PROPERLY

One of your most important jobs when you write a research paper is to document your use of source material carefully and clearly. Failure to do so causes confusion in your reader, damages the effectiveness of your paper, and perhaps makes you vulnerable to a charge of plagiarism. Proper documentation is more than just good form. It is a powerful indicator of your own commitment to scholarship and the sense of authority that you bring to your writing. Good documentation demonstrates your expertise as a researcher and increases your reader's trust in you and your work.

Unfortunately, as anybody who has ever written a research paper knows, getting the documentation right can be a frustrating, confusing job, especially if you are not familiar with the documentation system you are trying to use. Accurately positioning each element of a single reference citation can require a lot of time spent looking through the style manual. Even before you begin to work on the specific citations for your paper, there are important questions of style and format to answer.

What to Document

You must always credit direct quotes, as well as certain kinds of paraphrased material. Information that is basic—important dates, universally acknowledged facts, or commonly held opinions—need not be cited. Information that is not widely known, however, should receive documentation. This type of material includes ideas, evaluations, critiques, and descriptions original to your source.

What if you are unsure whether a certain fact is an academic "given" or sufficiently unique to warrant a citation? You are, after all, probably a newcomer to the field in which you are conducting your research. If in doubt, supply the documentation. It is better to overdocument than to fail to do justice to a source.

The Choice of Style

There are several documentation styles available, each designed to meet the needs of researchers in particular fields. The reference systems approved by the Modern Language Association (MLA) and the American Psychological Association (APA) are often used in the humanities and the social sciences and could serve the needs of the philosophy student. But perhaps the most universally approved of all documentation authorities is the *Chicago Manual of Style* (*CMOS*), and it is this authority, currently in its sixteenth edition (2010), that serves as the basis for the documentation models in this chapter.

The Importance of Consistency

The most important rule regarding documentation of your work is to *be consistent*. Sloppy referencing undermines your reader's trust and does disservice to the writers whose work you are using in your own argument. And from a purely practical standpoint, inconsistent referencing can severely damage your grade.

Using the Style Manual

Read through the guidelines in the following pages before trying to use them to structure your notes. Unpracticed student researchers tend to ignore this section of the style manual until the moment the first note has to be worked out, and then they skim through the examples looking for the one that perfectly corresponds to the immediate case in hand. But most style manuals do not include every possible documentation model, so the writer must piece together a coherent reference out of elements from several examples. Reading through all the examples before using them can give you a feel for the placement of information in citations for different kinds of sources—such as magazine articles, book chapters, government documents, and electronic texts—as well as for how the referencing system works in general.

The Documentary-Note System

General Format Rules   The sixteenth edition of *CMOS* describes two different source citation systems, the documentary-note system (chapter 14 of *CMOS*) and the author-date system (chapter 15 of *CMOS*), but notes the greater flexibility of the former system, whose notes may be used easily for a range of purposes. Perhaps for this reason the sixteenth edition of *CMOS* covers the documentary-note system somewhat more fully than the author-date system. This manual focuses exclusively on the documentary-note system, which requires the placement of a superscript (raised) number after a passage that includes source material in need of citation. The superscript number refers to a bibliographical citation given either at the foot of the page (a footnote) or in a numerically ordered list at the end of the paper (an endnote).

Numbering System for a College Paper   Number the notes consecutively throughout the entire paper, starting with 1. In other words, do not restart with 1 at the beginning of each new chapter or section of the paper, as many published works, including this manual, do.

Placement of Superscript Numeral   Whenever possible, the superscript numeral should go at the end of the sentence:

> Rorty's representation of Sellars as an eliminative materialist is radically mistaken.[1]

If it is necessary to place the reference within a sentence instead of at the end, position the numeral at the end of the pertinent clause.

> In his last editorial Bagley denounces the current city administration[13]— and thousands of others feel the same way.

Notice in the example above that the superscript numeral occurs before the dash. For all other pieces of punctuation—comma, semicolon, period, exclamation mark, question mark—the superscript numeral follows the punctuation. The numeral also follows the terminal quotation mark of a direct quote:

> "This clause," claimed Lindley, "is the most crucial one in the address."[20]

Multiple Notes   When a passage refers to more than one source, do not place more than one superscript numeral after the passage. Instead, use only one numeral, and combine all the references into a single footnote or endnote:

Separate studies by Lovett, Morrison, Collins, and the Anderson Group all corroborate the state's findings.[7]

Models for Documentary Notes and Bibliographical Citations

Each pair of models below include a documentary note followed by its corresponding bibliographical entry. Again, the note may appear either as a footnote or as an endnote. Many word processors are able to change notes from one style to the other.

Differences between Endnotes and Bibliography   In the paper's final draft, your endnotes will precede the bibliography, which is usually the final element in the paper. Because its entries are arranged alphabetically, the order of entries in the bibliography will differ from the order of the endnotes, which are arranged according to the appearance of the references within the text. Pay attention to the basic differences between the note format and the bibliography format. Notes are numbered; bibliographical entries are not. The first line of a note is indented; in a bibliography all lines are indented except the first, a format commonly called a *hanging indent*. Some word processing programs, including MS Word, provide a command for a hanging indent. It is always better to use such a command than to try to create a hanging indent manually by tabbing indentions for the second and all subsequent lines in a citation. This sort of "homemade" hanging indent will create unwanted gaps in your citation if you find you have to revise it.

While the author's name is printed in normal order in a note, the order is reversed in the bibliography—but only for the first author named—to facilitate alphabetizing.

If the note refers to a book or an article in its entirety, you need not cite specific page numbers in your references. If, however, you wish to cite material on a specific page or set of pages, give the page numbers in the note.

Books

One Author

Note:

1. Amanda Collingwood, *Metaphysics and the Public* (Detroit: Zane Press, 2017), 235–38.

Bibliography:

Collingwood, Amanda. *Metaphysics and the Public*. Detroit: Zane Press, 2017.

Two Authors

Note:

6. Delbert P. Grady and Jane Ryan Torrance, *Philosophers and Their Secrets* (New York: Holograph Press, 1989), 57.

Bibliography:

Grady, Delbert P., and Jane Ryan Torrance. *Philosophers and Their Secrets.* New York: Holograph Press, 1989.

Three Authors

Note:

2. Samuel Howard, William J. Abbott, and Jane Hope, *Powerbase: How to Increase Your Hold on Your Fellow Philosophy Students* (Los Angeles: Gollum and Smythe, 2015), 160–62.

Bibliography:

Howard, Samuel, William J. Abbot, and Jane Hope. *Powerbase: How to Increase Your Hold on Your Fellow Philosophy Students.* Los Angeles: Gollum and Smythe, 2015.

More Than Three Authors   In an in-text citation, the Latin phrase *et al.*, meaning "and others," appears, in roman type, after the name of the first author. Note that *al.* (an abbreviation for *alia*) must be followed by a period. In the bibliography, include all the authors' names, reversing the order of the first author's name.

Note:

21. Angela Genessario et al., *Religion and the Child* (Baltimore: Colgate, 2011), 16–18, 78–82.

Bibliography:

Genessario, Angela, Bette Freede, John Boland, Ransom Stoddard, and Elizabeth Bennett. *Religion and the Child.* Baltimore: Colgate, 2011.

Editor, Compiler, or Translator as Author

Note:

6. Dylan Trakas, comp., *Teaching Philosophy* (El Paso, TX: Del Norte Press, 2016).

Bibliography:

Trakas, Dylan, comp. *Teaching Philosophy.* El Paso, TX: Del Norte Press, 2016.

Editor, Compiler, or Translator with Author

Note:

15. Ezra Pound, *Literary Essays*, ed. T. S. Eliot (New York: New Directions, 1953), 48.

47. Philippe Aris, *Centuries of Childhood: A Social History of Family Life*, trans. Robert Baldock (New York: Knopf, 1962).

Bibliography:

Aris, Philippe. *Centuries of Childhood: A Social History of Family Life*. Translated by Robert Baldock. New York: Knopf, 1962.
Pound, Ezra. *Literary Essays*. Edited by T. S. Eliot. New York: New Directions, 1953.

Untranslated Book

Note:

8. Henri Cesbron, *Histoire critique de l'hystérie* (Paris: Asselin et Houzeau, 1909), 76.

Bibliography:

Cesbron, Henri. *Histoire critique de l'hystérie*. Paris: Asselin et Houzeau, 1909.

Untranslated Book with Title Translated, in Parentheses

Note:

53. Henryk Wereszyncki, *Koniec sojuszu trzech cesarzy* (The end of the Three Emperors' League) (Warsaw: PWN, 1977), 231–33.

Bibliography:

Wereszyncki, Henryk. *Koniec sojuszu trzech cesarzy* (The end of the Three Emperors' League). Warsaw: PWN, 1977.

Two or More Works by the Same Author   In the notes, subsequent works by an author are handled exactly as the first work. In the bibliography, the works are listed alphabetically, with the author's name replaced by a three-em dash (six strokes of the hyphen) in all entries after the first.

Bibliography:

Russell, Henry. *Famous Last Words*. New Orleans: Liberty Publications, 1978.
———. *Famous Philosophical Debates*. Denver: Axel and Myers, 1988.

Author with Different Coauthors   In a bibliography, multiauthor works with the same first author but different subsequent authors are alphabetized according to the last names of the coauthors.

Chizy, Robert, and Oleanna Stang. *Heuristics in the Classroom: A Workbook*. 3rd ed. New York: Barban and Golz, 2013.
Chizy, Robert, and Jacob Thewlis. *The Ghost of an Argument: Socrates and the Undergraduate Classroom*. New York: Routledge, 2010.

Chapter in a Multiauthor Collection

Note:

23. Alexa North Gray, "American Philosophers and the USIA," in *Current Media Issues*, ed. Barbara Bonnard (New York: Boulanger, 1994), 193.

Bibliography:

Gray, Alexa North. "American Philosophers and the Foreign Press." In *Current Media Issues*, edited by Barbara Bonnard, 189–231. New York: Boulanger, 1994.

You may, if you wish, place the inclusive page numbers in either the note, following the publication information, or in the bibliographical entry, following the name of the editor. If the author of the article is also the editor of the book, you must place her or his name in both locations. If the entire book is written by the same author, do not specify the chapter in the bibliographical reference.

Author of a Foreword or Introduction It is not necessary to cite the author of a foreword or introduction in the bibliography unless you have used material from that author's contribution to the volume.

Note:

4. Isaac Chilcote, foreword to *Athens and Chicago*, by Henry Roos (New York: Raphael, 2017), xviii.

Bibliography:

Chilcote, Isaac. Foreword to *Athens and Chicago*, by Henry Roos, xvii–xxxii. New York: Raphael, 2017.

Subsequent Editions If you are using an edition of a book other than the first, you must cite the number of the edition, or use *Rev. ed.* (for "Revised edition"), in roman type, if there is no edition number.

Note:

43. Sarah Hales, *The Coming Ethics Wars*, 2nd ed. (Pittsburgh: Blue Skies, 2013).

Bibliography:

Hales, Sarah. *The Coming Ethics Wars*. 2nd ed. Pittsburgh: Blue Skies, 2013.

Multivolume Work If you are citing a multivolume work in its entirety, use the following format:

Note:

49. Charles Logan August Graybosch, *Philosophers Still Write the Darnedest Things*, 3 vols. (New York: Starkfield, 2011–15).

Bibliography:

Graybosch, Charles Logan August. *Philosophers Still Write the Darnedest Things*. 3 Vols. New York: Starkfield, 2011–15.

If you are citing only one of the volumes in a multivolume work, follow the format below:

Note:

    9. Madeleine Ronsard, *Philosophers on Sabbatical*, vol. 2 of *A History of Philosophy*, ed. Joseph M. Sayles (Boston: Renfrow, 2013), 342–47.

Bibliography:

Ronsard, Madeleine. *Philosophers on Sabbatical*. Vol. 2 of *A History of Philosophy*, edited by Joseph M. Sayles. Boston: Renfrow, 2013.

Reprints of Older Works   Include original publication details if they are important, as in the second example below:

Note:

    8. Sterling R. Adams, *Debate Strategies* (1964; repr., New York: Starkfield, 1988).
    12. Stacy J. Mooring and Hester Billups, *On the Head of a Pin: Talk of Heaven in the Nineteenth Century*, rev. ed. (London: Happenstance, 1958; Los Angeles: Apocrypha Press, 1978), 114–16. Citations refer to the Apocrypha edition.

Bibliography:

Adams, Sterling R. *Debate Strategies*. 1964. Reprint, New York: Starkfield, 1988.
Mooring, Stacy J., and Hester Billups. *On the Head of a Pin: Talk of Heaven in the Nineteenth Century*. Rev. ed. Los Angeles, Apocrypha Press, 1978. First published 1958 by Happenstance.

Modern Editions of Classics   Source references for classic Greek and Latin works should be given either in the text or in notes. Remember that the numbers used to identify parts of a classical text never change from edition to edition or from original language to translation.

Note:

    34. Horace, *Odes* 1.23–1.25.

It is not necessary to give the date of original publication of a classic work.

Note:

    24. Edmond Burke, *Reflections on the Revolution in France*, ed. J. G. A. Pocock (Indianapolis: Hackett, 1987).

Bibliography:

Burke, Edmond. *Reflections on the Revolution in France*. Edited by J. G. A. Pocock. Indianapolis: Hackett, 1987.

Periodicals

Journals   Journals are periodicals, usually published either monthly or quarterly, that specialize in printing serious scholarly articles in a particular field. One significant distinction between the note format and the bibliographical format for a journal article is that in the note you cite only those pages from which you took material from the article, while in the bibliography you report the *inclusive* (first and last) pages of the article.

Note that the name of the journal, italicized, is followed without punctuation by the volume number, which is always given in arabic numerals, even if it appears in the journal itself in roman numerals. The issue number may follow the volume number, preceded by the abbreviation "no.," in roman. While it is permissible to leave out the issue number in a journal with continuous pagination throughout the volume, it is never wrong to include it. Likewise, it is permissible to include the month (abbreviated or spelled out in full) or season of publication, though neither is required if the issue number is present.

Following the volume and issue numbers comes, in parentheses, the year—sometimes preceded by the month or season of publication—and, after the closing parenthesis, a colon and then the page numbers. Do not use "p." or "pp." to introduce the page numbers.

While it is permissible, when listing a range of pages, to give the full form of both first and last numbers (260–262), according to *CMOS* (9.60), it is preferable, if the first number in the range is greater than 100, to abbreviate the last number of the range in the ways modeled in this chapter of the manual. Whichever format you use for recording ranges of pages, be consistent.

Note:

17. Joseph Conlin, "Teaching the Toadies: Cronyism in Academic Philosophy," *Reason Today* 4, no. 2 (Summer 1987): 260–62.

Bibliography:

Conlin, Joseph. "Teaching the Toadies: Cronyism in Academic Philosophy." *Reason Today* 4, no. 2 (Summer 1987): 249–62.

Magazines   Magazines, which are usually published weekly, bimonthly, or monthly, appeal to the popular audience and generally have a wider circulation than journals. *U.S. News and World Report* and *Scientific American* are magazines. Whether published weekly, bimonthly, or monthly, magazines, unlike journals, are usually cited only by date; the volume and issue number are excluded from the citation.

Monthly Magazine

Note:

10. Bonnie Staples, "I Ate Lunch with Attila the Hun," *Lifelike Magazine*, April 2017, 22–25.

Bibliography:

Staples, Bonnie. "I Ate Lunch with Attila the Hun." *Lifelike Magazine*, April 2017, 22–25.

Weekly or Bimonthly Magazine

Note:

37. James Parker, "A Saint for Difficult People," Culture File, *Atlantic*, March 2017, 32–34.

Bibliography:

Parker, James. "A Saint for Difficult People." Culture File. *Atlantic*, March 2017, 32–24.

As the example above demonstrates, for entries that cite magazine titles beginning with *The*, this word is dropped in the citation. Note also that the title of a regular department in a magazine is given before the name of the magazine and is neither put in quotation marks nor italicized.

Newspapers Note that, just as it is for magazine titles, *The* is omitted from a newspaper's title in all English-language newspapers. If the name of the city in which an American newspaper is published does not appear in the paper's title, it should be appended, in roman and in parentheses, as in the second model below. If the city is not well known, you may add the postal abbreviation for the name of the state.

Notes:

5. Editorial, *New York Times*, August 10, 2010.
14. Fine, Austin, "Hoag on Trial," *Tribune* (Carrollton, TX), November 24, 2010.

According to *CMOS* (14.206), bibliographies usually do not include entries for articles from daily newspapers, which are usually documented within the text instead. If you wish to include such material, however, you may do so. In the event that the author of the newspaper article is unknown, begin the citation with the name of the newspaper, followed by the relevant date(s):

Bibliography:

Hobart Democrat-Chief. "Revival Shatters Attendance Records at FBC." July 27, 2016.

Additional suggestions for citations of newspaper material are offered in *CMOS* (14.203–11).

Public Documents

CMOS (14.281) lists published guides for the formatting of citations of legal works. Most citation examples in *CMOS* itself are based on formats found in *The Bluebook: A Uniform System of Citation*, available online (currently in its eighteenth edition, published by the *Harvard Law Review* Association, 2015). According to *CMOS* (14.283), legal works tend to document their sources only in notes, not in bibliographies, and as a result there are few models of bibliographical citations for legal works given in *CMOS*.

Laws and Statutes   Bills and resolutions that have been signed into law (sometimes called *statutes*) are first published separately, as slip laws, and then collected in annual bound volumes of the *United States Statues at Large* (abbreviated, in roman, as Stat.). Eventually they are added to the *United States Code* (USC), a multivolume set that is revised every six years. You should use the latest publication.

Citing to the Statutes at Large

Note:

22. National Institutes of Health Reform Act of 2016, Pub. L. 109-482, 120 Stat. 3675 (2017).

Citing to the United States Code

Note:

42. Privacy Act of 1974, 5 USC § 552a (2016).

In the model above, the name of the bill is followed by the "title" (one of the fifty-one sections of the code, categorized according to areas of legislation), in this case "5." The symbol § means "section," which, in this entry, is 552a. Not all bills will have a name; in such a case, start the reference with the title number.

US Constitution   In the documentary-note format, according to *CMOS* (15.367), the Constitution is cited by article or amendment, section (§), and, if relevant, clause. The Constitution is not to be listed in a bibliography. Use roman numerals for the article and amendment numbers, and arabic numerals for all other numerals.

Note:

23. U.S. Const. art. I, § 4, cl. 2.

Legal References   According to *CMOS* (14.288), case names should appear in roman, and subsequent, shortened references should appear in italics.

Supreme Court

Note:

73. State of Nevada v. Goldie Warren. 324 U.S. 123 (1969).

The "US" in the entry refers to *United States Supreme Court Reports*, which is where decisions of the Supreme Court have been published since 1875. Preceding the *US* in the note is the volume number; following are the page number, and the year in parentheses. Before 1875, Supreme Court decisions were published under the names of official court reporters. The following reference is to William Cranch, *Reports of Cases Argued and Adjudged in the Supreme Court of the United States,* 1801–1815, 9 vols. (Washington, DC, 1804–1817). The number preceding the clerk's name is the volume number; following the clerk's name are the page number, and year in parentheses:

8. Marbury v. Madison, 1 Cranch 137 (1803).

Lower courts   Decisions of lower federal courts are published in the *Federal Reporter* (*F.*) or to the *Federal Supplement* (*F. Supp.*). As in the example that follows, the note should give the volume of the *Federal Reporter* (*F.*), the series, if it is other than the first series (2d), the page number, and, in parentheses, an abbreviated reference to the specific court (in this case, the Second Circuit Court) and the year.

Note:

58. United States v. Sizemore, 183 F. 2d 201 (2d Cir. 1950).

Electronic Sources: CD-ROM and Similar Databases

Indicate the medium.

Note:

2. Ella Staropolska, *Thinking in Wartime* (Krakow, Poland: Visla, 2011). CD-ROM, 2.16.

Bibliography:

Staropolska, Ella. *Thinking in Wartime*. Krakow, Poland: Visla, 2011. CD-ROM.

Online Sources

In general, a reference for an online source should include as much of the information that would be present in a printed citation as possible, followed by information sufficient to allow a reader to find the source on the Internet.

Online Book   For separate publications, such as books or pamphlets, include in parentheses the place of publication, publisher, and date for the printed version, if known, followed by the URL or, if available, the DOI (digital object identifier). A DOI provides a potentially more permanent way to locate a document than a URL (uniform resource locator) and so is the preferred locator in a citation.

Online Book Located with DOI

Note:

7. Cornell Gaffe and Elliott Sweiss, *A Trick of the Eye: Data in the Soft Sciences* (New York: Elbow and Elbow, 2011), 34-36, doi:10.1900/7977.31.5.304.

Bibliography:

Gaffe, Cornell, and Elliott Sweiss. *A Trick of the Eye: Data in the Soft Sciences*. New York: Elbow and Elbow, 2011. doi:10.1900/7977.31.5.304.

The abbreviation "doi" is not capitalized in a citation, and there is no space between the colon and the following number string.

Online Book Located with URL

Note:

6. Eric C. Withnall, *Wars Just and Unjust: A Catalog* (New York: Grenfell, 2010), 162, http: //www.utex.bartleby.justwar.com.

Bibliography:

Withnall, Eric C. *Wars Just and Unjust: A Catalog*. New York: Grenfell, 2010. http://www.utex.bartleby.justwar.com.

According to *CMOS* (14.12), you should avoid breaking a URL or DOI at the end of a line in the text you are creating. If, however, it is necessary to break a locator at the end of a line, make the break after a colon or double slash (//), before a single slash (/), a tilde (~), a period, a comma, a hyphen, an underline, a question mark, a number sign, or a percent symbol (%). A URL may be broken at the end of a line either before or after an equals sign (=) or an ampersand (&). Never add a hyphen to signal a line break, and never allow a hyphen that is part of the URL to appear at the end of a line.

Online Periodicals

Because the task of transmitting material from a print version to an electronic version may introduce errors into the text, you should always try to use the print version of a periodical that appears in both print and electronic versions. If the only version available to you is the electronic one, make sure to include in your citation as much information regarding the print version as possible before giving the publication information of the electronic version, the date you accessed it, and its URL or, if available, its DOI.

Online journal

Note:

9. Rachel Harnness and Bonnie Samuelson, "The Philosopher in the Family: William James and His Brother," *Journal of Philosophy and History* 10, no. 2 (2011): 143, accessed March 17, 2012, http://www.ucavola.edu/jphilohist/home.htm.

Bibliography:

Harnness, Rachel, and Bonnie Samuelson. "The Philosopher in the Family: William James and His Brother." *Journal of Philosophy and History* 10, no. 2 (2011): 138–57. Accessed March 17, 2012. http://www.ucavola.edu/jphilohist /home.htm.

While *CMOS* (14.185) does not require you to supply access dates for formally published electronic sources, many paper assignments still require them. If necessary, insert the date you accessed an electronic source immediately following the page number and before the URL or DOI, as indicated in the model above.

Online magazine

Note:

134. Nora Squires, "Interviewing a Vanishing Man: Richard Blankenship outside the Classroom," *Midbrain Magazine*, April/May 2017, 53, doi:10.1806/433782.

Bibliography:

Squires, Nora. "Interviewing a Vanishing Man: Richard Blankenship outside the
   Classroom." *Midbrain Magazine*. April/May 2017, 51–54. doi:10.1806/433782.

Email   According to *CMOS* (14.222), personal communications such as email messages are usually identified as personal communications in the text or given in a note.
They do not usually appear in a bibliography.

Note:

   14. Eustice Flannery, email message to author, July 23, 2017.

   You must never publish an email address belonging to an individual unless you
have received permission from that individual to do so.

Blog Entries   Start the citation with the name of the author of the entry, followed
by the name of the entry, in quotation marks, the title of the blog (or a description
of the blog, if there is no title), the posting date, and the URL. If the blog has a
title, set it in italics. If the word *blog* does not appear as part of the blog's name, add
the word, in parentheses, after the name of the blog. If the posting date cannot be
determined, include the date on which you accessed the source, placing the word
"accessed" before the date:

Note:

   37. George Smalltop, "Too Wonderful for Words," *Smalltop's Smallthoughts*
(blog), accessed February 27, 2017, http://smalltop.blogspot.com/2016/12/birth
rights.html.

Bibliography:

Smalltop, George. "Too Wonderful for Words." *Smalltop's Smallthoughts* (blog).
   http://smalltop.blogspot.com/2016/12/birthrights.html.

   To cite a comment, start with the commenter's identity and the date of the comment, if available. If you have cited the blog entry in an earlier note, use a shortened
form, as in the example below.

   38. Congolia Breckenridge, December 30, 2016, comment on *Smalltop*, "Too
Wonderful for Words."

Interviews

A citation for an interview usually begins with the name of the person interviewed
or the name of the person from whom the information in the text was received. The
name of the interviewer comes second, if at all.

Published or Broadcast Interviews   You should treat an interview that has
been published or broadcast as you would an article in a periodical or a book
chapter. If you found the interview online, include the URL or, if available, the
DOI.

Untitled Interview in a Book

Note:

30. Mary Jorgenson, interview by Alan McAskill, in *Hospice Pioneers*, ed. Alan McAskill (Richmond: Dynasty Press, 2012), 68.

Bibliography:

Jorgenson, Mary. Interview by Alan McAskill. In *Hospice Pioneers*,
    edited by Alan McAskill, 62–86. Richmond: Dynasty Press, 1994.

Titled Interview in a Periodical

Note:

7. Justinia Speake, "Picking Plato Apart: An Interview with Justinia Speake," interview by Selena Fox, *Cogitation*, March 14, 2017, 43–44.

Bibliography:

Speake, Justinia. "Picking the Patrons Apart: An Interview with Justinia Speake."
    By Selena Fox. *Cogitation*, March 14, 2017, 40–56.

Interview Broadcast on Television

Note:

4. Clarence Parker, interview by Clint Gordon, *Oklahoma Philosophers*, WKY Television, June 4, 2016.

Bibliography:

Parker, Clarence. Interview by Clint Gordon. *Oklahoma Philosophers*. WKY
    Television, June 4, 2016.

Unpublished Interviews   According to *CMOS* (14.222), references to interview material you collect personally is usually handled either in the text alone or in a note. Such material is rarely given a citation in the bibliography.

Note:

17. Olivia Staats, interview by author, April 23, 2012, tape recording, Chapel Hill, NC.

Unpublished Sources

For theses and dissertations accessed online, give the URL or, if available, the DOI. For those accessed through a database, give the name of the database and, in parentheses, any identifying phrase or number supplied by the database.

Dissertation

Note:

16. Robert Nisbaum, "Sidney Hook's Populism" (PhD diss., University of Virginia, 2011), 88–91, http://virginia.edu/artsandsciences/ph/rn/2011.pdf.

Bibliography:

Nisbaum, Robert. "Sidney Hook's Populism." PhD diss., University of Virginia, 1980. http://virginia.edu/artsandsciences/ph/rn/2011.pdf.

Thesis

Note:

5. Ellspeth Stanley Sharpe, "Black Women in Philosophy: A Troubled History" (Master's thesis, Oregon State University, 2015), 34, 36, 112–14. Philosopher's Index (PHL2256577).

Bibliography:

Sharpe, Ellspeth Stanley. "Black Women in Philosophy: A Troubled History." Master's thesis, Oregon State University, 2015. Philosopher's Index (PHL2256577).

Paper Presented at a Meeting

Note:

82. Kim Zelazny and Ed Gilmore, "Thought for Thought's Sake: Funding Freethought Organization in the Twenty-First Century" (paper presented at the Annual Conference of West Coast Philosophers, San Francisco, CA, April 2017), 4–7, 9.

Bibliography:

Zelazny, Kim, and Ed Gilmore. "Thought for Thought's Sake: Funding Freethought Organizations in the Twenty-First Century." Presented at the Annual Conference of West Coast Philosophers, San Francisco, CA, April 2017.

Subsequent or Shortened References in Notes

After you have given a complete citation for a source in a note once, it is possible to shorten the reference to that source in later notes. One convenient method of shortening later references to a source, described in *CMOS* (14.25), is to give only the last name of the author, followed by a shortened form of the title and the page numbers for the reference, if different from the page numbers of the earlier reference. In addition, you can use Ibid., an abbreviation of the Latin term *ibidem*, meaning "in the same place," to shorten a note that refers to the source in the immediately preceding note.

Shortened References

First Reference:

21. Angela Genessario et al., *Childhood as Metaphor from the New Testament to Rousseau* (Baltimore: Colgate, 2013), 16–18, 78–82.

Later Reference:

35. Genessario, *Childhood as Metaphor*, 46.

Use of Ibid.

First Reference:

14. Samuel Howard, William J. Abbott, and Jane Hope, *Powerbase: How to Increase Your Hold on Your Fellow Philosophy Students* (Los Angeles: Gollum and Smythe, 2015), 35–36.

Following Reference (citation of a new page):

15. Ibid., 38.

Following Reference (citation of the same page):

15. Ibid.

Read&Write 3.4 Create an Actually Usable Bibliography

Create a bibliography for a paper on a topic of your choosing using twelve or more high-quality, actually published print and online sources.

3.5 AVOID PLAGIARISM

Plagiarism is the use of someone else's words or ideas without proper credit. Although some plagiarism is deliberate, produced by writers who understand that they are guilty of a kind of academic thievery, much of it is unconscious, committed by writers who are not aware of the varieties of plagiarism or who are careless in recording their borrowings from sources.

Plagiarism includes:

- Quoting directly without acknowledging the source
- Paraphrasing without acknowledging the source
- Constructing a paraphrase that closely resembles the original in language and syntax

You want to use your source material as effectively as possible. This will mean that sometimes you should quote from a source directly, whereas at other times you will want to express such information in your own words. At all times, you should work to integrate the source material skillfully into the flow of your written argument.

When to Quote

You should quote directly from a source when the original language is distinctive enough to enhance your argument, or when rewording the passage would lessen its impact. In the interest of fairness, you should also directly quote a passage to which you will take exception. Rarely, however, should you quote a source at great length (longer than two or three paragraphs). Nor should your paper, or any substantial section of it, be merely a string of quoted passages. The more language you take from the writings of others, the more the quotations will disrupt the rhetorical flow of your own words. Too much quoting creates a choppy patchwork of varying styles and borrowed purposes in which your own sense of control over your material is lost.

Quotations in Relation to Your Writing

When you do use a quotation, make sure that you insert it skillfully. According to *CMOS* 16 (13.9–10), quotations of fewer than one hundred words (approximately eight typed lines) should generally be integrated into the text and set off with quotation marks:

> "In the last analysis," Alice Thornton argued in 2016, "we cannot afford not to embark on a radical program of curriculum reform."[24]

A quotation of one hundred words or longer (eight typed lines or longer) should be formatted as a *block quotation*; it should begin on a new line, be indented from the left margin, and not be enclosed in quotation marks:

> In a letter to the committee that voted to relieve Professor Givan of his tenure, citing moral turpitude, Rancherson barely managed to hold onto civility:
>
> > I am reminded that something very much like this was the charge levied successfully against Socrates, the charge that led not only to his discrediting but to his death. Now, as then, it is merely a cruel ploy to obscure the steady erosion of academic freedom perpetrated by small minds lit dimly by envy and hate. Why the board fears unfettered thought is a mystery to me and should be so to everyone on the campus and, indeed, in the community beyond. The problems that face this institution—problems whose components include a moral one as well as a financial one—cannot be overcome through cowardice, and they will not go away if we continue to ignore them as we have for the last several ignominious decades. Dr. Givan shares with his illustrious fellow outlaw a clarity of mind that allowed him to recognize the evils that perpetuated this rancid status quo and the courage to name them aloud and to propose remedies. It's a tragedy that his courage has met with the same result as Socrates'.[3]

Acknowledge Quotations Carefully

Failing to signal the presence of a quotation skillfully can lead to confusion or choppiness:

> The US secretary of labor believes that worker-retraining programs have failed because of a lack of trust within the American business culture. "The American business community does not visualize the need to invest in its workers."[12]

The first sentence in the above passage seems to suggest that the quote that follows comes from the secretary of labor. Note how this revision clarifies the attribution:

> According to reporter Fred Winn, the US secretary of labor believes that worker-retraining programs have failed because of a lack of trust within the American business culture. Summarizing the secretary's view, Winn writes, "The American business community does not visualize the need to invest in its workers."[12]

The origin of each quote must be indicated within your text at the point where the quote occurs as well as in the list of works cited, which follows the text.

Quote Accurately

If your transcription of a quotation introduces careless variants of any kind, you are misrepresenting your source. Proofread your quotations very carefully, paying close attention to such surface features as spelling, capitalization, italics, and the use of numerals.

Occasionally, in order to make a quotation fit smoothly into a passage, to clarify a reference, or to delete unnecessary material, you may need to change the original wording slightly. You must, however, signal any such change to your reader.

Some alterations may be noted by brackets:

> "Several times in the course of his speech, the philosopher said that his stand [on free will] remains unchanged."[7]

Ellipses indicate that words have been left out of a quote:

> "The last time students refused to endorse one of the professor's policies ... was back in 1982."[14]

When you integrate quoted material with your own prose, it is unnecessary to begin the quote with ellipses:

> Benton raised eyebrows with his claim that "nobody in the professor's office knows how to tie a shoe, let alone balance a budget."[8]

Paraphrasing

Your writing has its own rhetorical attributes, its own rhythms and structural coherence. Inserting several quotations into one section of your paper can disrupt the patterns of your prose and diminish its effectiveness. Paraphrasing, or recasting source material in your own words, is one way to avoid the choppiness that can result from a series of quotations.

Remember that a paraphrase is to be written in your language; it is not to be a near-copy of the source writer's language. Merely changing a few words of the original does justice to no one's prose and frequently produces stilted passages. This sort of borrowing is actually a form of plagiarism. To fully integrate another's material into your own writing, use your own language.

Paraphrasing may actually increase your comprehension of source material, because in recasting a passage you will have to think very carefully about its meaning—more carefully, perhaps, than if you had merely copied it word for word.

Avoiding Plagiarism When Paraphrasing   Paraphrases require the same sort of documentation as direct quotes. The words of a paraphrase may be yours, but the idea belongs to someone else. Failure to give that person credit, in the form of references within the text and in the bibliography, may make you vulnerable to a charge of plagiarism.

One way to guard against plagiarism is to keep careful notes of when you have directly quoted source material and when you have paraphrased—making sure that the wording of the paraphrases is your own. Be sure that all direct quotes in your final draft are properly set off from your own prose, either with quotation marks or in indented blocks.

What kind of paraphrased material must be acknowledged? Basic material that you find in several sources need not be documented by a reference. For example, it is unnecessary to cite a source for the information that Franklin Delano Roosevelt was elected to a fourth term as president of the United States shortly before his death, because this is a commonly known fact. However, Professor Smith's opinion, published in a recent article, that Roosevelt's winning of a fourth term hastened his death is not a fact, but a theory based on Smith's research and defended by her. If you wish to use Smith's opinion in a paraphrase, you need to credit her, as you should all judgments and claims from another source. Any information that is not widely known, whether factual or open to dispute, should be documented. This includes statistics, graphs, tables, and charts taken from sources other than your own primary research.

Read&Write 3.5   Properly Summarize an Article from *The Stone*

Select an article from a recent copy of *The Stone*, a philosophy forum published in the *New York Times,* and summarize it properly in your own words, without plagiarizing, in approximately five hundred words. Attach the article itself to your summary.

4

PRACTICE THE CRAFT
OF ARGUMENT

4.1 ARGUE EFFECTIVELY AND COGENTLY

A quality philosophy paper or essay will argue for a precise, clear, well-defined claim in a logically valid form. It will rely on true or well-supported premises. Any philosophical writing will be long enough to consist of many intermediate arguments with clear transitions. It will demonstrate concern for the reader by beginning with a map of what will follow and the steps to be taken on the journey through an extended argument. And it will close with an account of where its author thinks the journey has ended and, perhaps, an indication of what future journeys this one has inspired. It also will occasionally get off the road during the journey and take some time and space to summarize the trip from a rest stop. In this chapter and the next we will look at what should and should not occur in philosophical writing. But first, here are some remarks on the philosophical notion of an argument.

Argument: The Basic Tool of Philosophy

Arguments are discussions in which we strive to attain an objective. There are all sorts of objectives: selling our favorite political candidate, gaining a couple of points on an exam, selecting the movie we want to see, returning an item to a department store, or discovering the truth on an important matter. Verbal and nonverbal exchanges of reasons, threats, emotions, or even bricks in the interest of reaching an objective are normally called arguments. This ordinary sense of argument clashes with the philosophical notion. Some of the most effective tools of ordinary argument—appeal to authority, attacks on a person's character, traditional wisdom, affirming the consequent (explained below), and equivocation—will negatively affect your grade on a philosophy exam. You should not only avoid these nonphilosophical techniques but learn to recognize them when they occur in arguments. If you do become adept at recognizing formal and informal fallacies, then you will be in a better position to critique the arguments of others as well as your own first drafts. For instance, recognizing that you have cast your argument so that it appeals to a sufficient but not necessary condition or that you have formulated an argument relying on a false dilemma should lead you to significant revisions.

The language in which we talk about argument suggests that we conceive argument metaphorically as a war to be won. Words such as *demolished*, *overwhelmed*, *destroyed*, and *thrust* make frequent appearances in our accounts of arguments. And we know that all is fair in love and war. So the very idea that there are rules governing argument may seem questionable from the start, unless the rules are going to show us how to obtain our objectives more effectively.

The Components of a Philosophical Argument

An argument is not a squabble between people who disagree. In philosophy, an argument is a series of statements that include at least one premise, a conclusion, and connectives that link the premise(s) to a conclusion. A premise is a statement, offered as evidence for a conclusion, which is assumed or taken for granted in a context. For example, the statements "It is wrong to smoke around pregnant women" and "If it is wrong to smoke around pregnant women, then the unborn have rights" are premises. Some expressions that indicate premises are *if, since, because, on the basis of,* and *the following observation supports my claim.*

Philosophers use the expression *connective* to designate the basic linking expressions of logic. The basic connectives are *it's not the case that, and, or,* and *if . . . , then.* The first connective just mentioned, *it's not the case that,* does not really connect statements. Instead, it negates a statement or a group of statements connected by the other connectives. *And* joins two or more statements. *Or* also joins two or more statements and is understood in logic in its inclusive sense. A better rendering of this connective would be *at least one.*

The connective *if . . . , then* does double duty in arguments. In a conditional statement, it connects two statements. The statement before *then* is the antecedent; the statement after *then* is the consequent. Compound sentences formed by *if . . . , then* are called *conditionals.* Conditionals often are found as premises in arguments either expressly stated or implied. But *if . . . , then* also functions as the basic connective in any argument connecting the premises to the conclusion. An argument can always be translated into a long conditional sentence in which the conjunction of the premises forms the antecedent, and the conclusion is the consequent.

A conclusion is the statement or claim presented as resulting from the premise(s). For example, if we accept the premises that (1) it is wrong to smoke around pregnant women, and (2) if it is wrong to smoke around pregnant women, then the unborn have rights, we must reasonably conclude that the unborn have rights. The conclusion follows whether we like the practical consequences it would suggest or not.

The following are all linking expressions that indicate conclusions: *it follows that; therefore; if . . . , then; hence; my conclusion is; consequently; it is (probably) the case that;* and *so.*

Generally, arguments are expressed in a way that requires you to tease out the premises. Sometimes the arguments can be expressed offensively. In ordinary life, it takes a lot of patience and charity to reconstruct what others might mean.

Arguments call for us to take the truth or probable truth of the premises for granted for a moment so that we may determine whether the purported truth of the premises is sufficient to guarantee the truth or probability of the conclusion. In addition to premises and conclusions, arguments may contain extraneous material such as jokes, biographical data, or even personal attacks.

Philosophers generally avoid such distracting material, and in argument analysis you should simply disregard it. Some style manuals will tell you not to write in the first person. However, some philosophers find that occasional use of the first person serves to emphasize a point.

Narratives, which are simply chronological stories of actions or events, are not arguments. Yet narratives are effective devices for causing someone to accept a conclusion or causing a person to listen with more tolerance to an argument.

Deductive and Nondeductive Arguments

Arguments are either deductive or nondeductive. An argument is deductive if it claims that the conclusion must be true if the premises are true. The conclusion is therefore guaranteed by the truth of the premises. If the premises are true and the deductive form of the argument is valid, then the conclusion must also be true. The argument given above about the unborn is a valid deductive argument. It is an instance of the valid deductive form *modus ponens* (illustrated in table 4.1). Are the premises true?

The following argument is deductive because its conclusion, given its premises, is presented as being an unarguable matter of fact:

> Two million and thirty-seven lottery tickets were sold for Wednesday's drawing. I bought two tickets. So my chance of winning Wednesday is 2 in 2,000,037.

An argument is nondeductive if it claims only a high degree of probability for the conclusion. A nondeductive argument, then, allows for some doubt of the truth of the conclusion, and it bases its claim of accuracy on the very good chance that its premises are correct. Here is an example:

> All cats that I have ever seen will eat mice. Jake is a cat. Therefore, Jake will probably eat mice.

It is important to know the difference between deductive and nondeductive arguments because we must know what an argument demands of us. Does the argument ask us to accept the premises or the conclusion as true or only as probably true? The actions we take based upon certainty are different from the actions we take based upon probability, and we may hold deductive arguments liable for much stronger bases of proof. The level of evidence we ought to require for premises in nondeductive argument is less than that needed in deductive. Still, good writers do not offer conclusions that assert only faint degrees of probability with expressions such as *could be the case* or *might*.

An argument is deductively valid if it is deductive and if the truth of the premises would make it necessary that the conclusion is true also. In other words, an argument is deductively valid if it is deductive and if it cannot be the case that the premises are true and the conclusion is false.

Question: Is the following argument deductively valid?

> Premise 1: If God knows everything, then God knows what I will do tomorrow before I make up my mind.
> Premise 2: God knows everything.
> Conclusion: God knows what I will do tomorrow before I make up my mind.

Perhaps God does not know everything. Or perhaps there is nothing for God to know before I make up my mind. Still, the argument is deductively valid—that is, the deduction from the assumed true premises is valid. The argument is deductive because it claims certainty for the conclusion, and it is valid because its conclusion would have to be true if the premises were true.

Validity versus Truth

When you evaluate an argument for deductive validity, you do not yet check for the truth of the premises. *The factual truth of the premises is irrelevant to the validity of an argument.* Consequently, a deductively valid argument may have false premises and a true conclusion, or it may have false premises and a false conclusion.

In a deductively valid argument the relation between premises and conclusions is not a causal relationship. Premises do not cause a conclusion to be true; they often merely explain why, if they are true, the conclusion is also true.

If I claim "since my chances of winning the lottery are 2 million to 1, then I will probably lose the lottery," then I am making a nondeductive argument because I am claiming only the probability, not the certainty, of my conclusion. An argument is nondeductively valid if it is nondeductive and if the truth or high probability of its premises makes the conclusion highly probable also. My argument about the probability of my losing the lottery is nondeductively valid because the high odds against winning do indeed produce a high likelihood that I will lose.

Checking for validity is important because it is the first step in examining an argument in order to see if it is worthwhile to check the actual truth of the premises.

Consider the following deductive argument. Is it valid?

When I am in Memphis, I always go to the services at Al Green's church.

If I go to Al Green's church, then I will visit Graceland afterward, since it is nearby.

So, if I go to Memphis, then I will visit Graceland.

If you found yourself asking whether Al Green (soul and gospel singer) has a church or if Graceland (Elvis Presley's mansion) is indeed close to Al Green's church (it is), then you missed the point. It does not matter to the question of validity whether the statements you questioned are in fact true or false. It matters only whether, if they and the other premises were true, the truth of the premise would make it necessary that the conclusion be true also.

Is the following nondeductive argument nondeductively valid?

When people are transferred to Calvary Hospital, they usually die within a week or two. Helene's physician has transferred her to Calvary.

So, Helene is beyond recovery.

To recap: When evaluating a passage to test its credentials as an argument we must answer three questions:

1. Does it have the components of an argument (at least one premise and a conclusion)?
2. Is the argument type deductive or nondeductive?
3. Is the argument valid or invalid in the manner appropriate to the argument type?

Having answered those, we must ask a fourth question: Is the argument *cogent?*

Cogency

We may say that an argument is deductively cogent (or sound) if it is deductive and deductively valid and the premises are in fact true. An argument is nondeductively cogent (often called "strong" or "correct") if it is nondeductive and nondeductively valid and its premises are true or highly probable.

The following argument is deductively cogent:

> The electric company charges for electricity. I used electricity from the electric company last month. So, I will be charged for the use of electricity.

The following argument is nondeductively cogent:

> Millions of tickets are sold for each drawing of the California lottery. I bought only one ticket for the next drawing on Wednesday. So I will probably lose.

Learn the Forms of Argument

Table 4.1 presents a summary of some of the major forms of argument. As you read each one you will begin to understand some ways of constructing your arguments. Remember that these types of arguments may not always lead to conclusions that would seem to be "true" in real-world terms; see, for example, "Faulty Syllogism" in table 4.1. But while the faulty syllogism in the table doesn't lead to a statement that is true, it nevertheless names and articulates a form of argument that is of use in philosophy.

Arrange Your Philosophy Paper Logically

Let us agree that some philosophy papers, the most basic ones, will be expository papers, in other words, papers meant to explain or describe a particular subject. Here, your task will be to accurately present a position argued by a noted philosopher, being clear about the meaning of the philosophical terms key to that position. For example, if you are assigned an expository paper on William James's concept of freedom, your paper will involve an analytic step in which you explain what James meant by terms such as *determinism* and *indeterminism*. It will also involve exhibiting the structure of his argument against determinism.

Virtually any sort of paper written for a philosophy class will involve the process of exposition. Let's say you are assigned a compare-and-contrast paper in which your goal is to address the views of freedom held by William James, B. F. Skinner, and Jonathan Edwards. Such a paper will actually require three expository sections—one for each philosopher under examination. The critical parts of the compare-and-contrast paper will center on the validity or invalidity of each philosopher's argument, the defensibility of key definitions, and the truth of the premises offered for each thesis. So expository papers fall within the realm of compare-and-contrast papers.

Argumentative papers contain both expository and compare-and-contrast sections. It is very difficult to address a philosophical issue without considering the work

TABLE 4.1

Major Forms of Argument

Name	Symbolic Forms	Explanation	Example
Tautology	A or not A	A universally true statement.	It is raining or it is not raining.
Modus Ponens	If P, then Q. P. Therefore Q.	Latin for "method of putting."	When it rains it pours. It is raining. Ergo, it pours.
Hypothetical Syllogism	If P, then Q. If Q, then R. Therefore, if P, R.	Linking a first and third element.	When it rains it pours. When it pours it floods. Ergo, when it rains it floods.
Disjunctive Syllogism	P or Q. Not P, therefore, Q.	Uncombinable elements.	It either rains or shines. It rains not; ergo, it shines.
Faulty Syllogism	If P, then Q. If Q, then R. Therefore, if P, R.	Nonequivalent elements.	God is love. Love is blind. Ray Charles is blind. Ergo, Ray Charles is God.
Modus Tollens	If P, then Q. Not Q. Therefore not Q.	Latin for "method of removing."	When it rains it pours. It is not raining. Ergo, it is not pouring.
Dilemmas	P or Q. If P, then R. If Q, then S.	Two undesirable outcomes.	It rains or parches. If it rains it floods. If it parches we thirst.
Reductio ad Absurdum	To prove P: Suppose not P. If not P, then Q. If Q, then R. Not R. Therefore, not not P. Therefore, P.	Rejecting a false outcome.	I will prove that I have a car. Suppose I don't have a car. I must walk. If I must walk, I will be late. I will not be late. Therefore, I don't not have a car. Therefore, I have a car.
Contradiction	P and not P.	Negation of contradiction also true.	I hate salt and I love salt. I don't hate salt and I don't love salt.
Analogies	P is to Q as R is to S.	Similar things are always similar.	A frying pan is a chef's violin.
Induction by Elimination	X is a complete set of alternatives. X_1 is the best.	A complete set of choices produces the best.	I can walk, ride my bike, or take a bus to school. Taking the bus will ruin my reputation. Walking will make me late. I will ride my bike.
Induction by Enumeration	Y has always happened, so it will again.	Experience is the best guide.	Marge always makes me a cake on my birthday. She will this year, too.
Inference to Best Explanation	X causes Y, therefore Z.	The cause is the key.	Marge always makes me a cake on my birthday because I always buy her flowers on hers. Flowers bring cake.
Hypothetical-Deductive Method	You can never prove P, but you can prove not P.	Scientific experiments never prove universality, but they can negate it.	Just because we have never observed a cold star, we cannot be sure one does not exist.

of others. If you are working on the justification of making duties to family members a moral priority over duties to the state, it will be helpful to position your discussion within the context of reasons provided by philosophers who disagree with each other on the issue, among them Plato, Aristotle, Marx, Firestone, and Hobbes. The comments you make in comparing the positions of these philosophers will serve as reasons for the position you support in your argumentative paper. Marx, for instance, presented the sentimental family as a means of preserving economic classes through inheritance. If you find yourself objecting that this is rarely the reason why people choose to have children, this objection will serve both as a criticism of Marx and a reason in the position you develop.

Realizing the continuity in these three types of papers, we can map out the steps of a philosophical paper as follows. The different types of papers simply stop at different places.

I. Expository Step
   A. Explains key terms
   B. Exhibits the form of the argument under consideration

II. Compare-and-Contrast Step
   A. Addresses the validity of the arguments under consideration
   B. Addresses the cogency of the arguments by considering the evidence for the various premises and also by attempting to formulate counterexamples
   C. Repairs the arguments by recasting them in valid forms or adding premises to ensure that you address the best possible version of an argument

III. Argumentative Step
   A. States which alternative view seems more likely to be correct based on the premise available
   B. Uses the criticisms in the compare-and-contrast phase to state how close your own view is to the preferred alternative
   C. Develops your own view further, using the criticisms brought against other alternatives as your initial premises
   D. Recasts your own argument in a valid form
   E. Anticipates and addresses objections to your view
   F. Concludes by stating what has been accomplished and what remains to be investigated.

Read&Write 4.1   Write a Sound Argument

Select a topic of your choice and construct an argument in which you employ six of the forms of argument listed in the "Major Forms of Argument" table above (table 4.1). Structure your argument using the steps listed in the preceding outline.

4.2 AVOID FALLACIES

There is an infinite number of formal fallacies. The ability to recognize them may make your job as a critical writer easier. Table 4.2 below describes some of the more common ones.

TABLE 4.2

Common Fallacies

Name of Fallacy	Symbolic (where appropriate)	Example	Explanation of Fallacy
Denying the Antecedent	If P, then Q. Not P. Therefore, not Q.	If I get paid I will eat. I did not get paid; therefore I will not eat.	Maybe Mom will make me dinner.
Affirming the Consequent	If P, then Q. Q; therefore, P.	If I get paid I will eat. I ate; ergo, I got paid.	Maybe Mom made me dinner.
The Exclusive Fallacy	P or Q. P, therefore not Q.	I will eat beans or rice. I will eat beans; ergo, I will not eat rice.	At least one bad premise. I might eat beans and rice.
Informal Fallacies	If P, then Q.	Number 23 has not come up today in roulette. I will bet on 23.	Improper degree of probability.
Invalid Appeal to Authority	A confirms B.	General Grant will make a great president.	One type of authority does not necessarily transfer to another.
Straw Person	A refutes B.	Taxing the rich at a higher rate than the poor is unfair.	The rich receive many more benefits from the tax system and use of infrastructure to deliver their goods and services than the poor do.
Inconsistency	A and not A.	I approve of coal mining in West Virginia but not in Vermont.	An argument changes with its audience.
False Dilemma	Either A or B.	"Do you want to go to bed now or after your bath?"	Nonexclusive alternatives presented as exclusive.
Complex Question	Incorrect A leads to incorrect B or C.	"When are you going to become responsible?"	Maybe you are already responsible, even though the question implies you are not.
Begging the Question	"Don't you want to avoid going to hell?"		Does hell exist? Conclusion assumed in the premises.
Suppressed Evidence	"Son, the doctor will surely not hurt you."		Relevant facts deleted. Maybe okay for kids but not for philosophers.
Lack of proportion	"My convention will be HUGE."		Outsized estimates.

TABLE 4.2

Continued

Name of Fallacy	Example	Explanation of Fallacy
Appeal to Unknowable Statistics	"Battlefield deployment of tactical nuclear weapons has prevented 17 major wars in Europe since 1950."	Nobody can prove this statement.
Ad Hominem	"You could never keep on a budget."	Irrelevant or untrue attack, in this case in a dispute about buying a new car.
Guilt by Association	"Your mother is a Republican."	While attacking a young Democrat
Equivocation	Two meanings for the same word: "Determination leads to success."	Determining the right course, or staying the course?
Appeal to Ignorance	"You can't prove that chocolate is bad for your health."	The failure to prove is not a valid disproof.
Composition	"All illegal immigrants are dishonest."	Maybe few or none are dishonest.
Division	"Native Americans care about the environment."	Maybe some do not.
Hasty Conclusion	"He cheated me, so all cab drivers are dishonest."	Inadequate sample size.
Questionable Cause	"Obamacare sends jobs overseas."	Cheap labor sends jobs overseas.
Questionable Analogy	"Artificial intelligence is superior to human intelligence."	Can both forms of intelligence do all the same things?
Appeal to Pity	"If I don't get this teaching job, then my family will be homeless."	Even if true, does need equal merit?
Appeal to the Stick	"You will accept this policy if you know what's good for you."	Might makes right.
Appeal to Loyalty	"America's armed forces would never commit genocide."	Not even after firebombing more than three million Japanese civilians?
Appeal to Provincialism	"Before we came, these people all lived in teepees."	Does that mean they can't break complicated secret codes?
Popularity	"Everybody knows the Japanese and Cubans are good baseball players."	Popular stereotypes are often too durable.
Double Standard	"Men make better presidents than women."	Glass ceilings are common.
Invincible Ignorance	"I don't care what you say. I know better."	Refusing to listen is a common last resort.

Read & Write 4.2   Identify the Fallacies in the Arguments Provided

Practice the Five Fallacy Steps

Exercises to sharpen your argumentative skills are lying in wait for you everywhere. But newspapers and other media, especially those featuring politicians, are good places to look. Newspapers are especially reluctant to state conclusions. It is as if the news media believe that if the reader is left to draw the conclusion, then no bias has occurred. In real-world examples, it is not uncommon to find several fallacies and also to find fallacies committed by different parties.

The next section gives several real-world examples of arguments. Your task, to identify the fallacies within arguments, will be easier if you approach each example by taking the following steps, in this order:

1. Identify the conclusion that you are being asked to accept.
2. Identify the reasons (premises) that are offered for accepting the conclusion.
3. Determine the appropriateness of the premises—that is, the extent to which the premises lead to the conclusion.
4. Determine adequacy of the premises—that is, the extent to which the premises provide sufficient reason to accept the conclusion.
5. If the premises are inappropriate or inadequate, select the fallacy from the list above that most adequately explains the error in the argument.

Now that you know the steps in identifying fallacies, identify fallacies in the following sample situations and arguments:

- When interest rates eventually rise, prices of recently issued corporate bonds will fall. "The guy buying a [new] bond today is a guy buying a certain loss," said Anders Maxwell, a managing director at investment bank Peter J. Solomon Co. "Rates have to go higher, and when they do these low-coupon bonds will drop precipitously in value."[1]

- Against the flag-draped backdrop of the USS *Wisconsin*, Mitt Romney formally introduced Paul Ryan, the House Budget Committee chairman from Wisconsin, as his vice presidential running mate on Saturday. Ryan's budget-cutting ideas have the potential to transform the presidential race. Support for his proposed mix of spending cuts and tax cuts has become a litmus test on the right—and opposing them has become a rallying cry on the left.

   "A lot of people may disagree with Paul Ryan, but I don't know of anyone who doesn't respect his character and judgment," Romney said in announcing his running mate.

   In picking Ryan, the Romney campaign emphasized the congressman's local roots, releasing a bio that noted he was a fifth-generation Wisconsin native and the son of an attorney and a stay-at-home mom. Romney aides are hoping Ryan will help the Republican ticket win over working-class voters, who have been openly skeptical

---

[1]   Matt Wirz, "As Corporate-Bond Yields Sink, Risks for Investors Rise," *Wall Street Journal*, August 14, 2012, http://www.wsj.com/articles/SB10000872396390444042704577584792371582220.

of Romney's candidacy. In accepting the role of Romney's running mate on Saturday, Ryan made a direct appeal to that voting bloc.

"I represent a part of America that includes inner cities, rural areas, suburbs and factory towns," Ryan said. "Over the years I have seen and heard from a lot of families, from those running small businesses, and from people who are in need. But what I have heard lately troubles me the most. There is something different in their voice and in their words. What I hear from them are diminished dreams, lowered expectations, uncertain futures."

Ryan acknowledged that President Barack Obama "inherited a difficult situation" when he took office in 2009. But echoing the message Romney has emphasized on the trail for months, Ryan told supporters here Obama "didn't make things better."

"Whatever the explanations, whatever the excuses, this is a record of failure," Ryan said.[2]

- Our view: Butte County supervisors had the right idea on their first ordinance, but they also have to face reality about what voters will accept. We're not sure what point three Butte County supervisors are trying to make with the latest shot fired over medical marijuana. Maybe that they are poor losers. Or stubborn. Or maybe that they simply think they are doing the right thing. It doesn't matter. The only thing that matters is, what sort of restrictions on marijuana growing will pass muster with Butte County voters. Supervisors were delivered a firm message along those lines just two months ago—and apparently didn't get the hint. The county supervisors tried to pass restrictions on growing marijuana. Advocates of marijuana rose up and gathered enough signatures for a referendum measure to be put on the ballot. Voters then rejected the supervisors' restrictions with 55 percent of the vote. We hoped the supervisors would seek to craft a compromise—something that protected neighborhoods from growers who threaten, harass and intimidate, and from the skunky smell right before harvest, but also something that scaled back the more invasive parts of the previous ordinance. Instead, supervisors voted 3–2 to develop an even more restrictive ordinance. They want something modeled after Kings County in the San Joaquin Valley, where all outdoor medical marijuana growing is prohibited. Proposition 215 patients with a recommendation can only grow inside fully enclosed structures.

  Let us be clear: We supported the supervisors' original ordinance. We also endorsed Measure A on these pages because we believe the county needs restrictions on marijuana. We even believe an ordinance like the one in Kings County would be reasonable here—but that doesn't mean it ever will become reality. Supervisors should focus on constructing the most restrictive ordinance that will withstand a voter challenge. Anything more restrictive then [*sic*] their previous attempt is doomed to failure, which makes it a waste of staff time and money. Supervisors Maureen Kirk and Steve Lambert had the good sense to vote against the Kings County model. That's not because they support the marijuana lobby. It's because they are realists. Now the County Counsel's Office will try to help craft an ordinance that will ban all outdoor growing. The supervisors will get a chance to approve it in a month or more. Then the threats of lawsuits and referenda will start flying. We wish the supervisors would

---

[2] Holly Bailey, "Mitt Romney Introduces Paul Ryan as His VP Running Mate," Yahoo News, August 11, 2002, https://www.yahoo.com/news/blogs/ticket/live-video-mitt-romney-announces-vp-pick-123251121.html.

just skip that last step and instead focus on a measure that will be acceptable, not one that will lead to another drawn-out argument and contentious election.[3]

- Retired adult film actress Jenna Jameson voiced support for presumptive Republican presidential nominee Mitt Romney at a strip club Thursday, CBS San Francisco reports: "I'm very looking forward to a Republican being back in office," Jameson said while sipping champagne in a VIP room at Gold Club in the city's South of Market neighborhood. "When you're rich, you want a Republican in office."

  Jameson was being interviewed "exclusively" by a CBS reporter who was "on assignment" at "an event marking the 8th anniversary" of the San Francisco–area strip club.

  Jameson isn't the first in the business to praise Romney: Ron Jeremy recently called Romney "a good man" and "such an amazing father." In an interview with Yahoo News earlier this year, gay porn titan Michael Lucas said he would "of course" support the former Massachusetts governor.[4]

- I wonder how many of the 40% or so of U.S. households that don't pay federal income taxes have turned to an underground cash or barter economy to avoid taxation. . . . The rich may have plenty of loopholes and favorable tax regulation, but the middle and lower classes have their own: working off the books. There are many tiny elephants in the taxation room, but they add up to one huge elephant that no one seems willing, or able, to address.[5]

- Dave Mustaine of Megadeth: "Back in my country, my president . . . he's trying to pass a gun ban, so he's staging all of these murders, like the 'Fast And Furious' thing down at the border . . . Aurora, Colorado, all the people that were killed there . . . and now the beautiful people at the Sikh temple. I don't know where I'm gonna live if America keeps going the way it's going because it looks like it's turning into Nazi America."[6]

- "The panel notes your good conduct, program achievements, educational accomplishments, positive presentation, remorse, risk and needs assessment, letters of support, significant opposition to your release and all other statutory factors were considered," Thompson wrote. "However, parole shall not be granted for good conduct and program completions alone."[7]

- A prominent conservative writer would be hung out to dry for plagiarism comparable to Mr. Zakaria's. Maybe Mr. Zakaria did not commit a professional capital offense, as Mr. Stephens argues, but if he wasn't such a beloved member of the liberal media establishment, he would already be toast.[8]

3   "Editorial: Supervisors Take Curious Approach," *Chico Enterprise-Record*, August 2, 2012, http://www.chicoer .com/general-news/20120802/editorial-supervisors-take-curious-approach.

4   Chris Moody, "Retired Porn Star Jenna Jameson Supports Mitt Romney," Yahoo News, August 3, 2012, https:// www.yahoo.com/news/blogs/ticket/retired-porn-star-jenna-jameson-says-she-supports-143703925.html.

5   John Quilter, "Letter to the Editor: Taxes and Poor People's Loopholes," *Wall Street Journal*, August 21, 2012, http://www.wsj.com/articles/SB10000872396390444443504577601163646244278.

6   "Dave Mustaine Accuses President of Staging Recent Mass Killings," Punknews.org, August 15, 2012, https:// www.punknews.org/article/48516/dave-mustaine-accuses-president-of-staging-recent-mass-killings.

7   Michael Virtanen, "Mark David Chapman, John Lennon's Killer, Denied Parole Again," *Christian Science Monitor*, August 23, 2012, http://www.csmonitor.com/USA/Latest-News-Wires/2012/0823 /Mark-David-Chapman-John-Lennon-s-killer-denied-parole-again-video.

8   Rob Burke, "Letter to the Editor: It Would Be Worse if Zakaria Were More Conservative," *Wall Street Journal*, August 22, 2012, http://www.wsj.com/articles/SB10000872396390444443504577601181341795626.

- *The Book of Mormon*—a performance of which Hillary Clinton attended last year, without registering a complaint—comes to mind as the administration falls over itself denouncing *Innocence of Muslims*. This is a film that may or may not exist; whose makers are likely not who they say they are; whose actors claim to have known neither the plot nor purpose of the film; and which has never been seen by any member of the public except as a video clip on the Internet.[9]

[9]   Bret Stephens, "Muslims, Mormons and Liberals," *Wall Street Journal*, September 19, 2012, 17.

5

ARGUMENTS AND SUPPORTING DATA GALORE

Philosophy Information Sources

5.1 WELCOME TO THE APA AND THE APS

The American Philosophical Association (APA) and the American Philosophical Society (APS) are front doors to a large community of philosophy scholars and others interested in philosophy. As such, they are excellent first stops for many different sorts of philosophy research and writing projects. According to its website, the APS was founded, with the urging of Benjamin Franklin, in 1743. The "About" section of the site states:

> Early members included doctors, lawyers, clergymen, and merchants interested in science, and also many learned artisans and tradesmen like Franklin. Many founders of the republic were members: George Washington, John Adams, Thomas Jefferson, Alexander Hamilton, Thomas Paine, Benjamin Rush, James Madison, and John Marshall; as were many distinguished foreigners: Lafayette, von Steuben, Kosciusko.[1]

Many other famous people have been members since. An honorary society, the APS elects new members in April of each year, and in 2015 its membership totaled 1,023 scholars in five "classes" of disciplines:

Mathematical and Physical Sciences
Biological Sciences
Social Sciences
Humanities
The Arts, Professions, and Leaders in Public and Private Affairs[2]

Founded in 1900, the APA, with over nine thousand members, is the largest philosophical organization in the country. To present a discussion, paper, or other presentation at an APA annual meeting, you must be a member of APA as well as one of the following affiliated groups. The list of these groups, taken from the APA website, is presented here to provide you with an idea of how amazingly diverse the worldwide study of philosophy is today.

---

[1]   "About," APS: American Philosophical Society, https://amphilsoc.org/about.
[2]   "Members," APS: American Philosophical Society, https://amphilsoc.org/members.

APA Affiliated Groups

Academy for Jewish Philosophy

Alain L. Locke Society

American Association for the Philosophic Study of Society

American Association of Mexican Philosophers

American Association of Philosophy Teachers

American Catholic Philosophical Association

American Indian Philosophy Association

American Maritain Association

American Section of the International Association for Philosophy of Law and Social Philosophy (AMINTAPHIL)

American Society for Aesthetics

American Society for Political and Legal Philosophy

American Society for Value Inquiry

Association for Chinese Philosophers in America

Association for Informal Logic and Critical Thinking

Association for Liberty, Philosophy, and Society

Association for Philosophy of Education

Association for Philosophy of Judaism

Association for Philosophy of Liberation

Association for Symbolic Logic

Association for the Advancement of Philosophy and Psychiatry

Association for the Development of Philosophy Teaching

Association for the Philosophy of Judaism

Association for the Philosophy of the Unconscious

Association of Arab and Middle Eastern Philosophies

Association of Chinese Philosophers in North America

Association of Philosophy Journal Editors

Ayn Rand Society

Bay Area Continental Philosophy Association

Bertrand Russell Society

Central Division Sartre Circle

Charles S. Peirce Society

Committee on Institutional Cooperation

Concerned Philosophers for Peace

Conference of Philosophical Societies

Conference on Philosophical Societies

Consortium for Socially Relevant Philosophy of/in Science and Engineering (SRPoiSE)

Convivium: The Philosophy and Food Roundtable

David Kellogg Lewis Society

Descartes Society

Experimental Philosophy Society

Foucault Circle

Foundation for Philosophy of Creativity

G. E. Moore Society

Gabriel Marcel Society

Gandhi, King, Chavez, Addams Society

George Santayana Society

Hannah Arendt Circle

Hegel Society of America

Heidegger Circle

Hellenistic Philosophy Society

History of Early Analytic Philosophy Society

Hume Society

Indiana Philosophical Association

Institute for Humane Studies

Institute for the Advancement of Philosophy for Children

International Adam Smith Society

International Association for Computing and Philosophy

International Association for Environmental Philosophy

International Association for the Philosophy of Humor

International Association for the Philosophy of Sport

International Association of Japanese Philosophy

International Berkeley Society

International Development Ethics Association

International Economics and Philosophy Society

International Ernst Cassirer Society

International Hobbes Association

International Institute for Field-Being

International Philosophers for Peace

International Society for Buddhist Philosophy

International Society for Chinese Philosophy

International Society for Comparative Studies of Chinese and Western Philosophy

International Society for Environmental Ethics

International Society for Neoplatonic Studies

International Society for Universal Dialogue

International Society of Chinese Philosophy

John Dewey Society

Josiah Royce Society

Journal of the History of Philosophy

Karl Jaspers Society of North America

Leibniz Society of North America

Marxism and Philosophy Association

Max Scheler Society of North America

Max Scheler Society

Metanexus Institute

Metaphysical Society of America

Molinari Society

National Philosophical Counseling Association

Nicolai Hartmann Society

North American Division of the Schopenhauer Society

North American Kant Society

North American Korean Philosophy Association

North American Neo-Kantian Society

North American Nietzsche Society

North American Society for Philosophical Hermeneutics

North American Society for Social Philosophy

North American Spinoza Society

North American Wittgenstein Society

Pacific Hume Society

Pacific Society for Women in Philosophy

Personalist Discussion Group

Philosophers in Jesuit Education

Philosophers for Social Responsibility

Philosophy of Religion Group

Philosophy of Time Society

Pluralisms, Relativisms and Contextualisms Global Research Network

Polanyi Society

Political Theology Group

Radical Philosophy Association

Reid Society

Sartre Circle

Simone de Beauvoir Circle

Social Philosophy and Policy Society

Social Philosophy Research Institute

Society for Analytical Feminism

Society for Ancient Greek Philosophy

Society for Applied Philosophy

Society for Arab, Persian, and Islamic Philosophy

Society for Asian and Comparative Philosophy

Society for Business Ethics

Society for Empirical Ethics

Society for Ethics

Society for German Idealism and Romanticism

Society for German Idealism

Society for Iberian and Latin American Thought

Society for Indian Philosophy and Religion

Society for Lesbian and Gay Philosophy

Society for LGBTQ Philosophy

Society for Machines and Mentality

Society for Medieval and Renaissance Philosophy

Society for Modern Philosophy

Society for Moral Inquiry

Society for Natural Religion

Society for Neo-Kantianism

Society for Phenomenology and Analytic Philosophy

Society for Phenomenology and Existential Philosophy

Society for Philosophy and Disability

Society for Philosophy and Geography

Society for Philosophy and Public Affairs

Society for Philosophy and Technology

Society for Philosophy in the Contemporary World

Society for Philosophy of Agency

Society for Realist-Antirealist Discussion

Society for Realist/Antirealist Discussion

Society for Skeptical Studies

Society for Social and Political Philosophy: Historical, Continental, and Feminist Perspectives

Society for Student Philosophers

Society for Systematic Philosophy

Society for the Advancement of American Philosophy, Graduate Student Section

Society for the Advancement of American Philosophy

Society for the History of Political Philosophy

Society for the Metaphysics of Science

Society for the Philosophical Study of Education

Society for the Philosophical Study of the Paranormal

Society for the Philosophic Study of Genocide and the Holocaust

Society for the Philosophic Study of the Contemporary Visual Arts

Society for the Philosophy of Creativity

Society for the Philosophy of History

Society for the Philosophy of Human Life Issues

Society for the Philosophy of Sex and Love

Society for the Study of Ethics and Animals

Society for the Study of Husserl's Philosophy

Society for the Study of Indian and Tibetan Buddhist Philosophy

Society for the Study of Philosophy and the Martial Arts

Society for the Study of Process Philosophies

Society for the Study of the History of Analytical Philosophy

Society for the Study of Women Philosophers

Society for Women in Philosophy

Society of Christian Philosophers

Society of Humanist Philosophers

Society of Indian Philosophy and Religion

Society of Philosophers in America

Société Américaine de Philosophie de Langue Française

Société Internationale pour l'Étude de la Philosophie Médiévale

Southern California Epistemology Network

Søren Kierkegaard Society

The Society of Philosophers in America

US Midwest Society for Women in Philosophy

Western Phenomenology Conference

Wilfrid Sellars Society

William James Society

World Institute for Advanced Phenomenological Research and Learning

Young Philosophers' Society for International Exchange*

* "Affiliated Groups," American Philosophical Association, http://www.apaonline.org/page/affiliatedgroups.

The APA has three divisions, each with its own annual meeting. In 2017, for example, the Eastern Division meets in Baltimore, the Central Division meets in Kansas City, and the Pacific Division meets in Seattle.

While exploring the wonderful array of information on the APA website, check out its "Resources for Undergraduates" page (http://apaonline.org/?page =undergrad_resources), its "Guide to Graduate Programs in Philosophy" (http:// apaonline.org/?page=gradguide), and its "Publications" page (http://apaonline .org/?page=publications).

Read&Write 5.1 Write an Email to an APA Scholar

Your task here is simple and is based on your identifying a topic in philosophy in which you are interested. If you need an idea of where to start, browse the names of the APA affiliated groups. This may spark your interest in a particular research area. The next steps will be to narrow down to a topic and clearly explain in several sentences exactly what you are interested in researching.

Each APA division provides a downloadable PDF of its annual meeting program (e.g., http://apaonline.org/page/2017E_Program). In addition, it provides a link to the Guidebook mobile meeting app. Through this app, you can access the program on your smartphone or tablet.[3]

To help you narrow down to a topic, peruse the three division's annual meeting programs and find a paper or presentation in the subject area that interests you. Since the program lists each presenter's organizational affiliation (mostly colleges and universities), you can go to the organization's website and find the presenter's email address.

Compose an email to the listed author of the paper or presentation. Ask the author to provide you with: (1) guidance on researching the topic, (2) names of scholars in the United States (and abroad) who are knowledgeable in this subject, and (3) the names of journals, research institutes, university departments, and other sources of information on your topic. Be sure to thank the author for any information he or she may be able to provide. You may then present both the email you wrote to the author and the author's response to your course professor.

For example, let's suppose you are interested in the philosophy of creativity. After examining some articles on the topic in your library's online resources, you decide that you want to know more about the extent to which creativity is a learned skill. Now, choose an author who writes on the topic, request some information from that person, and write a summary of the information that person provides for you.

5.2   MINING DISSERTATIONS AND THINK TANKS

Dissertations and theses are papers written to fulfill requirements for master's and doctoral degrees. To be accepted by universities that issue graduate degrees,

---

[3]   See, for example, "2017 Eastern Division Meeting: Meeting Program," American Philosophical Association, http://www.apaonline.org/page/2017E_Program.

dissertations and theses normally must exhibit both (1) a demonstrated ability to meet widely recognized standards of scholarship, and (2) an original contribution to knowledge. In the United States the word *dissertation* normally refers to papers written to achieve the doctor of philosophy and other doctoral degrees, while the term *thesis* is most often attached to a paper written for a master's degree. In Europe and elsewhere, however, this distinction is less common. Dissertations are often published after graduation as monographs, articles, or books. While quantitative dissertations—papers dealing largely with statistics and statistical analyses—are often fewer than fifty pages in length, qualitative dissertations, which tend to use descriptive language to argue specific viewpoints, may run to several hundred pages.

A good place to start your search for dissertations is the search engine for the online catalog of the Global Resources Network's Center for Research Libraries (CRL), accessible from the center's home page (crl.edu). In "About CRL," you will find the following statement:

> The Center for Research Libraries (CRL) is an international consortium of university, college, and independent research libraries. Founded in 1949, CRL supports original research and inspired teaching in the humanities, sciences, and social sciences by preserving and making available to scholars a wealth of rare and uncommon primary source materials from all world regions.
>
> CRL's deep and diverse collections are built by specialists and experts at the major U.S. and Canadian research universities, who work together to identify and preserve unique and uncommon documentation and evidence, and to ensure its long-term integrity and accessibility to researchers in the CRL community.
>
> CRL is based in Chicago, Illinois, and is governed by a Board of Directors drawn from the library, research and higher education communities.[4]

Dissertations links, found on many college libraries' websites, will also provide databases of varied strengths depending upon the library's research capabilities.

Think Tanks

Private research institutes, popularly known as *think tanks,* provide a wealth of information on virtually any topic you can imagine. Your Google search will provide many lists of think tanks, but an excellent place to start is the Harvard Kennedy School's Think Tank Search (http://guides.library.harvard.edu/hks/think_tank_search). In the search engine, you can enter specific topics (e.g., "family") or specific institutes (such as the Hoover Institution).

Read&Write 5.2   Collect Dissertations and Research Institute Studies

Using the dissertation location services described above and the Harvard Kennedy School's search engine, (1) locate six dissertations and six research institute studies of importance to a research topic of your choice, and (2) write a summary of each one that describes the value of the study to the topic at hand.

---

[4]   "About," Center for Research Libraries Global Resources Network, http://www.crl.edu/about.

5.3 WELCOME TO THE NATIONAL ARCHIVES

Astronomer Carl Sagan became famous by expressing his awe of the universe by admiring a night sky full of "billions and billions of stars." When you explore the US National Archives online (archives.gov) you may well be awed by the range and variety of the billions of photographs, documents, and other items this remarkable institution has in store.

An increasing amount of material is online, yet there is much more at the archives headquarters in Washington, DC, and at other branch locations throughout the country. To find a branch location near you, visit http://www.archives.gov/locations.

Within the "Locations" section, you will find the following statements about what the archives can provide:

> We have historical documents that tell the stories of America's history as a nation and as a people, available to you in 33 locations nationwide. These valuable records are evidence of our national experience.
>
> Each year, our staff serves our visitors billions of letters, photographs, video and audio recordings, drawings, maps, treaties, posters, and other items that we have preserved. The materials are not for loan to the public, as a library loans material; they are protected, but are available for you to use in-person at our facilities and affiliated archives.
>
> You can visit the National Archives, nationwide, to:
>
> - View exhibits of historical records and presidential papers:
>   - The Public Vaults and the Charters of Freedom (the Declaration of Independence, The Constitution, and the Bill of Rights), located in Washington, D.C.
>   - Exhibits about American Presidents (each one since Herbert Hoover) in our Presidential libraries.
>   - Records of local importance to geographical regions of America in our regional facilities.
> - Request records for your examination in our research rooms. Please note: Records are located in specific facilities. Learn about how to determine which records are located where.
> - Attend public programs, including film presentations, workshops, and lectures. See our Washington D.C. Calendar of Events. For events around the country, see the calendars for each National Archives facility.
> - Review proposed Federal rules and regulations at the Federal Register, which is part of the National Archives and is located in Washington, D.C.[5]

Next, this website provides examples of what you can find at the National Archives:

- President Ronald Reagan's speech card from remarks made in Berlin, Germany in June 1987 (when the infamous Berlin Wall was still standing), which is marked up to indicate points of emphasis.

---

[5] "Why Visit the National Archives?" National Archives, last modified September 19, 2016, https://www.archives.gov/locations/why-visit.

- Photographs of child labor conditions at the turn of the 19th century. Children did everything from selling newspapers to shucking oysters to make a few pennies.
- The Zimmerman [*sic*] Telegram, named for German foreign minister Arthur Zimmermann, secretly offered U.S. lands to Mexico in exchange for Mexican support during World War I. The British were able to decipher the code. The telegram helped convince the United States to enter the war in 1917.
- The arrest warrant for Lee Harvey Oswald, the man who was accused of assassinating President John F. Kennedy in Dallas, Texas.[6]

Read&Write 5.3   Examine George Mason's Argument against the US Constitution

The National Archives offers wonderful collections of original documents. Through its search engine, locate letters written by Antifederalist George Mason (1725–1792) indicating his objections to the Constitution of the United States. Citing the original documents, summarize Mason's argument in a three-page essay.

5.4   WELCOME TO THE LIBRARY OF CONGRESS

Expect to be amazed once again at the phenomenal collections of the Library of Congress (loc.gov). Here you will find access to millions of documents of every conceivable source.

The manuscripts section alone declares: "The Library of Congress holds approximately sixty million manuscript items in eleven thousand separate collections, including some of the greatest manuscript treasures of American history and culture."[7]

Though massive today, the library's collections had a more modest beginning, as the website's history link describes:

> The Library of Congress was established by an act of Congress in 1800 when President John Adams signed a bill providing for the transfer of the seat of government from Philadelphia to the new capital city of Washington. The legislation described a reference library for Congress only, containing "such books as may be necessary for the use of Congress—and for putting up a suitable apartment for containing them therein."
>
> Established with $5,000 appropriated by the legislation, the original library was housed in the new Capitol until August 1814, when invading British troops set fire to the Capitol Building, burning and pillaging the contents of the small library.
>
> Within a month, retired President Thomas Jefferson offered his personal library as a replacement. Jefferson had spent 50 years accumulating books, "putting by everything which related to America, and indeed whatever was rare and valuable in every science"; his library was considered to be one of the finest in the United States. In offering his collection to Congress, Jefferson anticipated controversy over the nature of his

---

[6] Ibid.

[7] "Collections with Manuscripts/Mixed Material," Library of Congress, https://www.loc.gov/manuscripts/collections.

collection, which included books in foreign languages and volumes of philosophy, science, literature, and other topics not normally viewed as part of a legislative library. He wrote, "I do not know that it contains any branch of science which Congress would wish to exclude from their collection; there is, in fact, no subject to which a Member of Congress may not have occasion to refer."

In January 1815, Congress accepted Jefferson's offer, appropriating $23,950 for his 6,487 books, and the foundation was laid for a great national library. The Jeffersonian concept of universality, the belief that all subjects are important to the library of the American legislature, is the philosophy and rationale behind the comprehensive collecting policies of today's Library of Congress.[8]

Read&Write 5.4 Construct a Bibliography from the LOC Catalog

One of the featured items among the Library of Congress special collections, accessible through the search engine located at the top of the library's main page, is the Hannah Arendt collection, described as follows:

> The papers of the author, educator, and political philosopher Hannah Arendt (1906–1975) are one of the principal sources for the study of modem intellectual life. Located in the Manuscript Division at the Library of Congress, they constitute a large and diverse collection reflecting a complex career. With over 25,000 items (about 75,000 digital images), the papers contain correspondence, articles, lectures, speeches, book manuscripts, transcripts of Adolf Eichmann's trial proceedings, notes, and printed matter pertaining to Arendt's writings and academic career. The entire collection has been and is available to researchers in reading rooms at the Library of Congress, the New School University in New York City, and the Hannah Arendt Center at the University of Oldenburg, Germany. Parts of the collection and the finding aid are available for public access on the Internet.[9]

Your task in this exercise is to peruse this collection or a similar collection of materials related to another famous philosopher. Next, identify a theme in the materials (such as Arendt's views on totalitarianism). Finally, construct a properly formatted twelve-item (at least) bibliography of an aspect of your selected theme that would comprise your first selection of source materials for a research paper.

5.5   WELCOME TO THE *CONGRESSIONAL RECORD*

A 2008 government report describes the *Congressional Record* and gives tips on how to read it:

> The *Congressional Record* is the most widely recognized published account of the debates and activities in Congress. The *Record* often reflects the intent of Congress in enacting legislation. . . .

8 "History of the Library," Library of Congress, https://www.loc.gov/about/history-of-the-library.
9 "The Hannah Arendt Papers at the Library of Congress," Library of Congress, https://memory.loc.gov/ammem/arendthtml/arendthome.html.

The Constitution mandates that each house shall keep and publish a journal of its proceedings. Accordingly, the House and Senate *Journals*, which are summaries of floor proceedings, are the official accounts of congressional proceedings, but the *Record* is better known and the most useful.

The *Record* is published daily by the Government Printing Office (GPO) when either or both houses of Congress are in session. . . .

Each day's *Record* contains an account of the previous day's congressional activity. However, if a session extends past midnight, the *Record* is usually published in two parts with the first part printed the following day, and action after midnight included in the next day's edition. . . .

The *Record*, which averages about 200 pages a day, consists of four sections: the proceedings of the House; the proceedings of the Senate; the Extensions of Remarks, containing matter not part of the spoken debates and proceedings; and the Daily Digest of activity in Congress. It does not contain any text of committee proceedings.

Located at the back of the *Record,* the Daily Digest of activity in Congress is a key to using a daily *Record*. Separately for the House and Senate, it contains summary information on chamber action the preceding day, including measures introduced, reported, debated, and passed, and appointments made. It also summarizes committee activities, provides the time and location of committee and subcommittee meetings scheduled for the day the *Record* is delivered, and gives the time and date of the next convening of the House and Senate. . . .

The *Record* is also available online through GPO and the Library of Congress. It can be searched either by full text for a certain date, by Member of Congress, or by topic. The website through GPO is http://www.gpoaccess.gov/legislative.html. Once at the site, the user should click on the various options for viewing the *Congressional Record*, which is available from 1994 to the present. The website at the Library of Congress is available for the general public through THOMAS http://thomas.loc .gov and for congressional staff through the Legislative Information System http:// www.congress.gov. At these sites there are options for searching the full text of the *Record* from the 101st through 110th Congresses.[10]

The National Archives also provides detailed information on research strategies for using *CR* (http://www.archives.gov/legislative/guide/house/chapter-01-strategies .html). Perusing this site will provide you with an array of approaches to the *CR*. Our present purpose with respect to the *CR* is limited. We intend to show you how to make your voice heard to your representative or senator on current legislation.

Read&Write 5.5   Refute a Recent Speech in Congress

In this exercise, you will not only refute an argument made by a member of Congress, but you will also write a letter to that member presenting your argument. Not only is this good practice researching and writing arguments, but writing to your senator or representative may have more effect than you might think. There is an old political adage that states that for every letter a member of Congress receives, another one hundred people share the correspondent's opinion; they simply haven't taken time to write. Now you can take the time to write, and perhaps you will be the voice of 101 citizens.

---

[10] Mildred Amer, "*Congressional Record*: Its Production, Distribution, and Accessibility," Congressional Research Service, May 5, 2008, https://fas.org/sgp/crs/misc/98-266.pdf.

First, select a piece of legislation. On congress.gov, select the link for the Top 10 of the Most Viewed Bills. On October 6, 2016, this list included the following items:

1. S.2040 [114th]   Justice Against Sponsors of Terrorism Act
2. H.R.5325 [114th]   Continuing Appropriations and Military Construction, Veterans Affairs, and Related Agencies Appropriations Act, 2017, and Zika Response and Preparedness Act
3. H.R.213 [114th]   Fairness for High-Skilled Immigrants Act of 2015
4. H.R.6094 [114th]   Regulatory Relief for Small Businesses, Schools, and Nonprofits Act
5. S.3034 [114th]   Protecting Internet Freedom Act
6. H.R.5303 [114th]   Water Resources Development Act of 2016
7. H.R.2802 [114th]   First Amendment Defense Act
8. H.R.378 [114th]   Responsible Body Armor Possession Act
9. S.2848 [114th]   Water Resources Development Act of 2016
10. H.Res.896 [114th]   Recognizing the significance of the United States relationship with the Republic of Moldova and encouraging United States support for anti-corruption efforts and strengthening democratic institutions

A new top ten list appears every time Congress is in session. You can follow the links on the list to get more information about these bills. "H.R." bills are proceeding through the House of Representatives, and "S." bills through the Senate. If none of these topics interests you, or you have a favorite topic in mind, you can return to congress.gov and enter a topic of your choice into the search engine. Make sure that the bill you choose is still in Congress and has not been killed or sent to the president.

How Do I Go about Writing the Letter?

Toward the middle of the Congress.gov main page, you will find a link to "Current Members of Congress." Select your home state and then the representative or senator to whom you want to write. If you do not know who your representative is, go to http://www.house.gov/representatives/find, and enter your zip code in the search box. You can follow a link from this page to that person's web page, which contains a good deal of helpful information.

Address your letter properly. You may find a list of the proper forms of address for members of Congress in table 8 ("The Congress") of the Department of Defense Manual Number 5110.04-M-V2 (pages 16–17), published October 26, 2010, and located at this web address: http://execsec.defense.gov/Portals/34/Documents/511004m_v2.pdf.

Begin your letter by telling the representative exactly what you want him or her to do and which piece of legislation is affected. Locate the main page for that piece of legislation in the online *Congressional Record*, where a link to the right of the screen will take you to "All Bill Information (Except Text)," and be sure to include the following information:

- Short number and name of the bill (e.g., H.R.4269: "Assault Weapons Ban of 2015")
- Subtitle or full title of the bill ("To regulate assault weapons, to ensure that the right to keep and bear arms is not unlimited, and for other purposes")
- Current status of the bill ("Referred to the Subcommittee on Crime, Terrorism, Homeland Security, and Investigations," January 15, 2016)

Next, find out what members of Congress have already said about the bill so that you will have some arguments to use in your letter. In the search engine on Congress.gov, select *Congressional Record* from the pulldown menu next to the search box. Then enter the number of the bill. If members of Congress have made speeches on the bill, the speeches should appear here. Make up your own mind and take a stand.

In your letter, address two of the legislator's primary concerns. For every bill that comes to the representative's attention, he or she must answer two questions: (1) Is legislative action needed to deal with whatever problem or issue is at hand? and (2) if legislation is needed, is the specific legislation in question the best way to address the issue? To answer these two questions, you will need to make the following two arguments: (1) that the issue or problem warrants (or does not warrant) legislative action, and (2) that the specific proposed legislation appropriately deals (or does not appropriately deal) with the issue or problem.

Provide at least a few facts and examples or anecdotes. Include any personal experience or involvement that you have in the issue or problem. You do not need to provide all the information the legislator will need to make a decision, but provide enough to get him or her sufficiently interested in the issue to examine the matter further and give it serious thought.

Format the letter as you would a standard business letter and, of course, proofread your final draft carefully.

Sample Letter to a Representative

October 15, 2016

The Honorable Ben Ray Lujan
2446 Rayburn House Office Building
Washington, DC, 20515

Dear Representative Lujan:

I am writing to ask you to vote for the Environmental Justice Act of 2016 (H.R.2200, currently under consideration by the Subcommittee on Commercial and Administrative Law), an act "to require Federal agencies to develop and implement policies and practices that promote environmental justice, and for other purposes." Native Americans, Latinos, and Blacks have suffered too long under unhealthy environmental conditions on reservations and in substandard neighborhoods across the country. In my neighborhood, the toxic waste from old mining operations has caused illness in more than twenty children.

Across the country, Superfund sites and pockets of polluted air and water are affecting most the people with the fewest resources and the least political clout to deal with the problem. In Los Angeles, for example, more than 70 percent of African Americans and half of Latinos reside in the most highly polluted areas, while only a third of the local whites live in these areas. Workers in the meatpacking plants of South Omaha, Nebraska, are once again battling to restore the vitality of city parks and improve unsanitary conditions in the plants. Too often people in these communities face greater exposure to toxins and dangerous substances because waste dumps, industrial facilities, and chemical storage facilities take fewer precautions in low-income communities than they do in high-income communities. Sadly, the captains of industry view these communities as expendable, denying the human beings who live in them the dignity and respect that is their constitutional right as American citizens.

What can be done? The first step is to solve a problem in and among federal agencies. Recent environmental and health policy studies have determined that most federal agencies, including the Environmental Protection Agency, do not adequately understand that environmental justice is being continuously denied to American citizens. Furthermore, there is currently no mechanism in place to coordinate and therefore make effective the environmental justice efforts that are currently underway.

The Environmental Justice Act of 2016 does much to correct these problems. In addition to focusing federal agency attention on the environmental and human health conditions in low-income minority, including Native American, communities, this legislation takes several positive steps in the direction of securing environmental justice for Native Americans. The Environmental Justice Act of 2016:

- ensures that all federal agencies develop practices that promote environmental justice;
- increases cooperation and coordination among federal agencies;
- provides low-income minority, including Native American, communities greater access to public information and opportunity for participation in environmental decision making;
- mitigates the inequitable distribution of the burdens and benefits of federal programs having significant impact on human health and the environment; and
- holds federal agencies accountable for the effects of their projects and programs on all communities.

Your support in this urgent matter is much appreciated.

Sincerely,

P. Henry Gibson III
18 Lake Charles Way
Passamadumcott, SD 57003

6

BECOMING A PHILOSOPHER
Learning Scholarship Skills

6.1   HOW TO CRITIQUE AN ACADEMIC ARTICLE

When you read anything, especially scholarship, you will get more out of it if you ask yourself some questions as you begin: *What am I reading? Why am I reading it? What, exactly, do I expect to get out of it?*

First of all, when you read an academic article, you are reading scholarship. Scholars are people on a quest for knowledge. They want to know *what* exists (detecting, identifying, and categorizing phenomena), *how* it came to be or how it does what it does, and *why* it acts or reacts in a certain way. To qualify as scholarship accepted by the academic community, the article must make an *original contribution to knowledge*. When scholars achieve this goal, they participate in an ongoing discussion, becoming members of a community of people contributing to the ever-expanding universal storehouse of knowledge. Scholarship is rarely easy reading. Since its audience is other scholars, it assumes basic and sometimes advanced knowledge of the language(s) and practices employed in a particular discipline.

So, what is the best approach to reading scholarship? At this point it might be a good idea to revisit the reading tips given in chapter 1 of this manual. Here is a brief summary of those points, with new emphases geared specifically to the reading of scholarship:

- Before reading, check out the author. Find the author's web page and identify his or her specialty and credentials.
- Read slowly, carefully, deeply, and repeatedly.
- Read everything one section at a time.
- Reread everything one section at a time.
- Refuse to not understand anything you encounter:
    - Understand the article.
    - Understand the article's implications.
    - Imagine applications of the article's insights and discoveries.

- Question everything. Scholars are by no means infallible.
- Take lots of notes.
- Be sure to include in your notes important points, questions you can't answer, and interesting insights the article inspires.
- Create outlines as you go along that clarify for you the structure of the argument (its logic) and the process by which information in the article unfolds.

You will find that most if not all scholarly articles you read include the following elements:

- An *abstract*: a brief summary of what the article purports to have accomplished.
- An *introduction* that includes reasons for conducting the research.
- A *research question* that reveals what the article intends to discover.
- A discussion of the *methods* used to produce knowledge findings.
- A statement of the *outcomes* of applying the methods.
- A discussion of the *implications* of the findings.
- A conclusion that explains the *significance* of the findings.
- A list of *references*: sources of information used in the study.

Scholarship always has an agenda, something the scholar or scholars who have written the paper are trying to prove. Precisely identify the agenda. Then identify the sequence of points in the argument employed to support the agenda. Is the pattern of points logical? Is it biased?

To sum up, reading philosophy scholarship is all about identifying:

- What the author(s) attempted to do
- Why the author(s) wanted to do it
- How the author(s) went about doing it
- What the author(s) claimed to have discovered
- What the author(s) inferred about the importance and the benefits of knowing the discovery

Now that you know how to effectively *read* and *describe* an academic article, you can take your analysis a step further. An *article critique* is a paper that *evaluates* an article published in an academic journal. A good critique tells the reader what point the article is trying to make and how convincingly it makes that point. Writing an article critique achieves three purposes. First, it provides you with an understanding of the information contained in a scholarly article and a familiarity with other information written on the same topic. Second, it provides you with an opportunity to apply and develop your critical thinking skills as you attempt to evaluate a philosopher's work. Third, it helps you improve your own writing skills as you attempt to describe the selected article's strengths and weaknesses so that your readers can clearly understand them.

The first step in writing an article critique is to select an appropriate article. Unless your instructor specifies otherwise, select an article from a scholarly journal and not a popular or journalistic publication (such as *Time* or the *National Review*). Appendix A of this manual includes a substantial list of academic philosophy journals, but your instructor may also accept appropriate articles from academic journals in other disciplines, such as history, economics, or sociology.

Choosing an Article

Three other considerations should guide your choice of an article. First, having an interest in the topic will make writing a critique much more satisfying. Hundreds of interesting journal articles are published every year; browse article titles until you find a topic that interests you. The second consideration in selecting an article is your current level of knowledge. Many philosophy studies employ sophisticated statistical techniques. You may be better prepared to evaluate them if you have studied statistics.

The third consideration is to select a current article, one written within the last twelve months. Most material in philosophy is quickly superseded by new studies. Selecting a recent study will help ensure that you will be engaged in an up-to-date discussion of your topic.

Read&Write 6.1 Critique a Recent Article from a Philosophy Journal

Once you have selected and carefully read your article, you may begin to write your critique, which will cover five areas:

1. Thesis
2. Methods
3. Evidence of thesis support
4. Contribution to the literature
5. Recommendation

When writing this assignment, follow the directions for paper formats given in chapter 3 of this manual. Ask your instructor for directions concerning the length of the critique, but in the absence of further guidelines, your paper should not exceed five typed, double-spaced pages.

Thesis

Your first task is to find and clearly state the thesis of the article. The thesis is the main point the article is trying to make. In the abstract of an article published in the scholarly journal *Nietzsche-Studien* and titled "Nietzsche's Science of Love," Frank Chouraqui of Leiden University states his thesis very clearly:

> Abstract: In this paper, I examine the possibility of constructing an ontological phenomenology of love by tracing Nietzsche's questioning about science. I examine how the evolution of Nietzsche's thinking about science and his increasing suspicion towards it coincide with his interest for the question of love. . . . Although Nietzsche's concept of love has often been elucidated in terms of its object or its subject, I argue that such interpretations precisely defeat Nietzsche's point, which is to recover a ground that precedes the division of the world into subjects and objects. Love becomes the name of this intra-relationship of being, opening up to new perspectives on Nietzsche's ontology of the will to power.[1]

Some authors, however, do not present their theses this clearly. After you have read the article, ask yourself whether you had to hunt for the thesis. Comment about the clarity of the author's thesis presentation and state the author's thesis in your critique. Before proceeding

---

[1] Frank Chouraqui, "Nietzsche's Science of Love," *Nietzsche-Studien* 44, no. 1 (2015): 267–90, doi:10.1515 /nietzstu-2015-0131.

with the remaining elements of your critique, consider the importance of the topic. Has the author written something that is important for us as citizens or philosophers to read?

Methods

In your critique, carefully answer the following questions:

1. What methods did the author use to investigate the topic? In other words, how did the author go about supporting the thesis?
2. Were the appropriate methods used?
3. Did the author's approach to supporting the thesis make sense?
4. Did the author employ the selected methods correctly?
5. Did you discover any errors in the way he or she conducted the research?

Evidence of Thesis Support

In your critique, answer the following questions:

1. What evidence did the author present in support of the thesis?
2. What are the strengths of the evidence presented?
3. What are the weaknesses of the evidence?
4. On balance, how well did the author support the thesis?

Contribution to the Literature

This step will probably require you to undertake some research of your own. Identify articles and books published on the subject of your selected article within the past five years. Browse the titles and read perhaps half a dozen of the publications that appear to provide the best discussion of the topic. In your critique, list the most important other articles or books that have been published on your topic, and then, in view of these publications, evaluate the contribution that your selected article makes to a better understanding of the subject.

Recommendation

In this section of your critique, summarize your evaluation of the article. Tell your readers several things: Who will benefit from reading this article? What will the benefit be? How important and extensive is that benefit? Clearly state your evaluation of the article in the form of a thesis for your own critique. Your thesis might be something like the following:

> In a 2015 article published in *Nietzsche-Studien* and titled "Nietzsche's Science of Love," Frank Chouraqui of Leiden University provides a helpful correction of misconceptions about what Nietzsche was attempting to accomplish in writing a "science of love." Philosophers can now more accurately direct their focus to Nietzsche's "intra-relationship of being," which is a powerful ontological insight.

6.2 HOW TO WRITE A BOOK REVIEW

Successful book reviews answer three questions:

1. What did the writer of the book try to communicate?
2. How clearly and convincingly did he or she get this message across to the reader?
3. Was the message worth reading?

Capable book reviewers of several centuries have answered these three questions well. People who read a book review want to know if a particular book is worth reading, for their own particular purposes, before buying or reading it. These potential readers want to know the book's subject and its strengths and weaknesses, and they want to gain this information as easily and quickly as possible. Your goal in writing a book review, therefore, is to help people efficiently decide whether to buy or read a book. Your immediate objectives may be to please your instructor and get a good grade, but these objectives are most likely to be met if you focus on a book review's audience: people who want help in selecting books to buy or read. In the process of writing a book review that reaches this primary goal, you will also

- Learn about the book you are reviewing
- Learn about professional standards for book reviews in philosophy
- Learn the essential steps of book reviewing that apply to any academic discipline

This final objective, learning to review a book properly, has more applications than you may at first imagine. First, it helps you focus quickly on the essential elements of a book and draw from a book its informational value for yourself and others. Some of the most successful people in government, business, and other professions speed-read several books a week, more for the knowledge they contain than for enjoyment. These readers then apply this knowledge to substantial advantage in their work. It is normally not wise to speed-read a book you are reviewing because you are unlikely to gain enough information to evaluate it fairly from such a fast reading. Writing book reviews, however, helps you become proficient in quickly sorting out valuable information from material that is not. The ability to make such discriminations is a fundamental ingredient in management and professional success.

In addition, writing book reviews for publication allows you to participate in the discussions of the broader intellectual and professional community of which you are a part. People in law, medicine, teaching, engineering, administration, and other fields are frequently asked to write book reviews to help others assess newly released publications.

Before beginning your book review, read the following sample, a review of a book with substantial interest to political philosophers and philosophers of religion. It is Gregory M. Scott's review of a collection of essays edited by John L. Esposito, titled *Political Islam: Revolution, Radicalism, or Reform?* The review appeared in volume 26 of the *Southeastern Political Review* (June 1998) and is reprinted here by permission. The numerals in parentheses refer to page numbers from the book under review:

Behold an epitaph for the specter of monolithically autocratic Islam. In its survey of Islamic political movements from Pakistan to Algeria, *Political Islam: Revolution, Radicalism, or Reform?* effectively lays to rest the popular notion that political expressions of Islam are inherently violent and authoritarian. For this accomplishment alone John L. Esposito and company's scholarly anthology merits the attention of serious students of religion and philosophy, and justifies the book's own claim to making a "seminal contribution." Although it fails to identify how Islam as religious faith and cultural tradition lends Muslim philosophy a distinctively Islamic flavor, this volume clearly answers the question posed by its title: yes, political Islam encompasses not only revolution and radicalism, but moderation and reform as well.

Although two of the eleven contributors are historians, *Political Islam* exhibits both the strengths and weaknesses of contemporary philosophy with respect to religion. It identifies connections between economics and philosophy, and between culture and philosophy, much better than it deciphers the nuances of the relationships between philosophy and religious belief. After a general introduction, the first three articles explore political Islam as illegal opposition, first with a summary of major movements and then with studies of Algeria and the Gulf states. In her chapter titled "Fulfilling Prophecies: State Policy and Islamist Radicalism," Lisa Anderson sets a methodological guideline for the entire volume when she writes:

> Rather than look to the substance of Islam or the content of putatively Islamic political doctrines for a willingness to embrace violent means to desired ends, we might explore a different perspective and examine the political circumstances, or institutional environment, that breeds political radicalism, extremism, or violence independent of the content of the doctrine (18).

> Therefore, rather than assessing how Islam as religion affects Muslim philosophy, all the subsequent chapters proceed to examine philosophy, economics, and culture in a variety of Muslim nations. This means that the title of the book is slightly misleading: it discusses Muslim philosophy rather than political Islam. Esposito provides the book's conclusion about the effects of Islamic belief on the political process when he maintains that "the appeal to religion is a two-edged sword. . . . It can provide or enhance self-legitimation, but it can also be used as a yardstick for judgment by opposition forces and delegitimation" (70).

The second part of the volume features analyses of the varieties of political processes in Iran, Sudan, Egypt, and Pakistan. These chapters clearly demonstrate not only that Islamic groups may be found in varied positions on normal economic and ideological spectrums, but that Islam is not necessarily opposed to moderate, pluralist philosophy. The third section of the anthology examines the international relations of Hamas, Afghani Islamists, and Islamic groups involved in the Middle East peace process. These chapters are especially important for American students because they present impressive documentation for the conclusions that the motives and demands of many Islamic groups are considerably more moderate and reasonable than much Western political commentary would suggest.

The volume is essentially well written. All the articles with the exception of chapter two avoid unnecessarily dense philosophy jargon. As a collection of methodologically sound and analytically astute treatments of Muslim philosophy, *Political Islam: Revolution, Radicalism, or Reform?* is certainly appropriate for adoption as a supplemental text for courses in religion and philosophy. By way of noting what it does not cover, readers may consider that although it is sufficient for its purposes as it stands, the volume could be a primary text in a course on Islamic philosophy if it included four additional chapters:

1. An historical overview of the origins and varieties of Islam as religion
2. A summary of the global Islamic political-ideological spectrum (from liberal to fundamentalist)
3. An overview of the varieties of global Islamic cultures
4. An attempt to describe in what manner, if any, Islam, in all its varieties, gives philosophy a different flavor from the philosophy of other major religions[1]

Elements of a Book Review

Your first sentence should entice people to read your review. A crisp summary of what the book is about is inviting to your readers; it lets them know that you can quickly and clearly come to the point. They know that their time and efforts will not be wasted in an attempt to wade through your vague prose in hopes of finding out something about the book. Notice Scott's opening line: "Behold an epitaph for the specter of monolithically autocratic Islam." It is a bit overburdened with large words, but it is engaging and precisely sums up the essence of the review. Your opening statement can be engaging and "catchy," but be sure that it provides an accurate portrayal of the book in one crisp statement.

Your book review should allow the reader to join you in examining the book. Tell the reader what the book is about. One of the greatest strengths of Scott's review is that his first paragraph immediately tells you exactly what he thinks the book accomplishes.

When you review a book, write about what is actually in the book, not what you think is probably there or ought to be there. Do not explain how you would have written the book, but instead how the author wrote it. Describe the book in clear, objective terms. Tell enough about the content to identify the author's major points.

Clarify the book's value and contribution to philosophy by defining (1) what the author is attempting to do and (2) how the author's work fits within current similar efforts in the discipline of philosophy or scholarly inquiry in general. Notice how Scott immediately describes what Esposito is trying to do: "This volume clearly answers the question posed by its title." Scott precedes this definition of the author's purpose by placing his work within the context of current similar writing in political science; Scott states that "for this accomplishment alone John L. Esposito and company's scholarly anthology merits the attention of serious students of religion and politics, and justifies the book's own claim to making a 'seminal contribution.'"

The elucidation portion of book reviews often provides additional information about the author. Scott has not included such information about Esposito in his review, but it would be helpful to know, for example, if Esposito has written other books on the subject, has developed a reputation for exceptional expertise on a certain issue, or is known to have a particular ideological bias. How would your understanding of this book be changed, for example, if you knew that its author

---

[2] Gregory M. Scott, review of *Political Islam: Revolution, Radicalism, or Reform?* by John L. Esposito, ed., *Southeastern Political Review* 26, no. 2 (1998): 512–24.

was a leader of ISIS or the Taliban? Include information in your book review about the author that helps the reader understand how this book fits within the broader concerns of philosophy.

Once you explain what the book is attempting to do, you should tell the reader the extent to which this goal has been met. To evaluate a book effectively, you will need to establish evaluation criteria and then compare the book's content to those criteria. You do not need to define your criteria specifically in your review, but they should be evident to the reader. Your criteria will vary according to the book you are reviewing, and you may discuss them in any order that is helpful to the reader. Consider, however, including the following among the criteria that you establish for your book review:

- How important is the subject to the study of philosophy and government?
- How complete and thorough is the author's coverage of the subject?
- How carefully is the author's analysis conducted?
- What are the strengths and limitations of the author's methodology?
- What is the quality of the writing? Is it clear, precise, and interesting?
- How does this book compare with others on the subject?
- What contribution does this book make to philosophy?
- Who will enjoy or benefit from this book?

When giving your evaluations according to these criteria, be specific. If you write, "This is a good book; I liked it very much," you tell nothing of interest or value to the reader. Notice, however, how Scott's review helps clearly define the content and the limitations of the book by contrasting the volume with what he describes as an ideal primary text for a course in Islamic philosophy: "By way of noting what it does not cover, readers may consider that although it is sufficient for its purposes as it stands, the volume could be a primary text in a course on Islamic philosophy if it included four additional chapters."

Read&Write 6.2 Review a New Philosophy Book

Format and Content

The directions for writing papers provided in chapters 1 through 3 apply to book reviews as well. Some further instructions specific to book reviews are needed, however. List on the title page, along with the standard information required for philosophy papers, data on the book being reviewed: title, author, place and name of publisher, date, and number of pages. The title of the book should be in italics or underlined, but not both.

Reflective or Analytical Book Reviews

Instructors in the humanities and social sciences normally assign two types of book reviews: the *reflective* and the *analytical*. Ask your instructor which type of book review you are to write. The purpose of a reflective book review is for the reviewer to exercise creative analytical judgment without being influenced by the reviews of others. Reflective book reviews contain all the elements covered in this chapter—enticement, examination, elucidation, and evaluation—but they do not include the views of others who have also read the book.

Analytical book reviews contain all the information provided by reflective reviews but add an analysis of the comments of other reviewers. The purpose is, thus, to review not only the book itself but also *its reception in the professional community.*

To write an analytical book review, insert a review analysis section immediately after your summary of the book. To prepare this section, use the *Book Review Digest* and *Book Review Index* either in print or online to locate other reviews of the book that have been published in journals and other periodicals. As you read these reviews:

1. List the criticisms of the book's strengths and weaknesses that are made in the reviews.
2. Develop a concise summary of these criticisms, indicate the overall positive or negative tone of the reviews, and mention some of the most commonly found comments.
3. Evaluate the criticisms found in these reviews. Are they basically accurate in their assessment of the book?
4. Write a review analysis of two pages or less that states and evaluates steps 2 and 3 above, and place it in your book review immediately after your summary of the book.

Length of a Book Review

Unless your instructor gives you other directions, a reflective book review should be three to five typed pages long, and an analytical book review should be five to seven pages long. In either case, a brief, specific, and concise book review is almost always preferred over one of greater length.

6.3   HOW TO WRITE A LITERATURE REVIEW

Your goal in writing a research paper is to provide an opportunity for your readers to increase their understanding of the subject you are addressing. They will want the most current and precise information available. Whether you are writing a traditional library research paper, conducting an experiment, or preparing an analysis of a policy enforced by a government agency, you must know what has already been learned in order to give your readers comprehensive and up-to-date information or to add something new to what they already know about the subject. If your topic is immigration reform, for example, you will want to find out precisely what national, state, and local government policies currently affect immigration, and the important details of how and why these policies came to be adopted. When you seek this information, you will be conducting a *literature review*, a thoughtful collection and analysis of available information on the topic you have selected for study. It tells you, before you begin your paper, experiment, or analysis, what is already known about the subject.

Why do you need to conduct a literature review? It would be embarrassing to spend a lot of time and effort preparing a study, only to find that the information you are seeking has already been discovered by someone else. Also, a properly conducted literature review will tell you many things about a particular subject. It will tell you the extent of current knowledge, sources of data for your research, examples of what is *not* known (which in turn generate ideas for formulating hypotheses), methods that have been previously used for research, and clear definitions of concepts relevant to your own research.

Let us consider an example. Suppose that you have decided to research the following question: "How are personal beliefs affected by negative arguments?" First, you will need to establish a clear definition of "negative arguments"; then you will need to find a way to measure beliefs; finally, you will need to use or develop a method of discerning how beliefs are affected by arguments. Using research techniques explained in this and other chapters of this manual, you will begin your research by looking in the library, on the Internet, and through other resources for studies that address your research question or similar questions. You will discover that many studies have been written on personal beliefs and the effects of arguments on them. As you read these studies, certain patterns will appear. Some research methods will seem to have produced better results than others. Some studies will be quoted in others many times, some confirming and others refuting what previous studies have done. You will constantly be making choices as you examine these studies, reading very carefully those that are highly relevant to your purposes, and skimming those that are of only marginal interest. As you read, constantly ask yourself the following questions:

- How much is known about this subject?
- What is the best available information, and why is it better than other information?
- What research methods have been used successfully in relevant studies?
- What are the possible sources of data for further investigation of this topic?
- What important information is still not known, in spite of all previous research?
- Of the methods that have been used for research, which are the most effective for making new discoveries? Are new methods needed?
- How can the concepts being researched be more precisely defined?

You will find that this process, like the research process as a whole, is recursive. Insights related to one of the above questions will spark new investigations into others, these investigations will then bring up a new set of questions, and so on.

Read&Write 6.3 Write a Philosophy Literature Review

If you are writing a paper, your instructor may request that you include a literature review section in it. Your written literature review may be from one to several pages in length, but it should always tell the reader the following information:

1. Which previously compiled or published studies, articles, or other documents provide the best available information on the selected topic?
2. What do these studies conclude about the topic?
3. What are the apparent methodological strengths and weaknesses of these studies?
4. What remains to be discovered about the topic?

5. What appear to be, according to these studies, the most effective methods for developing new information on the topic?

Your literature review should consist of a written narrative that answers—not necessarily consecutively—the above questions. The success of your own research project depends in large part on the extent to which you have carefully and thoughtfully answered these questions.

PRELIMINARY SCHOLARSHIP

Research Effectively

7.1 INSTITUTE AN EFFECTIVE RESEARCH PROCESS

The philosophy research paper is where all your skills as an interpreter of details, an organizer of facts and theories, and a writer of clear prose come together. Building logical arguments on the twin bases of fact and hypothesis is the way things are done in philosophy, and the most successful philosophers are those who master the art of research.

Students new to the writing of research papers sometimes find themselves intimidated by the job ahead of them. After all, the research paper adds what seems to be an extra set of complexities to the writing process. As any other expository or persuasive paper does, a research paper must present an original thesis using a carefully organized and logical argument. But it also investigates a topic that is outside the writer's own experience. This means that writers must locate and evaluate information that is new, thus, in effect, educating themselves as they explore their topics. A beginning researcher sometimes feels overwhelmed by the basic requirements of the assignment or by the authority of the source material being investigated.

As you begin a research project, it may be difficult to establish a sense of control over the different tasks you are undertaking. You may have little notion of where to search for a thesis or how to locate the most helpful information. If you do not carefully monitor your own work habits, you may find yourself unwittingly abdicating responsibility for the paper's argument by borrowing it wholesale from one or more of your sources.

Who is in control of your paper? The answer must be you—not the instructor who assigned you the paper, and certainly not the published writers and interviewees whose opinions you solicit. If all your paper does is paste together the opinions of others, it has little use. It is up to you to synthesize an original idea from a judicious evaluation of your source material. At the beginning of your research project, you will, of course, be unsure about many elements of your paper. For example, you will probably not yet have a definitive thesis sentence or even much understanding of the shape of your argument. But you can establish a measure of control over the process you will go through to complete the paper. And if you work regularly and systematically, keeping yourself open to new ideas as they present themselves, your sense of control will grow. Here are some suggestions to help you establish and maintain control of your paper:

1. **Understand your assignment.** A research assignment can go wrong simply because the writer did not read the assignment carefully. Considering how much time and effort you are about to put into your project, it is a very good idea to make sure you have a clear understanding of what your instructor wants you to do. Be sure to ask your instructor about any aspect of the assignment that is unclear to you—but only after you have read it carefully more than once. Recopying the assignment in your own handwriting is a good way to start, even though your instructor may have already given it to you in writing. Before diving into the project, ask yourself these questions: *What is my topic? What is my purpose? Who is my audience? What type of research will I be doing?*

2. **What is your topic?** The assignment may give you a great deal of specific information about your topic, or you may be allowed considerable freedom in establishing one for yourself. In an ethics class in which you are studying ethical issues affecting American foreign policy, your professor might give you a very specific assignment—for example, a paper examining the difficulties of establishing an ethical foreign policy in the wake of the collapse of President Obama's moderate isolationism—or he or she may allow you to choose your own topic. You need to understand the terms, as set up in the assignment, by which you will design your project.

3. **What is your purpose?** Whatever the degree of latitude you are given in the matter of your topic, pay close attention to the way your instructor has phrased the assignment. Is your primary job to *describe* a current ethical issue or to *take a stand* on it? Are you to *compare* ethical options, and if so, to what end? Are you to *classify, persuade, survey,* or *analyze*? To determine the purpose of the project, look for such descriptive terms in the assignment.

4. **Who is your audience?** Your orientation to the paper is profoundly affected by your conception of the audience for whom you are writing. Of course, your main reader is your instructor, but who else would be interested in your paper? Are you writing for philosophy students, the general public, citizens in your community? A paper that includes symbolic logic may justifiably contain much more technical jargon for an audience of philosophy students than for the general public.

5. **What kind of research are you doing?** You will be doing one if not both of the following kinds of research:

   - *Primary research*, which requires you to discover information firsthand, often by reading works of published philosophers, conducting interviews of students, or surveying ethical positions underlying issues reported in the media. In primary research, you are collecting and sifting through raw data—data that have not already been interpreted by researchers—which you will then study, select, arrange, and speculate on. These raw data may be the positions of philosophers or opinions of people on the street, historical documents, the published letters of a famous philosopher, or material collected from other researchers. It is important to carefully set up the methods by which you collect your data. Your aim is to uncover and gather the most accurate information possible, from which you or other writers using the material will later make sound observations.

- *Secondary research*, which uses published accounts of primary materials. Although the primary researcher might poll a community for its opinion on the outcome of a recent bond election, the secondary researcher will use the material from the poll to support a particular thesis. Secondary research, in other words, focuses on interpretations of raw data. Most of your college papers will be based on your use of secondary sources.

Primary Source	Secondary Source
A published collection of David Hume's letters	A journal article arguing that the volume of letters illustrates Hume's epistemology
An interview with a philosopher	An analysis of the philosopher's positions based on the interview
Material from a questionnaire	A paper basing its thesis on the results of the questionnaire

6. **Keep your perspective.** Whichever type of research you perform, you must keep your results in perspective. There is no way that you, as a primary researcher, can be completely objective in your findings. It is not possible to design a questionnaire that will net you absolute truth, nor can you be sure that the opinions you gather in interviews reflect the accurate and unchanging opinions of the people you question. Likewise, if you are conducting secondary research, you must remember that the articles and journals you are reading are shaped by the aims of their writers, who are interpreting primary materials for their own ends. The farther you are removed from a primary source, the greater the possibility for distortion. Your job as a researcher is to be as accurate as possible, which means keeping in view the limitations of your methods and their ends.

In any research project, there will be moments of confusion, but you can prevent this confusion from overwhelming you by establishing an effective research procedure.

Give Yourself Plenty of Time

You may feel like delaying your research for many reasons: unfamiliarity with the library, the press of other obligations, a deadline that seems comfortably far away. But do not allow such factors to deter you. Research takes time. Working in a library seems to speed up the clock, so that the hour you expected it would take you to find a certain source becomes two. You must allow yourself the time needed not only to find material but also to read it, assimilate it, and set it in the context of your own thoughts. If you delay starting, you may well find yourself distracted by the deadline; having to keep an eye on the clock while trying to make sense of a writer's complicated argument is no easy task.

You need to design a schedule that is as systematic as possible, yet flexible enough so that you do not feel trapped by it. By always showing you what to do next, a schedule will help keep you from running into dead ends. At the same time, a schedule can help you retain the focus necessary to spot new ideas and new strategies as you work.

Do Background Reading

Whether you are doing primary or secondary research, you need to know what kinds of work have already been done in your field and that it is **NEVER APPROPRIATE** to rely on material that you find in general encyclopedias such as *Wikipedia* or *Encyclopedia Britannica*. You may wish to consult one for an overview of an unfamiliar topic, but you must not even import sections, let alone entire articles, from such volumes. This practice is not good scholarship. One major reason your instructor has assigned a research paper is to let you experience the kinds of books and journals in which the discourse of philosophy is conducted. Encyclopedias are good places for instant introductions to subjects; some even include bibliographies of reference works at the ends of their articles. But to write a useful paper, you will need much more detailed information about your subject. Once you have learned what you can from a general encyclopedia, move on to the academic articles that you will find by following links on your college library's web page. Once you find two or three good articles on your topic, you will find that the bibliographies at the end of the articles will be rich sources of other articles and books of academically acceptable quality.

Narrow Your Topic and Establish a Working Thesis

The process of coming up with a viable thesis for a paper involving academic research is pretty much the same as for a paper that doesn't require formal research. But the need to consult published sources in order to formulate a thesis may seem to make the enterprise more intimidating. (Chapter 1 offers general tips for finding a successful thesis for a paper.) For a research paper in a course in philosophy of religion, a student—we'll call her Charlotte—was given the topic category new religious movements (NRMs), from which she chose the specific topic of eschatology. Here is the path Charlotte took as she looked for ways to limit the topic effectively and find a thesis.

General Topic	Eschatology in NRMs
Potential Topics	The role of eschatology in NRM recruitment
	Themes in the eschatologies of NRMs
	Tendencies of NRMs to immanentize their eschatologies
	The role of eschatology in producing community solidarity within NRMs.
Working Thesis	Eschatologies are especially important in recruitment, but not in normal operations of NRMs.

As with any paper, it is unlikely that you will come up with a satisfactory thesis at the beginning of your research project. You need a way to guide yourself through the early stages of research as you work toward discovering a main idea that is both useful and manageable. If you have a *working thesis*—a preliminary statement of your purpose—in mind, it can help you select material that is of greatest relevance to you as you examine potential sources. The working thesis will probably evolve as your research progresses, and you should be ready to accept such change. You must not fix on a thesis too early in the process, or you may miss opportunities to refine it.

Conduct Interviews   Of particular importance to Charlotte's research is the value of personal interviews with NRM members. If you conduct interviews, first establish a purpose for each one, bearing in mind the requirements of your working thesis. In what ways might your interview benefit your paper? Write down your description of the interview's purpose. Estimate its length, and inform your subject. Arrive for your interview on time and dressed appropriately. Be courteous.

Before the interview, learn as much as possible about your topic by researching published sources. Use this research to design your questions. If possible, learn something about the backgrounds of the people you interview. This knowledge may help you establish rapport with your subjects and will also help you tailor your questions. Take with you to the interview a list of prepared questions. However, be ready during the interview to depart from your list in order to follow any potentially useful direction that the questioning may take.

Take notes. Make sure you have extra pens. Do not use a recording device because it will inhibit most interviewees. If you must use a recording device, *ask for permission from your subject* before beginning the interview. Follow up your interview with a thank-you letter and, if feasible, a copy of the paper in which you used the interview.

Draft a Thesis and Outline

No matter how thoroughly you may hunt for data or how fast you read, you will not be able to find and assimilate every source pertaining to your subject, especially if it is popular or controversial, and you should not unduly prolong your research. You must bring this phase of the project to an end—with the option of resuming it if the need arises—and begin to shape both the material you have gathered and your thoughts about it into a paper. During the research phase of your project, you have been thinking about your working thesis, testing it against the material you have discovered, and considering ways to improve it. Eventually, you must formulate a thesis that sets out an interesting and useful task, one that can be satisfactorily managed within the limits of your assignment and that effectively employs much, if not all, of the material you have gathered.

Once you have formulated your thesis, it is a good idea to make an outline of the paper. In helping you to determine a structure for your writing, the outline is also testing the thesis, prompting you to discover the kinds of work your paper will need to accomplish in order to complete the task set out by the main idea. Chapter 1 discusses the structural requirements of the formal and the informal outline. If you have used note cards, you may want to start outlining by organizing your cards according to the headings you have given them and looking for logical connections among the different groups of cards. Experimenting with structure in this way may lead you to discoveries that will further improve your thesis.

No thesis or outline is written in stone. There is still time to improve the structure or purpose of your paper after you have begun to write your first draft or, for that matter, your final draft. Some writers actually prefer to write a first draft before outlining, and then study the draft's structure to determine what revisions need to be made. *Stay flexible*, and always look for a better connection—a sharper wording of your thesis. All the time you are writing, the testing of your ideas continues.

Write a First Draft

Despite all the preliminary work you have done on your paper, you may feel a reluctance to begin your first draft. Integrating all your material and your ideas into a smoothly flowing argument is indeed a complicated task. It may help to think of your first attempt as only a rough draft, which can be changed as necessary. Another strategy for reducing reluctance to start is to begin with the part of the draft about which you feel most confident instead of with the introduction. You may write sections of the draft in any order, piecing the parts together later. But however you decide to start writing—START.

Obtain Feedback

It is not enough that you understand your argument; others have to understand it, too. If your instructor is willing to look at your rough draft, you should take advantage of the opportunity and pay careful attention to any suggestions for improvement. Other readers may also be of help, although having a friend or a relative read your draft may not be as helpful as having it read by someone who is knowledgeable in your field. In any event, be sure to evaluate any suggestions carefully. Remember, the final responsibility for the paper rests with you.

Read&Write 7.1 Write a Philosophy Research Proposal

Do you aspire to a professional career? Philosopher? Lawyer? Professor? Entrepreneur? Doctor? Engineer? School Principal? Nurse? Architect? Marketing Director? Executive Director, Nonprofit Organization? Research Director? The ability to write a high-quality research proposal may well be one of the most useful and profitable skills you acquire en route to your BA or BS degree. Research proposals are written by the hundreds in public and private agencies and by innovators and entrepreneurs every day. A long-standing motto of entrepreneurs of all sorts is a simple lead-in to commercial success: "Find a need and fill it." From the lightbulb to the iPhone, this principle has been a guiding motivation for thousands of successful inventors, entrepreneurs, CEOs, volunteers, and medical missionaries. Remember that a *need* is both a problem that someone wants to solve and an opportunity for you to make a contribution by solving it.

Why does writing a philosophy research proposal foster success in this process? Three good reasons. First, a research proposal is an excellent way to organize the flow of your logic, argument, and research process. This preliminary organization alone can save you a lot of time.

Second, a well-written research proposal can save you even more time and energy. Suppose your philosophy professor assigns a twenty-page research paper on a topic of your choice. If you ask your professor, early on in your research, to review a simplified proposal, basically a preliminary outline of your paper, you may receive feedback that strengthens your paper and saves you from running down blind alleys.

Third, as your philosophy studies advance to a doctoral dissertation, for example, your research may require funding. While most philosophy projects do not need the funding that experimental research in psychology or field research in anthropology require, you may still need to travel to find what you need. Suppose you want to study Spanish philosopher José Ortega y Gasset (1883–1955). You may need to examine some unpublished manuscripts at the Institute of Humanities in Madrid, an organization that Ortega y Gasset founded. A research proposal could be your key to a successful travel grant application.

Note: Even if your research is not as extensive as that required for a dissertation, many universities offer funds for undergraduate research.

The first step in acquiring funding of any sort is a *research proposal* to acquire funds and/or authorization to conduct the research. Research proposals, therefore, are sales jobs. Their purpose is to "sell" the belief that a research study will be beneficial to the academic community. Before conducting a research study for a government agency, you will need to convince someone in authority that a study is worthwhile by accomplishing the following seven tasks:

1. Document the benefits of the study.
2. Describe the objectives of the study.
3. Explain how the study will be done.
4. Describe the resources (time, travel, resources, etc.) that will be needed to do the job.
5. Construct a schedule that states when the project will begin and end, and gives important dates in between.
6. Prepare a project budget that specifies the financial costs and the amount to be billed (if any) to the government agency.
7. Carefully define what *product* your project will yield: what kind of document will be produced, how substantial it will be, and what it will contain.

The Content of Research Proposals

In form, research proposals contain the following four parts:

1. Title page
2. Outline page
3. Text (including a table of contents)
4. Reference page

The content of your research proposal will include

- A description of the nature of the materials being sought (books, manuscripts, interviews, letters, etc.)
- A description of the research methods to be employed
- A description of the information sources to be examined
- A budget for the research, writing, and publication (if any) process
- A schedule for the study
- A description of the final product of the study

7.2 FIND AND EVALUATE THE QUALITY OF ONLINE AND PRINTED INFORMATION

The saying "winning isn't everything; it's the only thing" may not have originated with Green Bay Packers coach Vince Lombardi, but he certainly popularized it. In terms of academic scholarship, it is no exaggeration to say "Credibility isn't everything; it's the only thing," because the importance of readers' acceptance of what is written cannot be underestimated. If your work lacks credibility, it has no value at all. With this in mind, understand that the credibility of your writing will depend, more than anything else, on the credibility of your sources.

You may have already read the news article appraisal checklist in section 1.3 of this manual. The principles involved with reading other sources of information are much the same as the ones you apply to news articles, but for more complex information sources you will find the following additional suggestions to be helpful.

Base Choice on Reputation

In general, reputation of information conforms to a clear hierarchy, described here in descending order of credibility. Here is a list of high-quality sources:

- *Articles in academic journals*, though not foolproof, have a huge credibility advantage. They conform to the research and writing standards explained throughout this manual. They often require months, if not years, to write, allowing for revision and refinement. They often employ a team of several authors, each of whom can assess the quality and accuracy of the others' work. Once submitted to a journal for publication they are "peer-reviewed"—that is, distributed (blind) to experts in the articles' topics—for review and comment. Once published they are exposed to widespread readership, providing an additional quality filter.

- *Research studies by recognized think tanks* (research institutes) are often of exceptionally high quality. They are not exposed to the same extent of external review prior to publication as academic journals, and the institutions that produce them often have a known ideological perspective. Yet whether they are conservative, liberal, or libertarian in orientation, their writers know that the credibility of their work depends on maintaining consistent high quality.

- *Research studies by government agencies* are much like think tank papers but are likely to be controversial because their findings will always annoy people who are unhappy with their conclusions. They can be very powerful, however, if they are used by the president or by Congress to adopt particular public policies.

- *Reports in high-quality nonpartisan magazines and television journalism* are often highly reliable in both research and reporting. Examples of sources include periodicals like the *Economist*, the *Atlantic*, the *New Yorker*, the *American Scholar*, *Foreign Affairs*, and *Foreign Policy*, and PBS journalism in features such as *Frontline* and *The American Experience*.

- *Articles in high-quality newspapers* like the *New York Times, Wall Street Journal, Washington Post,* and *Christian Science Monitor* cite authoritative sources.
- *Pieces in high-quality partisan magazines* like the *Nation* and the *National Review* can provide relatively reliable, if slanted and selective, information.

Low-quality sources are of several sorts, and all are to be read for quickly secured unverified "facts" and amusement rather than education. Here are some low-quality sources:

- *Wikipedia* provides much information quickly and some tolerable overviews of topics, but is notoriously vulnerable to contributors who provide unverified and even false information.
- Partisan blogs, such as the *Huffington Post,* are fun and provide an interesting array of perspectives and insights, but any information you find on them must be verified by more credible sources.
- Commercial TV news sources, like CNN and, especially, Fox News are so sensational and clearly biased that their value is little more than entertainment.

As with newspapers, the following elements of information sources for philosophy research are essential to assessing content quality.

- *Author.* What are the credentials and reputation of the author of the publication?
- *Information sources.* What sources of information does the author of a particular article use? Are these sources recognized individuals or institutions?
- *Writing quality.* Is the article well written? Is it clear and cogent? Does it use a lot of jargon? Can you understand it?
- *Quantity of information.* Is the article sufficiently comprehensive to substantiate its thesis?
- *Unsupported assumptions.* When an author writes, for example, "Statistics prove that hospitals in urban areas provide better care than rural facilities," does the author identify the statistics?
- *Balance.* Does the article cover all relevant aspects of a subject?

Develop a Working Bibliography

As you begin your research, you will look for published sources—essays, books, or interviews with experts—that may help you. This list of potentially useful sources is your *working bibliography.* There are many ways to develop this bibliography. The cataloging system in your library will give you sources, as will the published bibliographies in your field. The general references in which you did your background reading may also list such works, and each specialized book or essay you find will have a bibliography that its writer used, which may be helpful to you.

It is from your working bibliography that you will select the items for the bibliography that will appear in the final draft of your paper. Early in your research, you will not know which of the sources will help you and which will not. But it is important to keep an accurate description of each entry in your working bibliography so that you will be able to easily tell which items you have investigated and which you will need to consult again. Establishing the working bibliography also allows you to practice using the bibliographical format you are required to follow in your final draft. As you make your list of potential sources, be sure to include all the information about each one, in the proper format, using the proper punctuation. (Chapter 3 describes in detail the bibliographical formats most often required for philosophy papers.)

Request Needed Information

In the course of your research, you may need to consult a source that is not immediately available to you. Working on a textbook censorship paper, for example, you might find that a packet of potentially useful information may be obtained from a government agency or public interest group in Washington, DC. Or you may discover that a needed book is not owned by your university library or by any other local library, or that a successful antidrug program has been implemented in the school system of a city of comparable size in another state. In such situations, it may be tempting to disregard potential sources because of the difficulty of consulting them. If you ignore this material, however, you are not doing your job.

It is vital that you take steps to acquire the needed data. In the first case mentioned above, you can simply write to the Washington, DC, agency or interest group; in the second, you may use your library's interlibrary loan procedure to obtain the book; in the third, you can track down the council that manages the antidrug campaign by email, phone, or Internet, and ask for information. Remember that many businesses and government agencies want to share their information with interested citizens; some have employees or entire departments whose job is to facilitate communication with the public. Be as specific as possible when asking for such information. It is a good idea to outline your own project briefly—in no more than a few sentences—to help the respondent determine the types of information that will be useful to you.

Never let the immediate unavailability of a source stop you from trying to consult it. And be sure to begin the job of locating and acquiring such long-distance material as soon as possible, to allow for the various delays that often occur.

Read&Write 7.2   Locate a Dozen High-Quality Sources

Assume you are going to write a ten-page paper on a topic of your choice. Locate and list, in proper *Chicago Manual of Style* bibliographical format, a dozen high-quality sources for your paper.

8

PRACTICE VARIETIES
OF PHILOSOPHY

8.1 PRACTICE POLICY ANALYSIS

What Is Policy Analysis?

When President Obama took office in 2008 he faced a long list of problems, some of which seemed almost overpowering. The nation was in the trough of its deepest recession since the Great Depression of the 1930s. America was fighting wars in both Iraq and Afghanistan. The health care system was the worst among the world's great powers. Hundreds of thousands of medical bankruptcies, gaps in health insurance coverage, and soaring medical costs were three more of the many challenges to be faced. Governments solve problems by formulating *policies*, which are sets of principles or rules that guide government agencies in creating and running programs aimed at dealing with the problems. Confronted with a vast array of serious national predicaments, President Obama's administration developed and proposed to Congress a set of policies, some of which were eventually passed and became law.

Policy analysis is the examination of a policy (domestic or international) to determine its *effectiveness* (how well it solves the problem it was designed to solve) and its *efficiency* (the extent to which the cost of implementing the policy is reasonable, considering the size and nature of the problem to be solved).

Who does policy analysis? Let's start with a group of people who may not immediately come to mind. A *lobbyist* is a person hired to influence legislators to embrace particular public policies. Did you know that local, state, and national governments are swarmed with around 250,000 lobbyists today? Did you also know that the stereotypical lobbyist—a cigar-smoking good ol' boy—is relatively uncommon? Effective lobbying has for several decades been primarily a product of campaign contributions and policy analysis. Legislators need cash to get elected and strong arguments with which to press their agendas on the Hill and back home. Policy analysts provide these arguments.

And lobbying firms dominate only one corner of the public-policy playing field. Armies of policy analysts cross the Potomac daily. Legislators hire staff people who continually investigate public-policy issues and seek ways to improve legislation—most often to make it more beneficial to their particular constituents. At the national level, the Congressional Research Service continually finds information for representatives and senators. Each committee of Congress employs staff members who help it review current laws and define options for making new ones. State legislatures also employ their own research agencies and committee staff. Legislators and other policy makers are also given policy information by hundreds of consultants, public interest groups, and research institutes.

Public officials are constantly challenged to initiate new policies or change old ones. If they have a current formal policy at all, they want to know how effective it is. They then want to know what options are available to them, what changes they might make to improve current policy, and what the consequences of those changes may be. Policies are reviewed under a number of circumstances, including annual agency budgeting processes. They help decision makers determine what policies should be continued or discontinued. These policies under scrutiny may be very narrow in scope, such as deciding the hours of operation of facilities at state parks. Or they may be very broad, such as deciding how the nation will provide health care or defense for its citizens.

A good example of an organization that conducts policy analysis is the US Office of Management and Budget (OMB), an agency within the White House that provides information to the president and public servants in the president's administration. Within the OMB is the Office of Information and Regulatory Affairs (OIRA), which conducts policy analyses on many subjects. On the OIRA web page now archived from the Obama administration (https://obamawhitehouse.archives.gov /omb/policy_analyst), you will find this explanation of what OIRA analysts do:

Policy Analyst

Office of Information and Regulatory Affairs

Policy analysts oversee the Federal regulatory system so that agencies' regulatory actions are consistent with economic principles, sound public policy, and the goals of the President. They also review requests by agencies for approval of collections of information (including surveys, program evaluations, and applications for benefits) under the Paperwork Reduction Act of 1995. In addition, policy analysts review and analyze other Administration and Congressional policy initiatives. Policy analysts in OIRA work directly with high-level policy officials and have a great deal of responsibility in a wide array of policy areas. Major topic areas include virtually every domestic policy area including environment, natural resources, agriculture, rural development, energy, labor, education, immigration, health, welfare, housing, finance, criminal justice, information technology, and other related domestic policy issues.

Specifically an OIRA policy analyst:

Oversees and evaluates the regulatory, information policies, and other policy initiatives of one or more government agencies, applying economics, statistics, and risk assessment.

Analyzes agency regulations prior to publication to ensure that the regulations adhere to sound analytical principles, and that agencies evaluate the need for, societal costs and benefits of, and alternatives to new regulations.

Reviews and approves agency collections of information in accordance with the Paperwork Reduction Act (PRA) of 1995. Ensures that agency collections reduce, minimize and control paperwork burdens and maximize the practical utility and public benefit of the information created, collected, disclosed, maintained, used, shared and disseminated by or for the Federal government.

Coordinates the review of regulations and collections of information within OMB and the Executive Office of the President, as well as among other relevant Federal agencies.

Monitors and analyzes legislative and policy proposals and testimony for conformance with the policies and priorities of the President.

Performs special analyses and advises senior policy officials on specific issues.[1]

Why Should Philosophy Students Practice Policy Analysis?   Logic, argument, and ethics, the primary tools of philosophy, are the primary instruments of policy analysis as well. Precision, efficiency, and effectiveness are the blood flow of public policy's anatomy, and philosophy graduates are especially well transfused. And so, many "college philosophers" become policy analysts. It's a natural fit and a financially rewarding one as well. One more point: Baby Boomer retirements are already opening tens of thousands of policy analysis jobs, a trend good for at least a decade or more to come.

Become Familiar with Policy Analysis Institutions

In general, policy analysis institutions are of two sorts, public (government) and private (mostly nonprofit). Virtually every federal government agency conducts some sort of policy analysis, and there are many that specialize in this activity. Among the most important *federal* policy analysis organizations are:

- Congressional Budget Office (CBO)
- Congressional Research Service (CRS)
- National Council for Science and the Environment (NCSE)
- US Department of State Office of Economic Policy Analysis and Public Diplomacy
- Office of Management and Budget (OMB)
- US General Accountability Office (GAO)

Every state also has its own policy analysis offices. California's agencies, for example, include:

- California Senate Office of Research (SOR)
- California Office of the Governor, Legislative Analyst's Office

Private research institutes (think tanks) provide a great deal of often influential policy analysis and research upon which policy analysis can be conducted. Some of the most important are:

- American Enterprise Institute
- American Foreign Policy Council
- Battelle Memorial Institute

---

[1]   "Policy Analyst: The White House," Office of Management and Budget, accessed February 23, 2017, https://obamawhitehouse.archives.gov/omb/policy_analyst.

- Brookings Institution
- Carnegie Endowment for International Peace
- Cato Institute
- Center for Strategic and International Studies
- Claremont Institute

Read&Write 8.1   Write a Brief Domestic Policy Analysis

In writing a policy analysis paper, you should take the following steps:

1. Select and clearly define a specific government policy.
2. Carefully define the social, governmental, economic, or other problem that the policy is designed to solve.
3. Describe the economic, social, and political environments in which the problem arose and in which the existing policy for solving the problem was developed.
4. Evaluate the effectiveness of the current policy or lack of policy in dealing with the problem.
5. Identify alternative policies that could be adopted to solve the selected problem, and estimate the economic, social, environmental, and political costs and benefits of each alternative.
6. Provide a summary comparison of all policies examined.

Successful policy analysis papers all share the same general purpose: to inform policy makers about how public policy in a specific area may be improved. A policy analysis paper, like a position paper, is an entirely practical exercise. It is neither theoretical nor general. Its objective is to identify and evaluate the policy options that are available for a specific topic.

The Contents of a Policy Analysis Paper

Policy analysis papers contain six basic elements:

1. Title page
2. Executive summary
3. Table of contents, including a list of tables and illustrations
4. Text
5. References to sources of information
6. Appendices

Parameters of the Text   Ask your instructor for the number of pages required for the policy analysis paper assigned for your course. Such papers at the undergraduate level often range from twenty to fifty typed, double-spaced pages.

Two general rules govern the amount of information presented in the body of the paper. First, content must be adequate to make a good policy evaluation. You must include all the facts necessary to understand the significant strengths and weaknesses of a policy and its alternatives. If your paper omits a fact that is critical to the decision, a poor decision will likely be made.

Never omit important facts merely because they tend to support a perspective other than your own. It is your responsibility to present the facts as clearly as possible, not to bias the evaluation in a particular direction.

Second, the paper should not contain extraneous material. Include only the information that is helpful in making the particular decision at hand. If, for example, you are analyzing the policy by which a municipal government funds a museum dedicated to the history of fishing in area lakes, how much information do you need to include about the specific exhibits in the museum?

The Format of a Policy Analysis Paper

Title Page   The title page for a policy analysis paper should follow the format provided for title pages in chapter 3.

Executive Summary   A one-page, single-spaced executive summary immediately follows the title page. The carefully written sentences of the executive summary express the central concepts to be explained more fully in the text of the paper. The purpose of the summary is to allow the decision maker to understand, as quickly as possible, the major facts and issues under consideration. The decision maker should feel that he or she is getting a clear, thorough overview of the policy problem, together with the value and costs of available policy options, by reading the one-page summary.

Table of Contents   The table of contents of a policy analysis paper must follow the organization of the paper's text and should conform to the format shown in chapter 3.

Text   The structure of a policy analysis paper's text may be outlined as follows:

   I. Description of the policy currently in force
     A. A clear, concise statement of the policy currently in force
     B. A brief history of the policy currently in force
     C. A description of the problem the current policy was aimed at resolving, including an estimate of its extent and importance
   II. Environments of the policy currently in force
     A. A description of the physical factors affecting the origin, development, and implementation of the current policy
     B. A description of the social factors affecting the origin, development, and implementation of the current policy
     C. A description of the economic factors affecting the origin, development, and implementation of the current policy
     D. A description of the political factors affecting the origin, development, and implementation of the current policy
  III. Effectiveness and efficiency of the current policy
     A. How well the existing policy does what it was designed to do
     B. How well the policy performs in relation to the effort and resources committed to it

IV. Policy alternatives
   A. Possible alterations of the present policy, with the estimated costs and
      benefits of each
   B. Alternatives to the present policy, with the estimated costs and benefits
      of each
V. Summary comparison of policy options

Note: Most public-policy analysis textbooks describe in detail each of the policy analysis components listed in the above outline. The following sections of this chapter, however,
provide further information with respect to section II of this outline. Be sure to discuss the
outline with your instructor to ensure that you understand what each item entails.

References   You must be sure to cite properly all sources of information in a
policy analysis paper. Follow the directions for proper citation in chapter 3.

Appendices   Appendices can provide the reader of policy analysis papers with
information that supplements the important facts contained in the text. For many
local development and public works projects, a map and a diagram are often very
helpful appendices. You should attach them to the end of the paper, after the reference page. You should not append entire government reports, journal articles, or
other publications, but feel free to include selected charts, graphs, or other similar
pages. The source of the information should always be evident on the appended
pages.

8.2   DEFINE AND APPLY ETHICS

There are two different types of ethics courses: ethical theory and applied ethics.
Ethical theory courses probe the depths of ethical philosophies, whereas applied
ethics courses normally focus on contemporary moral issues or ethics of the professions. The wide world of ethics spans the topic of a good many courses, and your
introductory ethics text will provide a sample. The objective here is to provide you
with a brief sample of approaches to ethics as either an introduction or a refresher,
so that you can tackle some topical ethics exercises.

Perhaps a good place to begin is the *is-ought* dichotomy.

The word *ought* has several meanings. One sense is prudence. If I want to avoid
an early loss in chess, I ought to castle. If I do not want to pay for a hotel reserva-
tion I have guaranteed, I ought to cancel it before 6 p.m. A second sense of *ought* is
that of politeness or etiquette. It does not matter if I suck the juice from corncobs
at home. That is not proper behavior at Popeye's Louisiana Kitchen; I ought not to
do it. The *ought* of ethics conveys a special type of obligation, usually to someone
or something outside oneself. It is more than personal prudence, and the relevant
matters are, at least in the view of the person who feels the obligation, more serious
than those covered by etiquette.

In the eighteenth century, David Hume pointed out that ethicists tended to
move tacitly from statements of fact to statements of value without justifying the
transitions. Examples of statements of fact are "pain is to be avoided," "pleasure

is regarded as a good," and "business depends upon the keeping of contracts." Value statements, according to Hume, look quite a bit like statements of fact, except they include the word *ought*, or a synonym. Examples are "you ought to choose actions that maximize pleasure and minimize pain," and "you ought to keep your contracts." Hume doubted that we could derive *ought* statements, also called normative statements, from statements of fact. For Hume, moral statements cannot be based upon facts, only upon our emotive reactions to the effects of facts: "[V]irtue is distinguished by the pleasure, and vice by the pain, that any action, sentiment, or character, gives us by mere view and contemplation."[2]

Your writing should be sensitive to the distinction of fact and value when you are arguing in support of a position in applied ethics. People disagree both about the facts of the cases discussed and about what the important values are. If you find yourself realizing that a disagreement is based upon what happened in a case or the statistics about a social practice, then your disagreement is one of fact. Disagreements of fact are more easily settled because, for one thing, they do not have to be settled. You can treat your disagreement as two different hypothetical cases and discuss each in turn. This way, your discussion focuses on the ethical issues.

When you write a paper or an exam, make sure you give a descriptive exposition of your understanding of a case or social practice before launching an evaluative discussion. This will prevent misunderstanding of your position by the instructor when there may not be the opportunity to clear it up at a later time.

Ethical theory is perhaps the means of answering Hume's objection that *ought* cannot be derived from *is*. Ethical theory argues that some aspects of action are morally relevant, and different theories are best viewed as offering different hierarchies of morally relevant characteristics. Hume ultimately placed ethics on the foundation of sentiment, not reason, and so Hume would regard rational ethical theory as a rationalization of the ways in which we are naturally and socially conditioned to feel about actions.

Some Traditional Approaches to Ethics

Starting with the opposition between consequentialism and deontology will facilitate our discussion of ethical theory. *Consequential* theories propose that actions are right or wrong depending upon their outcome. For a consequentialist, an action is good if we reasonably expect it to have good results. *Deontological* theories hold that the rightness or wrongness of an action depends upon the intent of the actor, and the word *deontologist* comes from a Greek word meaning "having to do with assuming responsibility." For a deontologist, an action is good if my intentions when I commit the act are good.

Suppose that I promise to have dinner with you on Saturday night, but then I am offered a chance to go to the opera with a new friend. I decide to lie and tell you that I had already been invited to the opera; I simply forgot. You and I will have dinner Sunday night instead of Saturday. Is it moral to lie, to break my promise? Other things being equal, one type of consequentialist says it is not only morally permissible but also morally mandatory because it promotes the greatest happiness

---

[2]   David Hume, *Treatise of Human Nature* (New York: Dutton, 1974), 183.

for the greatest number. But a deontologist would say that lying is always or generally morally impermissible regardless of consequences.

Consequentialism Among the important varieties of consequentialists are hedonists, eudaemonists, and egoists.

- Hedonists believe the only intrinsic good is pleasure, and by pleasure they mean the pleasant feelings associated with our senses.
- Eudaemonists (a term derived from the Greek word for "living well") believe that pleasure is part of happiness but insist that the intrinsic good is more complicated than just pleasure. For instance, they might include intellectual happiness and the companionship of friends as important elements in achieving a good life.
- Psychological egoists believe that humans always choose what appears to be the greatest good for themselves. In other words, they believe that humans act only in their own interests. Psychological egoists deny that humans can act from altruistic motives, but they do not deny that they can commit altruistic actions.

Jeremy Bentham, one of the founders of utilitarianism, wrote, "Nature has placed mankind under the governance of two sovereign masters, pain and pleasure. It is for them alone to point out what we ought to do, as well as to determine what we shall do."[3] Bentham was a hedonist. Another utilitarian, John Stuart Mill, observed that a beast's pleasures do not satisfy a human being's conception of happiness.[4] Mill was a hedonist also, but remarked that the pleasures of human beings were not equivalent to those of other living beings.

Ethical egoism maintains that we ought to act only in our own interests and that we have a responsibility to maximize our own concept of what is good. There are at least three types of ethical egoism: personal, individual, and universal. All three types believe that people have the right to decide on "good" for themselves. In regard to the acts of others, however, they differ.

1. A personal egoist makes no claim and has no opinion about what someone else should do.
2. An individual egoist assumes that it is your responsibility to maximize his or her expected good.
3. A universal egoist declares that everyone has the responsibility to maximize his or her own happiness.

Just imagine that these individuals were on your basketball team. Whenever any one of them got the ball, the individual would shoot it. But the expectations each of them has of your behavior when you get the ball are very different. The first player does not care what you do. The second wants you to pass it back so that he or she can shoot. And the third envisions a basketball game in which everyone has a ball and everyone shoots.

---

[3]   Jeremy Bentham, *An Introduction to the Principles of Morals and Legislation* (Garden City, NY: Doubleday, 1961), 17.

[4]   John Stuart Mill, *Utilitarianism* (Kitchener, ON: Batoche Books, 2001), 11, http://socserv.mcmaster .ca/econ/ugcm/3ll3/mill/utilitarianism.pdf.

Utilitarianism is based on the principle of utility, or usefulness. Utilitarianism tells me that my moral duty is to select, from the available alternatives, the action that would lead to the greatest amount of happiness for the greatest number of all those with an interest in a matter. The two major historical figures in the development of utilitarianism were nineteenth-century British philosophers Jeremy Bentham and John Stuart Mill. It must be noted in passing that the first claim of utilitarianism is that pleasure is intrinsically valuable. Both Bentham and Mill were hedonists in that they believed the pleasure of any one person is worth as much or as little as anyone else's pleasure.

There are two kinds of utilitarianism:

- *Act utilitarians* calculate benefits for each specific situation and are guided by rules of thumb or the needed calculus.
- *Rule utilitarians* attempt to define general policies that, if consistently followed, would lead to the greatest good for the greatest number, and they follow that policy in each situation.

Deontology: Kant   A deontologist is a person who studies moral obligation. The most famous deontologist is Immanuel Kant, who believed that we could derive the correct ethical theory from reason alone. In Kant's view the only unconditional and hence intrinsic good is the good intention sometimes called "the good will." Pleasure or happiness is not intrinsically good. Kant understands "good intention" to mean something like respect for duty and law. Yet the law in question is not the law of the state, but moral law. Moral actions are those done with good intention, with respect for duty and love of the moral law.

> For it is not sufficient to that which should be morally good that it should conform to the law; it must also be done for the sake of the law. Otherwise the conformity is merely contingent and spurious; because though the unmoral ground may indeed now and then produce lawful actions, more often it brings forth unlawful ones.[5]

Imagine, for example, that you inherit a large sum of money. Kant would commend you if you decide to donate some of it to your college (and maybe some of it to the philosophy department). But Kant would not be sure that your action fits within the moral dimension. It may be the case that you made the donation for the purpose of maximizing your own happiness. Maybe you need the tax deduction. A moral action, for Kant, is one you are obligated to do regardless of the consequences. Now, if the good will is an intention that compels action regardless of consequences, it is not going to be governed by our personal inclinations. And if not from personal inclination, where, then, does our sense of moral duty come from? Kant's position is that morality is based in what he calls the *categorical imperative*—an absolute command, not dependent upon one's inclinations or personal desires or goals. The categorical imperative is the product of reason alone and is capable of being formulated in three ways, the first two of which are calls to action:

---

[5]   Immanuel Kant, *Foundations of the Metaphysics of Morals*, trans. Lewis White Beck (Indianapolis: Bobbs-Merrill, 1959), 6.

1. Act so that the maxim of your action could be a universal law.

2. Treat all humans as ends in themselves and never merely as means.

3. All humans are universal lawgivers.

According to the categorical imperative, when I consider an action, I should not calculate its consequences to society or myself. Rather, I should submit the action in question to the *universalization test*: I should ask myself if the maxim (the rule) on the basis of which I am acting could be followed by all rational creatures. For example, if I think of breaking a promise, I should ask myself if I could logically imagine a world in which all people broke promises when it suited them.

The second formulation of the categorical imperative is commonly referred to as the *respect for persons principle*. Kant calls attention to the special worth of human beings as possessors of the good will. Since humans are the source of moral goodness, they should never be treated as merely a means to an end.

The third formulation of the categorical imperative is the one that is most often misunderstood. It does not say that every human creates his or her own ethics. Nor does it say that each human legislates an ethics that he or she wishes to be binding on all others, as the individual ethical egoist might argue. Instead, this third formulation says that each human has reason and that, on the basis of reason alone, a person can discover the categorical imperative. The categorical imperative gives people access to the objective moral law that applies to every rational creature. There is one morality that can be discovered by every rational creature.

It probably has not escaped your notice that Kant's morality is similar to the golden rule. There are two ways of stating the golden rule, one positive and the other negative. Some people say, "Do unto others as you would want them to do unto you." Others advise us, "Don't do unto others what you would not want done to you."

Read & Write 8.2   Compare Consequential and Deontological Arguments

We propose that good applied ethics papers will:

1. Address a significant moral issue.

2. Address a difficult theoretical conflict of values.

3. Develop a solution sensitive to the need to accommodate other value hierarchies.

4. Place the issue in the context of values based in ethical theory.

5. Discriminate between questions of morality and questions of legal regulation.

For this particular exercise, apply what you know about ethics to the following situations.

Scenario 1

Bob's high school required students to perform forty hours of volunteer work before graduation. One very hot summer he started at Habitat for Humanity and was put to work on the roof. After a couple weeks, he found an opening at the Boys and Girls Club where he would be playing basketball with children outside in the mornings only and then moving into the air-conditioned indoor facility in the afternoons to play pool and video games. Would Kant have considered his volunteer work morally praiseworthy if he made the switch? Would Bentham?

Scenario 2

On October 5, 2016, President Obama made the following remarks on the Paris Agreement. At the heart of the president's argument is America's ethical responsibility to address climate change. Write an essay in which you argue that the president's underlying ethical argument is either consequential or deontological.

The White House
Office of the Press Secretary
For Immediate Release   October 05, 2016

Remarks by the President on the Paris Agreement

Rose Garden

**Please see below for a correction, marked with an asterisk.

3:30 P.M. EDT

THE PRESIDENT: Good afternoon, everybody. Today is a historic day in the fight to protect our planet for future generations.

Ten months ago, in Paris, I said before the world that we needed a strong global agreement to reduce carbon pollution and to set the world on a low-carbon course. The result was the Paris Agreement. Last month, the United States and China—the world's two largest economies and largest emitters—formally joined that agreement together. And today, the world has officially crossed the threshold for the Paris Agreement to take effect.

Today, the world meets the moment. And if we follow through on the commitments that this agreement embodies, history may well judge it as a turning point for our planet.

Of course, it took a long time to reach this day. One of the reasons I ran for this office was to make America a leader in this mission. And over the past eight years, we've done just that. In 2009, we salvaged a chaotic climate summit in Copenhagen, establishing the principle that all nations have a role to play in combating climate change. And at home, we led by example, with historic investments in growing industries like wind and solar that created a steady stream of new jobs. We set the first-ever nationwide standards to limit the amount of carbon pollution that power plants can dump into the air our children breathe. From the cars and trucks we drive to the homes and businesses in which we live and work, we've changed fundamentally the way we consume energy.

Now, keep in mind, the skeptics said these actions would kill jobs. And instead, we saw—even as we were bringing down these carbon levels—the longest streak of job creation in American history. We drove economic output to new highs. And we drove our carbon pollution to its lowest levels in two decades.

We continued to lead by example with our historic joint announcement with China two years ago, where we put forward even more ambitious climate targets. And that achievement encouraged dozens of other countries to set more ambitious climate targets of their own. And that, in turn, paved the way for our success in Paris—the idea that no nation, not even one as powerful as ours, can solve this challenge alone. All of us have to solve it together.

Now, the Paris Agreement alone will not solve the climate crisis. Even if we meet every target embodied in the agreement, we'll only get to part of where we need to go. But make no mistake, this agreement will help delay or avoid some of the worst consequences of climate change. It will help other nations ratchet down their dangerous carbon emissions over time, and set bolder targets as technology advances, all under a strong system of transparency that allows each nation to evaluate the progress of all other nations. And by sending a signal that this is going to be our future—a clean energy future—it opens up the floodgates for businesses, and scientists, and engineers to unleash high-tech, low-carbon investment and innovation at a scale that we've never seen before. So this gives us the best possible shot to save the one planet we've got.

I know diplomacy *can be [isn't always] easy, and progress on the world stage can sometimes be slow. But together, with steady persistent effort, with strong, principled, American leadership, with optimism and faith and hope, we're proving that it is possible.

And I want to embarrass my Senior Advisor, Brian Deese—who is standing right over there—because he worked tirelessly to make this deal possible. He, and John Kerry, Gina McCarthy at the EPA, everybody on their teams have done an extraordinary job to get us to this point—and America should be as proud of them as I am of them.

I also want to thank the people of every nation that has moved quickly to bring the Paris Agreement into force. I encourage folks who have not yet submitted their documentation to enter into this agreement to do so as soon as possible. And in the coming days, let's help finish additional agreements to limit aviation emissions, to phase down dangerous use of hydrofluorocarbons—all of which will help build a world that is safer, and more prosperous, and more secure, and more free than the one that was left for us.

That's our most important mission, to make sure our kids and our grandkids have at least as beautiful a planet, and hopefully more beautiful, than the one that we have. And today, I'm a little more confident that we can get the job done.

So thank you very much, everybody.

END

3:35 P.M. EDT[6]

8.3   APPLY ETHICS TO PUBLIC POLICY

In some ways, life in the second decade of the twenty-first century is simple. For example, we still live as the ancients did, easily differentiating animal, mineral, and vegetable. We are animal, our iPhones are mineral, and our cell phone cases are vegetable. Despite some elementary advances to the contrary, like artificial limbs

---

[6]   Barack Obama, "Remarks by the President on the Paris Agreement," The White House, October 5, 2016, https://obamawhitehouse.archives.gov/the-press-office/2016/10/05/remarks-president-paris-agreement.

that respond directly to brain signals, we still easily distinguish between biology and technology. All this is about to change radically. Imagine a time in the not-so-distant future when biology and technology are so interwoven that we are unable to distinguish between the two. Blood cells will be programmed to fight disease. Artificial fossil-fuel human organs will provide us an endless supply of spare body parts. And these events are only the beginning.

The preeminent prophet of this great metamorphosis is computer scientist and futurologist Ray Kurzweil, whose 2006 book *The Singularity Is Near* has predicted processes already well under way.[7] The "Singularity" is the unified identity of biology and technology: Biology will be technologized and technology will be biologized. A website for the book describes the Singularity as follows:

> That merging is the essence of the Singularity, an era in which our intelligence will become increasingly nonbiological and trillions of times more powerful than it is today—the dawning of a new civilization that will enable us to transcend our biological limitations and amplify our creativity. In this new world, there will be no clear distinction between human and machine, real reality and virtual reality. We will be able to assume different bodies and take on a range of personae at will. In practical terms, human aging and illness will be reversed; pollution will be stopped; world hunger and poverty will be solved. Nanotechnology will make it possible to create virtually any physical product using inexpensive information processes and will ultimately turn even death into a soluble problem.[8]

In addition to the fascinating book, *The Singularity Is Near* is also a movie that can be accessed, for a fee, from this website: http://singularity.com /themovie/#.V_-zROArKhc. And you can hear a good summary of trends in technology from Kurzweil himself in a TED talk.[9]

Read&Write 8.3 Construct an Ethics for the Singularity

For ethicists, the twenty-first century will present phenomenal challenges, among them the transformative potential of the singularity. During his TED Talk, Kurzweil says, "When I was a student it [a powerful computer] was across campus. Now it's in our pockets. What used to take up a building now fits in our pockets. What now fits in our pockets would fit in a blood cell in 25 years."[10]

Let that last statement sink in: "What now fits in our pockets would fit in a blood cell in 25 years." If a single blood cell can become as technologically powerful as today's iPhone, what are the possible consequences?

Let's take an initial stab at it. The Paralympics provides an opportunity for physically disadvantaged people to participate in athletic competitions. Improvements in artificial limbs will soon allow their users to exceed the physical abilities of the world's greatest "normal" athletes. How can this development be managed?

---

[7]   Ray Kurzweil, *The Singularity Is Near: When Humans Transcend Biology* (New York: Viking, 2005).
[8]   "About the Book," Singularity.com, accessed October 29, 2016, http://singularity.com/aboutthebook.html.
[9]   Ray Kurzweil, "A University for the Coming Singularity," TED, February 2009, accessed October 29, 2016, http://www.ted.com/talks/ray_kurzweil_announces_singularity_university.
[10]   Ibid.

But articulating the comparative abilities of different classes of athletes is a minor problem compared to other potential future developments. At the rate the Singularity is advancing, for example, your children may well be able to determine the IQs of their children. Suppose your grown child and his or her partner wish to have a child. This child's attributes can either be left to chance—to the parents' combined DNAs—or else the parents can decide their child should be a genius, a superior athlete, or a being more handsome or more beautiful than any mythological deity. What should the parents do? Allow the child to be ordinary while his or her classmates proceed to MIT? Will the parents actually have a choice? Perhaps Nietzsche's prediction was accurate: "What is the ape to a man? A laughing-stock, a thing of shame. And just so shall a man be to the Superman: a laughing-stock, a thing of shame."[11]

Nietzsche's Zarathustra looked forward to the day when human beings will have evolved so far beyond their present state that we in the present moment would seem as apes to them. What we are now will be laughingstocks to our great-grandchildren.

Scary? Keep going. The future will hold two classes of people, the upper class, with minds as powerful as those of the gods, and the lower class, biological robots that will run both the organic and inorganic machineries of the day.

Will humanity, as a whole, determine its fate? Will the inescapable march of technology make ethics superfluous? Or can we form for ethics a viable role in our species' future? Write an essay in which you engage one or more of the ethical challenges arising from the Singularity that are beginning to arrive even now. Conclude your essay by formulating specific public-policy recommendations that address the ethical issues you identify.

8.4   PRACTICE THE PHILOSOPHY OF THE MIND

Plants lean toward the sun. Single cells divide to become two. Quartz crystals grow inside geodes. Are these phenomena forms of consciousness?

The concept of consciousness has long been controversial. An ancient controversy still alive today is, "Does the brain *create* consciousness, *perceive* consciousness, or *both*?" If the brain can perceive consciousness, can it perceive spiritual phenomena?

Perhaps today's most pressing consciousness controversy is "Will artificial intelligence ever duplicate or supersede human consciousness?" The basic question that underlies all these controversies is "What is consciousness?" Asking this question draws one into the depths of ontology, epistemology, psychology, and neurology, and answering it requires a still unachieved precise knowledge of how the brain works, and what, exactly, is "mind." Pursuit of such knowledge has spawned a number of interdisciplinary conferences.

At a May 2016 panel sponsored by the New York Academy of Sciences, NYU researcher David Chalmers declared, "The scientific and philosophical consensus is

---

[11]   Frederick Nietzsche, "Zarathustra's Prologue," in *Thus Spake Zarathustra*, trans. Thomas Common (Adelaide, Australia: University of Adelaide), last modified January 2, 2016, https://ebooks.adelaide.edu.au/n/nietzsche/friedrich/n67a/index.html.

that there is no nonphysical soul or ego, or at least no evidence for that."[12] Princeton University neuroscientist Michael Graziano maintained:

> Consciousness is a kind of con game the brain plays with itself. The brain is a computer that evolved to simulate the outside world. Among its internal models is a simulation of itself—a crude approximation of its own neurological processes. . . . The result is an illusion. Instead of neurons and synapses, we sense a ghostly presence—a self—inside the head. But it's all just data processing. The machine mistakenly thinks it has magic inside it, . . . And it calls the magic consciousness. It's not the existence of this inner voice he finds mysterious. The phenomenon to explain, . . . is why the brain, as a machine, insists it has this property that is non-physical.[13]

Chalmers and Graziano are two voices on one side of the great divide in consciousness studies, those who believe that the brain *manufactures* its own phenomena. Theorists on the other side of the controversy believe that the brain *perceives* phenomena so far undetected by scientific instruments. A fascinating discussion of conscious is unfolding as scholars in the disciplines of religion and theology employ science to react to dismissive posturing with respect to other potential forms of consciousness.

In their book *The Mystical Mind*, Eugene d'Aquili and Andrew Newberg, drawing in part on their own pioneering work with SPECT (Single Photon Emission Computed Tomography) imagery of meditating subjects, present a detailed neurological analysis of the human brain at work during a prototypically *religious* activity. D'Aquili and Newberg build on their findings and related research to propose a "neurotheology" that in many ways turns the classic reductionist critique of mind and soul on its head. Rather than explaining *away* religious experiences as *epiphenomena*, the authors propose that brain science provides powerful support for the "reality" and epistemological utility of spiritual phenomena.[14]

D'Aquili and Newberg describe how the human brain goes about producing meditative states. They find that higher mental functioning, whether it relates to logic, emotions, imagination, or willful action, involves an almost infinitely complex series of interactions across a host of neural structures. As a result, it is impossible to simplistically assign any given mental state to a particular brain part or function. Instead, higher mental states must be seen as the activity of the *whole* brain interacting in a dynamic process within an encompassing human physical and mental environment.[15]

This understanding leads them to at least entertain the possibility that unverified forms of consciousness may exist. While d'Aquili and Newberg do not claim to prove that a "higher reality" exists in fact, they do find support for the possibility that "a mind can exist without an ego and that awareness can exist without a self."[16] At this point, we may want to admit that a discussion of potential higher realities at

---

[12] George Johnson, "Consciousness: The Mind Messing with the Mind," *New York Times*, July 4, 2016, http://www.nytimes.com/2016/07/05/science/what-is-consciousness.html.

[13] Ibid.

[14] Eugene d'Aquili and Andrew B. Newberg, *The Mystical Mind: Probing the Biology of Religious Experience* (Minneapolis: Fortress Press, 1999).

[15] Ibid.

[16] D'Aquili and Newberg, *The Mystical Mind*, 126.

least produces some interesting research. But this writing exercise will now turn to a different sort of emerging reality: artificial intelligence (AI).

University of Connecticut professor Susan Schneider says, "The problem of AI consciousness asks whether AI, being silicon-based, is even capable of consciousness"[17]—that is, consciousness as we commonly understand it. "A superintelligent AI could solve problems that even the brightest humans are unable to solve, but being made of a different substrate, would it have conscious experience? Could it feel the burning of curiosity, or the pangs of grief?"[18] Another problem. Science fiction has already warned us of such horrors as AI beings replacing human beings altogether. And Schneider notes, "This would be an unfathomable loss. Even the slightest chance that this could happen should give us reason to think carefully about AI consciousness."[19]

Other possibilities, Schneider suggests, are also worth considering:

First, a superintelligent AI may bypass consciousness altogether. In humans, consciousness is correlated with novel learning tasks that require concentration, and when a thought is under the spotlight of our attention, it is processed in a slow, sequential manner. Only a very small percentage of our mental processing is conscious at any given time. A superintelligence would surpass expert-level knowledge in every domain, with rapid-fire computations ranging over vast databases that could encompass the entire internet. It may not need the very mental faculties that are associated with conscious experience in humans. Consciousness could be outmoded.[20]

Schneider concludes, "We should regard the problem of AI consciousness as an open question."[21] And her final admonition is well worth considering:

Of course, from an ethical standpoint, it is best to assume that a sophisticated AI may be conscious. For any mistake could wrongly influence the debate over whether they might be worthy of special ethical consideration as sentient beings. As the films *Ex Machina* and *I, Robot* illustrate, any failure to be charitable to AI may come back to haunt us, as they may treat us as we treated them.[22]

Read&Write 8.4 Explore Problems and Potentials of Artificial Intelligence

Applying the methods and formats described in previous chapters of this manual, write a research paper that discusses the relationship of consciousness to the development of artificial intelligence. Be sure to include among your sources a dozen scholarly articles, including at least three from the discipline of philosophy.

---

[17] Susan Schneider, "The Problem of AI Consciousness," *Kurzweil Accelerating Intelligence* (blog), March 28, 2016, http://www.kurzweilai.net/the-problem-of-ai-consciousness.
[18] Ibid.
[19] Ibid.
[20] Ibid.
[21] Ibid.
[22] Ibid.

8.5 PRACTICE THE PHILOSOPHY OF RELIGION

Philosophy is on the rise. Once the canopy for all science and knowledge, philosophy is slowly emerging from its modern secular ivory-tower exile, effectively addressing the public square. Abandoning the cul-de-sacs of philology and deconstruction, philosophers now mine the data of evolutionary psychology and neurology. Addressing ethics in public policy, philosophers influence the directions of social science. A contemporary example of this leadership is religion professor Todd Tremlin's influential book *Minds and Gods*.[23]

Minds and Gods applies the cognitive science of religion to the data of evolutionary psychology to explain how and why people invent gods. A caveat is in order here: Tremlin's work addresses human behavior, not the existence of God. It in no way attempts to prove or disprove the objective existence of any god. He does make a powerful argument, however, for the proposition that human beings are evolutionarily inclined to perceive deities because doing so satisfies natural proclivities that prove to be powerful instruments for survival.

We present here a brief and informal elaboration of the fundamentals of Tremlin's findings. Let us begin by recalling that, according to archaeology and anthropology, the human brain assumed its current capacity around fifty thousand years ago. We may therefore infer that a baby, snatched from its family five millennia ago and brought up in an adequately supportive family today, could reasonably be expected to graduate from college. We may also assume that our current mental structure retains sufficient "primitive" capabilities that a baby snatched today from a hospital nursery in Chicago and taken back five millennia to a family on an African savanna could survive there as well.

Survival, Tremlin reminds us, requires group life. Among the mental faculties required for group life are "cognitive capacity" (the mental equipment to recognize the requirements of social life) and "strategic thinking" (the ability to use cognitive capacity to contribute to and compete in social life). Next, we encounter what evolutionary psychologists call "theory of mind," more simply, "mind-reading" or "the ability to put oneself in the mind of another." Theory-of-mind capacity is essential in social life because it allows us to perceive the intentions of others.

Remember a point made a little earlier about the time frame of the brain's development: While our human mental capacities evolved within a "primitive" environment far different from what we experience today, our brains still operate with those same mechanisms developed in primitive times. Tremlin explains that a basic reason people survive successfully is that their brains evolved in the form of "mental modules," including capacities to detect predators; select appropriate foods; choose mates; raise children; and establish kinship, alliances, and friendship.

According to Tremlin, the brain has intuitive capacities (in other animals we call them *instincts*). Humans have *intuitive biology* (we can distinguish various sorts of plants and animals), *intuitive physics* (we can handle basic modes of solidity and fluidity, motion, and causality), and *intuitive psychology* (we can attribute attitudes and motives of other animals and people, and we can discern various sorts of patterns in our social and physical environments).

---

[23] Todd Tremlin, *Minds and Gods: The Cognitive Foundations of Religion* (Oxford: Oxford University Press, 2006).

At this point in Tremlin's book the discussion shifts from environments to gods. Two more concepts are put in play: Agency Detection Device (ADD) and Theory of Mind Mechanism (ToMM). Tremlin's discussion of these two fascinating concepts is lengthy and detailed. The following scenario attempts, in the interest of brevity, to summarize this part of Tremlin's argument:

Imagine two savanna dwellers we shall call Yves and Maddie, in the fiftieth century BCE. Each day they emerge from their rock shelter with one preeminent goal: survival. Most immediately, survival requires safety and food. Their brains are equipped with ADD, the ability of a phenomenon to make its own decisions. They see a stream and know that, even though in the monsoon season it can be dangerous, it lacks agency; in other words, the stream follows its course of least resistance, making no decisions for itself. This morning the current is low and slow and therefore safe. Maddie spots a lion, a beast that *has* agency, because it can make its own decisions, and motive, because it hunts for its pride. Yves and Maddie's brains instantly engage ToMM, a set of assumptions our brains make about phenomena with agency. Yves and Maddie note that the pride is yet unfed, so it will be wise to avoid the lions until after lunch. Through ToMM, Yves and Maddie know to avoid coming between an elephant and her calf, to hide their supply of berries from their neighbors' kids, and to fight hyenas with fire.

In today's world we understand that some people possess an incredibly keen sense of ToMM. Politicians like former president Bill Clinton and former British prime minister Margaret Thatcher, for example, seem to be able to read voters like an open book. On the opposite extreme are people afflicted with autism, a condition creating a "mind-blindness." Though often brilliant in other ways, autistic people appear incapable of intuitively perceiving the thoughts and feelings of others.

Back to intuition. Our minds are both intuitive and counterintuitive. While navigating the practicalities of life depends upon accurate intuitions, our minds enjoy imagining the counterintuitive: mice who govern magic kingdoms, horses that talk, men who fly, inventors who go back or forward in time. Gods are counterintuitive in this way, most often imagined as having supernatural qualities and talents. People are also social animals, and religions are social constructs. As such, minds and religions provide mechanisms to manage *conditions of exchange* (how we shall share), *reciprocity* (mutuality in sharing), *fairness* (whom we can trust) and *identity of interested parties* (who's in the group). Religions provide human beings a discernable woven fabric of consciousness. They connect each of us with one another and connect our intuitive beings (our clearly perceptive practical selves) with our counterintuitive natures (our yearning for transcendence, truth, justice, salvation, and magic).

Okay, so how do we connect gods to ADD and ToMM? Through religion. Here, once again, is a loose interpretation of Tremlin's substantial argument. Let's return once more to Yves and Maddie. Within their clan, they consciously navigate the flow of social interactions with vibrant, intuitive ToMMs. They get their needs met through subtle or abrupt gestures. They negotiate their status and secure their share of the savanna's resources. But a part of their intuitive natures (everyday life on earth) intersects with their counterintuitions (their grasp of the mysterious beyond). While the cosmos at times appears chaotic (floods, fires, earthquakes), its dependable rhythms (dawn, day, dusk, night; spring, summer, winter, fall; new moon, half moon, full moon) suggest a cosmic order that requires an intelligent agent. That agent is a god. It can be nothing less. And if we are relational, so is our God. When we initiate relations with God (ceremony, ritual, sacrifice, prayer) we perceive a cosmic agent. When our counterintuitive ToMM kicks in, we perceive an agent that first reflects ourselves, providing and demanding, soothing and frightening, provoking and responding. We further perceive an agent who transcends our capacities with faculties sufficient for cosmic management. Yves and Maddie's counterintuitions, therefore, supply them with the comfort of relationship and a source of hope-inspiring strength.

Read&Write 8.5   Encounter *Minds and Gods*

Read and review *Minds and Gods* (see section 6.2, "How to Write a Book Review"). Conclude your review with additional comments: Provide some personal reflections concerning how *Minds and Gods* has affected your personal beliefs.

8.6   PRACTICE POLITICAL PHILOSOPHY

Consider Some Options for Political Philosophy Papers

Undergraduate and graduate programs in both philosophy and political science offer courses and concentrations in political philosophy, each discipline placing particular emphasis on its broader interests and objectives. Philosophers and political scientists often distinguish between political philosophy, a qualitative and normative examination of the writings of the great political thinkers throughout human history, and political theory, which is the contemporary, nonnormative, and qualitative effort to understand political behavior. Political philosophy, the subdiscipline of philosophy addressed in this chapter, mines the history of the great ideas that not only provide rich insights into political behavior, but have often shaped politics itself. John Locke's *Two Treatises of Government* (1690) helped pave the way for democratic movements leading to British parliamentary monarchy and for America's Declaration of Independence and Constitution. When Karl Marx and Friedrich Engels wrote *The Communist Manifesto* (1848) and a series of other works, they set the stage for the regimes that controlled more than a third of the world's population at the peak of communist influence in the twentieth century.

Reading the works of political philosophers is a deeply enriching and satisfying experience. For example, contrasting the political regimes preferred by Plato and his student Aristotle provide many observations that echo their cogency down through the centuries and provide grist for arguments made around the world today.

Since many instructors assign papers with page limits but with maximum freedom of content for students, this chapter contains suggestions for writing short papers (fewer than ten pages) and long papers (more than ten pages) in college political philosophy courses. First, be sure to write your paper according to the highest standards of the discipline of political science as explained in previous chapters of this manual. Research thoroughly. Cite sources accurately. Make your paper plagiarism free. Say something meaningful to yourself and others. Carefully establish and systematically support a definite thesis. Write clearly. Write well.

Suggestions for Short Papers

Short political philosophy papers are normally (1) topical essays, (2) book reviews, or (3) article critiques. Book reviews provide many interesting options. Be sure to check with your instructor before you begin writing. Consider the following approaches.

Option 1: Focus on Philosophers You can select one or more ancient, medieval, or modern political philosophers from the "canon" lists, which tend to include everyone from Plato to Nietzsche. But don't forget the marvelous works of twentieth-century authors like Oakeshott, Popper, Rand, Aron, Sartre, Arendt, Berlin, Aron, Rawls, Foucault, Baudrillard, Habermas, and Wolin. And also consider some of the important philosophers alive and writing today: Michael Walzer (b. 1935), Giacomo Marramao (b. 1946), James Tully (b. 1946), Slavoj Žižek (b. 1947), Olavo de Carvalho (b. 1947), Judith Butler (b. 1956), Rae Helen Langton (b. 1961).

Here are three philosopher-centered short paper options:

- Review a new book or critique a new article.
- Compare scholarly interpretations of a major work by a particular philosopher.
- Apply an author's theory to a new or different political problem or challenge.

Option 2: Focus on Ideas or Issues Here are five topic-centered short paper options:

- Explain Plato's definition of justice.
- Describe Aristotle's political ethics.
- Explain Marx's concept of "species-being."
- Explain Foucault's notion of the political power inherent in "normal."
- Evaluate the logic of Rawls's concept of a "veil of ignorance."

Topics for longer political philosophy papers include the following:

- Explain how political and economic conditions in eighteenth-century Scotland influenced the political philosophies of David Hume and Adam Smith.
- Compare the reactions of Jean-Jacques Rousseau and Edmund Burke to the French Revolution.
- Describe the contribution of Epictetus to Stoic political thought.
- Compare the concepts of political freedom in the works of John Stuart Mill, Isaiah Berlin, and Ayn Rand.
- Identify the most important challenges facing political philosophers in the twenty-first century.
- Explain the importance of the contributions of Michel Foucault to understanding the subtle operations of social and political power in society.
- In *The End of History and the Last Man*, published in 1992, Francis Fukuyama argued that history, in the sense of a process of evolving forms of society, had ended, because the best society (capitalist democracy) was at that time making strong progress to dominating the entire world. Now, a quarter of a century later, to what extent do world events support Fukuyama's thesis?

- In 1996 Samuel P. Huntington published *The Clash of Civilizations and the Remaking of World Order*, arguing that future world conflicts will not be based on ideology or economics, but on the conflicting ambitions of civilizations. Among the important rising and competing civilzations that the United States will need to deal with are nations with large Islamic populations. To what extent do current world events support Huntington's thesis?

Read&Write 8.6 Behold the Panopticon

A particularly stimulating topic to introduce you to the depth and variety of the contributions of contemporary political thought to life in society today is Michel Foucault's concept of the panopticon.

French philosopher Michel Foucault (1926–1984) wrote several volumes of what he called "genealogy." He was not interested in tracing family trees. Instead, he attempted to trace patterns of political power as they emerged in society. He was most interested in identifying how political power is created and wielded and how people perceive it and are affected by it. His studies led him to conclude that political power is much more pervasive than many people assume. To illustrate this principle, he borrowed the concept of the panopticon, a curiously designed building proposed by the eighteenth-century British utilitarian philosopher Jeremy Bentham.

Bentham wanted to reform the British penal system. As foucault notes in his book *Discipline and Punish* (1991), in 1791 Bentham proposed a new, more humane, and more efficient prison design than was in use in the eighteenth and nineteenth centuries: a building designed in such a way that all its inhabitants could be observed at all times by a supervisor. In his book, Foucault explains how Bentham's panopticon is a metaphor for the instruments of political power in our lives today:

> Bentham's Panopticon is the architectural figure of this composition. We know the principle on which it was based: at the periphery, an annular building; at the centre, a tower; this tower is pierced with wide windows that open onto the inner side of the ring; the peripheric building is divided into cells, each of which extends the whole width of the building; they have two windows, one on the inside, corresponding to the windows of the tower; the other, on the outside, allows the light to cross the cell from one end to the other. All that is needed, then, is to place a supervisor in a central tower and to shut up in each cell a madman, a patient, a condemned man, a worker or a schoolboy. By the effect of backlighting, one can observe from the tower, standing out precisely against the light, the small captive shadows in the cells of the periphery. They are like so many cages, so many small theatres, in which each actor is alone, perfectly individualized and constantly visible. The panoptic mechanism arranges spatial unities that make it possible to see constantly and to recognize immediately. In short, it reverses the principle of the dungeon; or rather of its three functions—to enclose, to deprive of light and to hide—it preserves only the first and eliminates the other two. Full lighting and the eye of a supervisor capture better than darkness, which ultimately protected. Visibility is a trap.
>
> To begin with, this made it possible—as a negative effect—to avoid those compact, swarming, howling masses that were to be found in places of confinement, those painted by Goya or described by Howard. Each individual, in his place, is securely confined to a cell from which he is seen from the front by the supervisor; but the side walls prevent him from coming into contact

with his companions. He is seen, but he does not see; he is the object of information, never a subject in communication. The arrangement of his room, opposite the central tower, imposes on him an axial visibility; but the divisions of the ring, those separated cells, imply a lateral invisibility. And this invisibility is a guarantee of order. If the inmates are convicts, there is no danger of a plot, an attempt at collective escape, the planning of new crimes for the future, bad reciprocal influences; if they are patients, there is no danger of contagion; if they are madmen there is no risk of their committing violence upon one another; if they are schoolchildren, there is no copying, no noise, no chatter, no waste of time; if they are workers, there are no disorders, no theft, no coalitions, none of those distractions that slow down the rate of work, make it less perfect or cause accidents. The crowd, a compact mass, a locus of multiple exchanges, individualities merging together, a collective effect, is abolished and replaced by a collection of separated individualities. From the point of view of the guardian, it is replaced by a multiplicity that can be numbered and supervised; from the point of view of the inmates, by a sequestered and observed solitude (Bentham, 60–64).

Hence the major effect of the Panopticon: to induce in the inmate a state of conscious and permanent visibility that assures the automatic functioning of power. So to arrange things that the surveillance is permanent in its effects, even if it is discontinuous in its action; that the perfection of power should tend to render its actual exercise unnecessary; that this architectural apparatus should be a machine for creating and sustaining a power relation independent of the person who exercises it; in short, that the inmates should be caught up in a power situation of which they are themselves the bearers. To achieve this, it is at once too much and too little that the prisoner should be constantly observed by an inspector: too little, for what matters is that he knows himself to be observed; too much, because he has no need in fact of being so. In view of this, Bentham laid down the principle that power should be visible and unverifiable. Visible: the inmate will constantly have before his eyes the tall outline of the central tower from which he is spied upon. Unverifiable: the inmate must never know whether he is being looked at at any one moment; but he must be sure that he may always be so. In order to make the presence or absence of the inspector unverifiable, so that the prisoners, in their cells, cannot even see a shadow, Bentham envisaged not only venetian blinds on the windows of the central observation hall, but, on the inside, partitions that intersected the hall at right angles and, in order to pass from one quarter to the other, not doors but zig-zag openings; for the slightest noise, a gleam of light, a brightness in a half-opened door would betray the presence of the guardian. The Panopticon is a machine for dissociating the see/being seen dyad: in the peripheric ring, one is totally seen, without ever seeing; in the central tower, one sees everything without ever being seen.

It is an important mechanism, for it automatizes and disindividualizes power. Power has its principle not so much in a person as in a certain concerted distribution of bodies, surfaces, lights, gazes; in an arrangement whose internal mechanisms produce the relation in which individuals are caught up. The ceremonies, the rituals, the marks by which the sovereign's surplus power was manifested are useless. There is a machinery that assures dissymmetry, disequilibrium, difference. Consequently, it does not matter who exercises power. Any individual, taken almost at random, can operate the machine: in the absence of the director, his family, his friends, his visitors, even his servants (Bentham, 45). Similarly, it does not matter what motive animates him: the curiosity of the indiscreet, the malice of a child, the thirst for knowledge of a philosopher who wishes to visit this museum of human nature, or the perversity of those who take pleasure in spying and punishing. The more numerous those anonymous and temporary observers are, the greater the risk for the inmate of being surprised and the greater his anxious awareness of being observed. The Panopticon is a marvellous machine which, whatever use one may wish to put it to, produces homogeneous effects of power.

A real subjection is born mechanically from a fictitious relation. So it is not necessary to use force to constrain the convict to good behaviour, the madman to calm, the worker to work, the schoolboy to application, the patient to the observation of the regulations. Bentham was surprised that panoptic institutions could be so light: there were no more bars, no more chains, no more heavy locks; all that was needed was that the separations should be clear and the openings well arranged. The heaviness of the old "houses of security," with their fortress-like architecture, could be replaced by the simple, economic geometry of a "house of certainty." The efficiency of power, its constraining force, have, in a sense, passed over to the other side—to the side of its surface of application. He who is subjected to a field of visibility, and who knows it, assumes responsibility for the constraints of power; he makes them play spontaneously upon himself; he inscribes in himself the power relation in which he simultaneously plays both roles; he becomes the principle of his own subjection. By this very fact, the external power may throw off its physical weight; it tends to the non-corporal; and, the more it approaches this limit, the more constant, profound and permanent are its effects: it is a perpetual victory that avoids any physical confrontation and which is always decided in advance.[24]

Let's now apply Foucault's observations to life on college campuses today. Surely, traditional college life provides liberties unknown in other areas of life (e.g., corporations, the military, congregational membership). One viewing of the National Lampoon movie *Animal House* makes the point. But is life in college unrestricted bliss? Certainly it requires passing exams, required courses, and other proficiencies. But beyond these obligations, consider campus life as a panopticon. Every student is both prisoner and guard. If you are a male student, for example, you will not likely wear a tutu to your American history class. There are possible conditions under which it might work: If you are advertising your role in a school play or making a presentation on the history of ballet, a tutu might be an acceptable part of your outfit. But otherwise your behavior will appear unusual, if not odd. Worst of all, repeated instances of this behavior could cost you the one thing for which you are investing four years and thousands of dollars: credibility. What is a diploma, after all? Credibility. Why is admission to the Ivy League so competitive? Credibility. What does it take to land a job at Goldman Sachs? Credibility. Eccentricity is tolerated in normal life, even encouraged if your career goal is to join the cast of *SNL*. But most of us are not headed there.

Most of us want acceptance, even admiration, so much so that, if you think about it, everything we do from waking up in the morning until going to sleep at night is conditioned by what others may think of us. Sure, you can get drunk and fall asleep on the lawn of the administration. Once, maybe twice. But if you make a habit of it, your pool of quality friends and sexual partners will diminish. College teaches you a lot of things, one of the foremost of which is how to conform.

You are a guard in college's panopticon for two primary reasons. You want to know who is potentially emotionally or physically dangerous and who cannot be trusted. And you want to know who is among those whose association will bring you what you want in life. Conversely, you are also a prisoner in college's panopticon for the mirror of these assets. You want acceptance, admiration, and a piece of the pie.

Matters for Elaboration in Your Essay

1. Foucault's allegorical Panopticon, unlike Bentham's actual panopticon, is not a prison, but society itself.

---

[24] Michel Foucault, *Discipline and Punish*, trans. Alan Sheridan (New York: Vintage, 1995), 200–203. The page numbers Foucault cites from Bentham come from "Panopticon; or, The Inspection-House," in *The Works of Jeremy Bentham*, ed. John Bowring, vol. 4 (Edinburgh: William Tait, 1838–1843).

2. To what extent am I, as a member of my society, an inmate of a panopticon?

3. To what extent am I a guard in my college panopticon?

4. Although we are members of a "free" society, how much freedom do we actually have to express our individuality?

5. To what extent are freedom and success zero-sum values?

8.7   PRACTICE LEGAL ARGUMENTATION

Learn the Rules for Writing Briefs for the US Supreme Court

When people are parties to disputes before the US Supreme Court, the attorneys representing each side prepare written documents called *briefs on the merit*, which explain the nature of the dispute and present an argument for the side each attorney represents. The justices read the briefs, hear oral arguments, hold conferences to discuss the case, and then write opinions to announce both the Court's decision and the views of justices who disagree in whole or in part with that decision. Cases that come before the Supreme Court are usually important to many people who are not actually parties to the specific case being presented, because the Court's decisions contain principles and guidelines that all lower courts must follow in deciding similar cases. *Roe v. Wade*, for example, did not become famous because it allowed one person to have an abortion free from the constraints of the laws of Texas, but because it set forth the principle that state law may not restrict abortions in the first three months of pregnancy to protect the fetus.

Because Supreme Court cases are important to people other than those directly involved in a case, sometimes groups and individuals outside the proceedings of a specific case want their views on cases to be heard by the Court before it makes a decision. It is not proper, however, to go to the justices directly and try to influence them to decide a case in a particular way. Influencing government officials directly through visits, phone calls, or letters is called *lobbying*. When people want to influence the way Congress handles a law, they lobby their representatives by writing letters or talking to them personally. The lobbying of Supreme Court justices, however, is considered improper, because the Court is supposed to make decisions based on the content of the Constitution and not on the political preferences of one or more groups in society.

There is a way, however, for outsiders to submit their views to the Supreme Court. The Court invites interested parties, most often organizations, to submit briefs of *amicus curiae* (a Latin phrase meaning "friend of the court"). A party that submits an amicus curiae brief becomes a friend of the Court by giving it information that it may find helpful in making a decision. As the Court explains, "An *amicus curiae* brief that brings to the attention of the Court relevant matter not already brought to its attention by the parties may be of considerable help to the Court. An amicus curiae brief that does not serve this purpose burdens the Court, and its filing is not favored."[25]

---

[25]   "Rule 37: Brief for an *Amicus Curiae*," *Rules of the Supreme Court of the United States*, Legal Information Institute, Cornell University Law School, accessed October 30, 2016, https://www.law.cornell.edu/rules/supct/rule_37.

In the summer of 1971, the Supreme Court began its review of *Roe v. Wade*. Roe, who was arrested for violating a Texas law forbidding abortions except to save the mother's life, argued that the Texas law was a governmental violation of the right to privacy guaranteed to her by the Constitution. Many national organizations filed amicus curiae briefs in this case. Acting as attorneys on behalf of the National Legal Program on Health Problems of the Poor, the National Welfare Rights Organization, and the American Public Health Association, Alan F. Charles and Susan Grossman Alexander filed a brief of amici curiae (*amici* is the plural of *amicus*) in support of the right to an abortion. The Summary of Argument that Charles and Alexander included in that brief appears below as an example to assist you in writing your own amicus curiae brief:

BRIEF OF *AMICI CURIAE*

Summary of Argument

A woman who seeks an abortion is asserting certain fundamental rights which are protected by the Constitution. Among these are rights to marital and family privacy, to individual and sexual privacy; in sum, the right to choose whether to bear children or not. These rights are abridged by the state's restriction of abortions to saving the mother's life. To justify such an abridgment, the state must demonstrate a compelling interest; no such compelling interest exists to save the Texas abortion law.

The state's interest in protecting the woman's health no longer supports restrictions on abortion. Medical science now performs abortions more safely than it brings a woman through pregnancy and childbirth. Any state interest in discouraging non-marital sexual relationships must be served by laws penalizing these relationships, and not by an indirect, overly broad prohibition on abortion. There is no evidence, in any case, that abortion laws deter such relationships. The state's purported interest in expanding the population lacks any viability today; government policy in every other area is now squarely against it. And any purported interest in permitting all embryos to develop and be born is not supported anywhere in the Constitution or any other body of law.

Because of its restriction, the Texas statute denies to poor and non-white women equal access to legal abortions. It is an undeniable fact that abortion in Texas and in virtually every other state in the United States is far more readily available to the white, paying patient than to the poor and non-white. Studies by physicians, sociologists, public health experts, and lawyers all reach this same conclusion. The reasons for it are not purely economic, i.e., that because abortion is an expensive commodity to obtain on the medical marketplace, it is therefore to be expected that the rich will have greater access to it. It is also because in the facilities which provide health care to the poor, abortion is simply not made available to the poor and non-white on the same conditions as it is to paying patients. As a result, the poor resort to criminal abortion, with its high toll of infection and death, in vastly disproportionate numbers.

Largely to blame are restrictive abortion laws, such as the Texas statute, in which the legislature has made lay judgments about what conditions must exist before abortions can be legally performed, and has delegated the authority to make such decisions to physicians and committees of physicians with the threat of felony punishment if they err on the side of granting an abortion. Unlike more privileged women, poor and non-white women are unable to shop for physicians and hospitals sympathetic to their applications, cannot afford the necessary consultations to establish that their conditions qualify them for treatment, and must largely depend upon public hospitals and physicians with whom they have no personal relationship, and who operate under the government's eye, for the relief they seek. The resulting discrimination is easily demonstrated.

Restricting abortion only to treatment necessary to save the mother's life irrationally excludes those classes of women for whom abortion is necessary for the protection of health, or because they will bear a deformed fetus, or who are pregnant due to sexual assault, or who are financially, socially or emotionally incapable of raising a child or whose families would be seriously disrupted by the birth of another child, and these exclusions bear most heavily on the poor and non-white.

In the absence of any compelling state interest, the harsh discriminatory effect on the poor and the non-white resulting from the operation of the Texas abortion law denies to poor and non-white women the equal protection of the laws in violation of the Equal Protection Clause of the Fourteenth Amendment.[26]

Scope and Purpose

Your task in this chapter is to write an amicus curiae brief for a case that is being considered by the US Supreme Court. You will write your own brief, making your own argument about how the case should be decided. Of course, you do not have to be entirely original. You will examine the arguments used in others' briefs, add new arguments of your own, and write the entire brief in your own carefully chosen words. In completing this assignment, you will also be meeting five more personal learning objectives:

1. You will become familiar with the source, form, and content of legal documents.
2. You will become acquainted with the procedures of brief preparation.
3. You will become familiar with the details of a selected case currently before the Court. As you follow the news reports on this case, you will eventually learn the Court's decision.
4. You will come to understand a Supreme Court case in sufficient depth to be able to integrate the arguments of actual amicus curiae briefs into your own argument.
5. You will learn how to write a clear, logical, effective, and persuasive argument.

---

[26] Alan F. Charles, *Motion for Leave to File Brief Amici Curiae in Support of Appellants and Briefs Amici Curiae*, Roe v. Wade, 70-18 U.S. at 5-7 (1971).

Remember that your goal is to *persuade* the Supreme Court to make a certain decision. Before you begin, reread part 1 of this manual, especially the sections on how to write clearly and persuasively.

General Considerations and Format

Briefs provide the Supreme Court with the facts in a particular case and make arguments about how the case should be decided. The *Rules* of the Court state that "a brief must be compact, logically arranged with proper headings, concise, and free from burdensome, irrelevant, immaterial, and scandalous matter. A brief not complying with this paragraph may be disregarded and stricken by the Court."[27] The Court also requires those who submit an amicus curiae brief to provide a statement of permission, which may be (1) the evidence that either permission to submit the amicus curiae brief has been granted by both parties to the dispute or the permission of both parties has not been granted and (2) the reason for the denial and the reason that the Court should consider the amicus brief in spite of the absence of permission of the parties.

Of course, as a student writing an amicus brief for a class in political science, you will not actually submit your brief to the Supreme Court, so you need not write a statement of permission. Information on such statements is provided here so that you will understand their purpose when you encounter them in your research.

Ask your instructor about the page limit for your assignment. The Supreme Court's limit for the actual text of amicus curiae briefs (exclusive of the questions-presented page, subject index, table of authorities, and appendix) is thirty pages, single-spaced. Your brief, however, will be double-spaced for the convenience of your instructor and as few as fifteen pages, depending on your instructor's requirements. Because a central purpose of this assignment is for you to understand the arguments to be made in the case, your brief will be shorter than actual amicus briefs submitted to the Court, which require much more detail than you will need to know. As you read actual amicus briefs, use your own judgment to select the material that you believe is most important for the Court to understand, and include this information, in your own words, in your brief.

The proper presentation of briefs is essential. Briefs to the Supreme Court are normally professionally printed, and the *Rules* of the Court include directions for this process. The Court does, however, also accept typed briefs, and your amicus curiae brief will conform to the Court's instructions for typed briefs in most respects, with modifications to allow your instructor sufficient space to write comments. You must therefore prepare your amicus curiae brief according to the following specifications:

- Black type on 8.5" × 11" white paper, double-spaced, printed on one side only
- Text and footnotes in 12-point type
- A typeface as close as possible to that used in actual briefs
- Margins of 1.5" on the left and 1" on all other sides
- A binding that meets your instructor's requirements

---

[27] "Rule 37: Brief for an *Amicus Curiae*," Rules of the Supreme Court.

You will submit one copy of your brief to your instructor. It is always wise, when submitting any paper, to retain a copy for yourself in case the original is lost. (The Supreme Court requires that sixty copies of a brief be submitted for a case coming to it directly under its original jurisdiction, and forty copies for a case coming to it under appellate jurisdiction from lower courts.)

Read&Write 8.7 Write an Abridged Amicus Brief for the US Supreme Court

In this assignment, after reading the materials available on the Cornell and Supreme Court websites (see below), you will write only a relatively short argument and then a summary of an argument you wish to make. Although you can use and elaborate on arguments others have made, you must make your own argument in your own words.

Select a Case and a Side

To find cases on the Internet that are currently before the Supreme Court, go to Cornell University's Legal Information Institute (LLI; http://www.law.cornell.edu/supremecourt /text/home). On this page select "Cases Pending Oral Argument." This link will give you a list of cases in which briefs and other essential documents have been submitted to the court, documents that will provide the information you need to complete this exercise. Peruse the list of cases pending oral argument and select one that generates some personal interest for you.

Write an Argument Outline

Read the arguments in the materials you find on the Cornell site, and then construct an outline of an argument that makes the points you believe are most important. Your outline should normally have from two to six main points. Follow the directions for constructing outlines that you find in chapter 3 of this manual very carefully. Submit your outline to your instructor for advice before continuing.

Write the Argument

Following the outline you have constructed, write your argument. Your writing needs to be clear and sharply focused. Follow the directions for writing in the first part of this manual. The first sentence of each paragraph should state its main point.

The *Rules* of the Court state that the argument of a brief must exhibit "clearly the points of fact and of law being presented and [cite] the authorities and statutes relied upon"; it should also be "as short as possible."[28] In addition to conforming to page limitations set by your instructor, the length of your argument should be guided by two considerations. First, content must be of adequate length to help the Court make a good decision. All the arguments necessary to making a decision must be present. Write this paper as if you were an officer of the Court. Under no circumstances should you make a false or misleading statement. Be persuasive, but be truthful. You do not need to make the opponents' argument for them, but the facts that you present must be accurate to the best of your knowledge.

---

[28] Ibid.

The second guideline for determining the length of your argument is to omit extraneous material. Include only the information that will be of help to the Court in making the decision at hand.

The *Rules* of the Court require that an amicus brief include a "conclusion, specifying with particularity the relief which the party seeks."[29] Read the conclusions of the briefs you collect and then write your own, retaining the same format but combining the arguments for the groups you are representing, and limiting your conclusion to two pages.

Write the Summary of Argument

After you have written the argument, write the summary, which should be a clearly written series of paragraphs that include all the main points. It should be brief, not more than three double-spaced, typed pages. The Summary of Argument written for *Roe v. Wade* that is included in this chapter provides an example.

According to the *Rules* of the Court, briefs should contain a "summary of the argument, suitably paragraphed, which should be a succinct, but accurate and clear, condensation of the argument actually made in the body of the brief. A mere repetition of the headings under which the argument is arranged is not sufficient."[30]

The summary of your argument may be easily assembled by taking the topic sentences from each paragraph and forming them into new paragraphs. The topic sentences contain more information than your subject headings. As complete sentences arranged in logical order, they provide an excellent synopsis of the contents of your brief. Your argument summary should not exceed two double-spaced pages. Your summary should include the types of information found in the abridged version of the Supreme Court's own summary in the case of *Supreme Court of the United States District of Columbia et al. v. Heller* (No. 07-290; argued March 18, 2008; decided June 26, 2008), printed below:

District of Columbia law bans handgun possession by making it a crime to carry an unregistered firearm and prohibiting the registration of handguns; provides separately that no person may carry an unlicensed handgun, but authorizes the police chief to issue 1-year licenses; and requires residents to keep lawfully owned firearms unloaded and dissembled or bound by a trigger lock or similar device. Respondent Heller, a D. C. special policeman, applied to register a handgun he wished to keep at home, but the District refused. He filed this suit seeking, on Second Amendment grounds, to enjoin the city from enforcing the bar on handgun registration, the licensing requirement insofar as it prohibits carrying an unlicensed firearm in the home, and the trigger-lock requirement insofar as it prohibits the use of functional firearms in the home. The District Court dismissed the suit, but the D. C. Circuit reversed, holding that the Second Amendment protects an individual's right to possess firearms and that the city's total ban on handguns, as well as its requirement that firearms in the home be kept nonfunctional even when necessary for self-defense, violated that right.

[The Supreme Court] *Held:*

1. The Second Amendment protects an individual right to possess a firearm unconnected with service in a militia, and to use that arm for traditionally lawful purposes, such as self-defense within the home. . . .

2. Like most rights, the Second Amendment right is not unlimited. It is not a right to keep and carry any weapon whatsoever in any manner whatsoever and for whatever purpose . . .

---

[29] Ibid.
[30] Ibid.

3. The handgun ban and the trigger-lock requirement (as applied to self-defense) violate the Second Amendment. The District's total ban on handgun possession in the home amounts to a prohibition on an entire class of "arms" that Americans overwhelmingly choose for the lawful purpose of self-defense. Under any of the standards of scrutiny the Court has applied to enumerated constitutional rights, this prohibition—in the place where the importance of the lawful defense of self, family, and property is most acute—would fail constitutional muster. Similarly, the requirement that any lawful firearm in the home be disassembled or bound by a trigger lock makes it impossible for citizens to use arms for the core lawful purpose of self-defense and is hence unconstitutional. Because Heller conceded at oral argument that the D. C. licensing law is permissible if it is not enforced arbitrarily and capriciously, the Court assumes that a license will satisfy his prayer for relief and does not address the licensing requirement. Assuming he is not disqualified from exercising Second Amendment rights, the District must permit Heller to register his handgun and must issue him a license to carry it in the home.[31]

---

[31] District of Columbia et al. v. Heller 07-290 U.S. (2008), http://www.supremecourt.gov/opinions/07pdf/07-290.pdf.

LIST OF PHILOSOPHY PERIODICALS

The Philosophy Documentation Center (pdcnet.org) is an excellent place to find information about philosophy journals dedicated to specific issues or time periods. Also well worth a visit is Peter Suber's Guide to Philosophy on the Internet (http://legacy.earlham.edu/~peters/philinks.htm), to consult his list of journals. Following are journals that are appropriate for introductory students (indicated by an asterisk) and journals dedicated to topics generally addressed in introductory, interdisciplinary, or applied philosophy.

This is just a selection from a much larger number of philosophy journals.

American Philosophical Quarterly. This journal irregularly runs review articles of current research in areas of philosophy, such as relativism and foundationalism.

*Auslegung. The Philosophy Graduate Student Association at the University of Kansas is the sponsor of this journal, which publishes the work of new PhDs and graduate students.

*Business and Professional Ethics

*Business Ethics

*Business Ethics Quarterly

*Canadian Journal of Philosophy

*Carleton University Student Journal of Philosophy

Criminal Justice Ethics

Eidos: The Canadian Graduate Student Journal of Philosophy

*Environmental Ethics

*Ethics

Film and Philosophy

*Foreign Affairs. Primarily a political science journal, this publication contains cogent discussions of current foreign policy issues and can be especially helpful to students of just-war theory and international politics.

*Foreign Policy

*Free Inquiry

*Hastings Center Report. This is an excellent source for case studies in ethics and the professions.

History of Philosophy Quarterly

Hypatia: A Journal of Feminist Philosophy

*Informal Logic

*International Journal of Applied Philosophy

Journal of Aesthetics and Art Criticism

Journal of Agricultural and Environmental Ethics

Journal of Business Ethics

*Journal of Social Philosophy

Journal of the History of Ideas

Journal of the History of Philosophy

Journal of Value Inquiry. This journal covers ethics, social and political philosophy, and aesthetics.

Kennedy Institute of Ethics Journal

Kinesis: Graduate Journal in Philosophy. This journal publishes papers by graduate students.

Monist. Published quarterly, this journal arranges each issue around a specific topic.

Philosophic Exchange

Philosophical Books. This is a journal of book reviews.

Philosophical Forum

Philosophy and Literature

Philosophy and Public Affairs

Philosophy and Rhetoric

Philosophy and Social Criticism

Philosophy and Theology

Philosophy East and West

Philosophy of Science

Philosophy of the Social Sciences

Professional Ethics

Public Affairs Quarterly

Reason Papers. This journal focuses on social and political philosophy.

Review of Metaphysics.

Social Epistemology

Social Philosophy and Policy

Social Theory and Practice

Transactions of the Charles S. Peirce Society. Peirce is often the focus, but essays on all the classical American philosophers are included. Sometimes the editor also prints essays on contemporary philosophy.

APPENDIX B
GLOSSARY OF PHILOSOPHIC TERMS

act utilitarianism

The belief that the expected consequences of an action should be weighed in each situation before embracing one option as the moral one (see *rule utilitarianism*)

ad hoc

Latin for "to this" or "to this purpose"; in philosophy, a part of an argument that is fabricated only to serve an immediate purpose and has not been demonstrated to have independent value through added explanatory power or testable predictions

ad hominem

Latin for "to the man"; an informal fallacy committed in an argument by attacking one's opponent personally instead of attacking his or her position

aesthetics

The branch of philosophy that attempts to define, describe, and evaluate art

agape

In Christian philosophy, the term describing the unconditional love that God feels toward humanity; contrasts with other forms of love

agnosticism

The conviction that, while a deity may exist, there can be no absolute proof of the deity's existence or nonexistence; an *agnostic* suspends judgment on the existence or nonexistence of God as opposed to an *atheist*, who denies God's existence

akrasia

Greek for "lack of self-control"; an inability to do what one knows is right, due to lack of will

altruism

The belief that one should do what is best for others; usually accompanied by the belief that humans may have altruistic motives; holds that unselfish acts are accomplished for unselfish, rather than selfish, reasons

anarchism

The belief that no organized government has the right to coerce its citizens into any action; a rejection of all forms of externally imposed authority

animism

The belief, found in many primitive religions and some philosophical religions, that all things, animate and inanimate, possess a soul

a posteriori

Latin for "from what follows"; arrived at from experience and observation; a method of reaching a conclusion through reasoning from particular facts to general principles (see also *a priori*)

a priori

Latin for "from before"; a method of reaching a conclusion independently of experience; sometimes a priori knowledge is based on the meanings of terms, as when one knows from the meaning of the word *triangle*—independently of experiencing an actual triangle—that it has three angles and three sides; such tacit knowledge is constitutive of experience (see also *a posteriori*)

Aristotle	384–322 BCE; Plato's student, thought by some to be the greatest philosopher; concerned with formalizing the approach to argument begun by Plato and Socrates; a major influence on medieval Christian thought
artificial intelligence	Also commonly known as AI; a field of study that builds or theorizes about machines capable of thought; some AI advocates believe that intelligent machines must exhibit human thought; others believe that machines are intelligent if they exhibit any kind of problem-solving ability
atheism	The belief that there is no deity; opposite of *theism*
begging the question	Another term for "circular reasoning," a type of faulty argument in which a form of the conclusion to be established is used in the premises (see *circular reasoning*)
behaviorism	An approach to the study of the mind that focuses on the observation of external behavior
best of all possible worlds	A phrase from the German mathematician and philosopher Gottfried Leibniz (1646–1716), who argued that since the world was created by a deity who was perfect and whose works were perfect, then despite all appearances the world is the best of all possible worlds—an idea often treated with derision, as in Voltaire's fantasy novel *Candide*; Leibniz believed that free will was a condition of the best of all possible worlds and explained why the best world contained suffering and evil
bioethics	Ethical positions and arguments concerning biological and medical issues, such as abortion and genetic engineering
Buddha	Siddhartha Gautama, the Buddha, 563–483 BCE; founder of the philosophical and religious tradition known as Buddhism, based on the *Four Noble Truths*; Buddhism seeks to transcend the suffering and contingency of human life through the elimination of the individual self and human desires to attain the state of enlightenment or nirvana
Buridan's ass	The central actor in a story designed to illustrate a problem inherent in the concept that one should do only what seems to be of the greatest good: the hungry ass who, finding itself equidistant from two sources of hay, finds neither source more desirable and so, unable to move in either direction, starves to death
Cartesian doubt	Referring to Descartes's process of assuming that any belief capable of being doubted is false—the first step toward discovering a point of certainty (see *Descartes, René*)
categorical imperative	Immanuel Kant's phrase for an absolute command, such as "Tell the truth," something one must always do regardless of circumstance, since the moral law deserves the highest respect
circular reasoning	Reasoning that is faulty because it assumes without reasonable evidence the truth of the statement, in whole or in part, which it is trying to defend (see *begging the question*)
civil disobedience	An act contrary to the law, performed in the belief that it is morally acceptable to disobey civil authority in matters where it comes in conflict with one's perceived notions of the moral law, which is generally held to follow from the authority of God or personal conscience
consequentialism	An ethical position that holds that the consequences of an action determine whether that action is morally right or wrong

contemplation	The act of meditating in a manner that reveals ultimate reality and value
cosmology	Theorizing about the origins, the elements, and the structure of the cosmos
creationism	A would-be theory, common to many fundamentalist religions, that the world was created by a deity who intended its elements to be as they are, in opposition to the theory of *evolution*, which argues for the random beginning and development of life through natural selection
deduction	A form of argument that holds that if the premises of an argument are true, its conclusion must be true, in contrast to inductive arguments where the conclusion is claimed to be only probably true; example of deduction: All bulldogs breathe air, Iris is a bulldog, therefore, Iris breathes air; example of induction: All bulldogs heretofore observed breathe air, Iris is a bulldog, therefore Iris probably breathes air
deontology	A system of ethical theories that emphasize the importance of duty to making the moral choice
Descartes, René	1596–1650; French philosopher who, by contending that philosophy, independently of revealed religion, could discover the foundations of truth, founded modern philosophy (see *Cartesian doubt*)
determinism	The position that all things (actions, personality traits, natural phenomena) are caused by antecedent factors that are, perhaps, knowable but beyond mediation, so that all things must be as they are
dilemma	A problem in which there is a choice between two or more unacceptable alternatives; a form of argument in which an opponent is offered undesirable alternatives implied by views the opponent advocates
dualism	A belief in the existence of two and only two separate classes of phenomena: spirit and matter, for example; most dualists are really committed to three substances: matter, mind, and abstract objects such as numbers (see also *monism* and *pluralism*)
dystopia	An imagined society in which conditions are as bad as they can be; the reverse of a *utopia*
Eightfold Path	In Buddhism, the practice of life that aids in the attainment of enlightenment: Right View, Right Aim, Right Speech, Right Action, Right Living, Right Effort, Right Mindfulness, Right Contemplation
empiricism	A belief that experience alone generates all knowledge and that there is no such thing as inherent or innate knowledge; opposed to *rationalism*
ends versus means	An argument that holds that there are some actions that, as means, are themselves so morally wrong or bad that their consequences, no matter how good, cannot compensate
epistemology	The study of the nature and origins of knowledge
ethics	The collection of beliefs by which a person determines whether an action is right or wrong; a person's set of moral principles; *philosophical ethics* inquires into the foundation of such principles and seeks to offer rational justification for them
eudaemonia	Greek for "living well"; refers to the Aristotelian belief that the true aim of life is happiness, attained by the proper balance of intellectual and moral virtues

euthanasia	Greek for "a happy death"; the act of killing someone for his or her own good, for example, to relieve suffering due to a fatal illness
existentialism	A modern philosophy that argues for the total freedom of the individual from external or inherited controls on his or her behavior, and, therefore, for the complete responsibility of the individual for his or her own action; you must figure this philosophy out for yourself—we will not explain it to you
foundationalism	The view that there is a privileged class of belief from which springs the justification of all other beliefs or statements in a particular belief system
Four Noble Truths	From Buddhist teachings: (1) Suffering exists, (2) Suffering has identifiable causes, (3) There is a way to end suffering, (4) The way is to follow the *Eightfold Path*
freedom	In terms of political freedom, the degree to which the actions of people within a society are allowed by law and sometimes facilitated by government; philosophers generally refer to *negative freedom* as those areas of human activity allowed by law, and they use the term *positive freedom* to mark areas in which government facilitates human action by offering assistance—for instance, most people would agree that you have a right to pursue a college degree (negative freedom) without suffering discrimination; fewer people would agree that the government has a right to tax society to provide free college educations (positive freedom)
free will	A characteristic, assumed in certain philosophies, by which people may choose their actions without the influence of internal or external constraints; a troublesome term, since philosophers sometimes redefine free will in a manner that makes it difficult to separate it from the account of choice given in determinism
happiness	In some philosophies, the single basic element necessary for living the good life; usually a pluralistic concept involving a variety of intrinsic goods such as knowledge and pleasure; there are monistic eudaemonists, called hedonists, who argue that happiness is ultimately reducible to pleasure
hedonism	A philosophic position that the pursuit of pleasure is the highest aim in life
historicism	The view that it is impossible to arrive at an understanding of human behavior without understanding its historical context; also, the understanding that one's interpretation of reality is conditioned to an extent by one's historical environment
humanism	Any philosophical position that centers on the innate worthiness of humans and human values
hypothetico-deductive model	A three-step model of scientific justification in which (1) a hypothesis is developed in response to an unexpected observation; (2) statements about reality are deduced from the hypothesis, initial conditions, and other background knowledge; and (3) the hypothesis is confirmed through observation
idealism	The theory that ultimate reality exists only in a nonphysical realm of ideas, and that physical objects in the world are imperfect copies of ideal objects; also, a theory that ultimate reality exists only in the mind
ideal observer theory	A process of ethical reasoning that subjects conclusions to the views of an ideal (and imagined) observer who, possessed of all the facts relating to the conclusion, should be able to make judgments about it that are free of bias

ideology	Any systematic collection of beliefs infected with ethical or religious values, but especially one relating to politics or sociological matters
induction	See *deduction*
infinite regress	A system in which one event is caused by a past event, which in turn was caused by an earlier past event, and so on, backward into eternity, showing that an opponent's position is committed to an infinite regress, a demonstration generally considered an effective refutation of the position
innateness	The condition of being inherent or inborn, as opposed to originating externally, as through experience or education; an intrinsic quality or object; in philosophy, a term generally referring to questions about the mind, such as whether ways of classifying objects or the ability to learn a language or to reason are innate or learned
intrinsic	Partaking of the essential nature of a thing; also, the quality of having value for itself, rather than for its relationship to something else
introspection	Deep exploration of one's own consciousness, looking for self-knowledge; some introspectionists hold that one cannot be mistaken about the contents of one's own mind; you can lie to others about what you think and feel, but not to yourself
intuition	The human faculty of believing something, often suddenly, without subjecting it to argumentation or testing; in philosophy, a general term referring to the having of an experience—whether it be sensory, religious, aesthetic, rational, or a combination of these—that conveys certainty
mean	A center point between two extremes; in ethics, a term referring to Aristotle's view that a virtue is always the mean between two extremes, as courage is halfway between cowardice and foolhardiness
metaphysics	The branch of philosophy that focuses on the ultimate components of existence, such elements as time, free will, and the nature of matter
Mill, John Stuart	1806–1873; classical liberal English philosopher who defended and popularized utilitarianism; his father, John Mill, and Jeremy Bentham were the major proponents of utilitarianism before him
mind–body problem	The focal point for any attempt to understand the relationship between the physical and the mental substances
monism	A belief in the existence of only one ultimate kind of substance; for example, a belief that existence is composed of one organic spiritual whole, with no independent elements; a tenet argued in the work of Spinoza (see *dualism* and *pluralism*)
mysticism	Any belief system that relies on direct experience as a means of connecting with ultimate reality, which is usually held to be supernatural truth or God
natural law	In some philosophies, the set of innate constraints that should govern human action; note that unnatural does not mean in violation of the laws of nature in a physical sense: one cannot violate the laws of nature unless, of course, one is God; unnatural means in violation of the proper purposes of nature, as exhibited in nature and apprehended through reasoning; St. Thomas did not claim that sex outside of marriage was physically impossible, but he did claim that it was unnatural, since it did not attend to the proper function of sex: procreation in a context that provides for the raising of children to adulthood

nihilism

The position that all traditional beliefs and belief systems are unfounded and that life itself is meaningless

nothing

Emptiness, complete void, nonexistence; a philosophical puzzle, since the naming of "nothing" confers upon it an existence; in non-Western philosophy, the term names the unnameable and undifferentiated source of all being and has a positive role to play: The usefulness of the bowl is accounted for by the material out of which it is constructed and the emptiness that provides its shape; consider the haiku:

> No one spoke.
> Not the host.
> Nor the guest.
> Nor the pink chrysanthemum.

omnipotent

All powerful; capable of any action; a characteristic often assigned to God regardless of such paradoxical facts as that God cannot build a stone so heavy that God cannot pick it up

paternalism

A system in which an authority provides for the needs of its constituents and regulates their conduct, thus, in effect, assuming responsibility for them; even libertarians such as John Stuart Mill argue for instances in which paternalism is justified

personal identity

The combination of personal elements that distinguishes one person from all other people; those characteristics that provide a person with his or her individuality over time

Plato

428?–348 BCE; a student of Socrates and thought by some to be the greatest philosopher of all time; author of the Socratic dialogues and famous for his three theories of forms, which consistently hold that physical reality is composed of imperfect copies of ideal forms of which we can become conscious only through the mystical leap at the penultimate step of the dialectic process of reasoning

pluralism

A belief that there are many equally valid, though incompatible, classes of ultimate ethical or political values; in metaphysics, the belief that there is more than one type of substance, which leads to such questions as the mind–body problem, which questions how the substances interact (see *dualism* and *monism*)

problem of evil

The question of why evil exists in a world built by a benevolent God who has the power to eliminate evil and the knowledge that it will occur

problem of induction

A reference to the difficulty of proving the "principle of reasoning," which holds that it is reasonable to believe that past and present observable properties of nature will continue into the future; inductive proofs of induction are question-begging; deductive proofs of induction are lacking

Pyrrhonism

Skeptical philosophy that draws its name from Pyrrho (306–270 BCE) and is preserved in the writings of Sextus Empiricus (second–third centuries CE), who advocates the attainment of happiness through the suspension of judgment; Pyrrhonists engage in philosophical argument to cure others of the sickness of belief

rationalism

A belief that some knowledge is attainable through the processes of reason alone, unaided by experience or education; opposed to *empiricism*

rule utilitarianism	The belief that general policies should be the focus of our attempt to determine which options will have the best overall consequences; rule utilitarians generally argue against allowing exceptions in contexts where the consequences would be better if we broke the generally beneficial rules (see *act utilitarianism*)
sense-data	Those impressions, received through the senses, that according to empirical philosophers may serve as the bases of all our understanding of external objects; sense-data philosophers usually emphasize visual presentations
skepticism	The doctrine that knowledge in general or knowledge in certain areas, such as ethics or the question of existence of the external world, cannot be considered certain beyond a doubt; some skeptics deny that humans have knowledge, thus seeming to refute themselves with the knowledge claim; others suspend judgment about whether there is knowledge
social contract	The actual or hypothetical agreement between the government or ruler and the governed that outlines the rights and duties of citizens and the government; social contract theorists differ on the question of whether the governmental authorities are parties to the contract or are constituted as authorities on the basis of a contract between citizens; the concept is often invoked as a way of legitimizing a government
Socrates	470?–399 BCE; teacher of Plato and the principal speaker in the earliest Socratic dialogues; a master of the dialectical method of argument in which opponents are led by a series of questions into revealing the weaknesses in their own positions
Solipsism	The theory that the only thing in existence is the self, or the only thing we can know for sure is our self or mind
state of nature	The real or hypothetical condition in which humanity existed before the establishment of government or laws regulating behavior
Tao	Originating in Chinese thought, the name for the unnameable and ineffable unity of all existence and nonexistence
Taoism	The philosophical tradition, originating in China, that believes that humans can find peace and tranquility through following the Tao; major figures in Taoism are Lao Tzu (sixth century BCE) and Chuang-Tzu (fourth century BCE)
Theism	The belief in a deity; opposite of *atheism*
utilitarian ethics	A philosophical tradition that places the ultimate moral justification of an action in the overall balance of good consequences over bad ones; utilitarians differ over the nature of the good: some believe that the only good is pleasure; others prefer the more pluralistic term *happiness*, but they all accept the principle of equality of interests embodied in Jeremy Bentham's statement that each counts for one, and no one counts for more than one
utopia	Greek for "nowhere"; an imagined society of ideal perfection; the reverse of a *dystopia*

"About." APS: American Philosophical Society. https://amphilsoc.org/about.

"About." Center for Research Libraries Global Resources Network. http://www.crl.edu/about.

"About the Book." Singularity.com. Accessed October 29, 2016. http://singularity.com/aboutthebook .html.

"Affiliated Groups." American Philosophical Association. http://www.apaonline.org/page/affiliatedgroups.

Amer, Mildred. "*Congressional Record*: Its Production, Distribution, and Accessibility." Congressional Research Service, May 5, 2008. https://fas.org/sgp/crs/misc/98-266.pdf.

Aristotle. *Politics* 1.1253a. http://www.perseus.tufts.edu/hopper/text?doc=Perseus:text:1999.01.0058.

Associated Press. "Stray Bullet That Killed Long Island Girl Was Fired in Retaliation for Hoverboard Theft, Police Say." *New York Times*, January 11, 2016. http://www.nytimes.com/2016/01/12/nyregion /stray-bullet-that-killed-long-island-girl-was-fired-in-retaliation-for-theft-police-say.html.

Babb, Drew. "LBJ's 1964 Attack Ad 'Daisy' Leaves a Legacy for Modern Campaigns." *Washington Post*, September 5, 2014. https://www.washingtonpost.com/opinions/lbjs-1964-attack-ad-daisy-leaves-a -legacy-for-modern-campaigns/2014/09/05/d00e66b0-33b4-11e4-9e92-0899b306bbea_story.html.

Bailey, Holly. "Mitt Romney Introduces Paul Ryan as His VP Running Mate." Yahoo News, August 11, 2002. https://www.yahoo.com/news/blogs/ticket/live-video-mitt-romney-announces-vp-pick-123251121 .html.

Bentham, Jeremy. *An Introduction to the Principles of Morals and Legislation*. Garden City, NY: Doubleday, 1961.

Brooks, David. "The Minimum-Wage Muddle." *New York Times*, July 24, 2015. http://www.nytimes .com/2015/07/24/opinion/david-brooks-the-minimum-wage-muddle.html.

Bulwer-Lytton, Edward. *Richelieu: or, The Conspiracy, a Play in Five Acts*. New York: Samuel French, [186-?]. In *Making of America*, accessed February 23, 2016, http://name.umdl.umich.edu/AAX3994.0001.001.

Burke, Rob. "Letter to the Editor: It Would Be Worse if Zakaria Were More Conservative." *Wall Street Journal*, August 22, 2012. http://www.wsj.com/articles/SB10000872396390444443504577601181 341795626.

Charles, Alan F. *Motion for Leave to File Brief Amici Curiae in Support of Appellants and Briefs Amici Curiae*. Roe v. Wade, 70-18 U.S. at 5-7 (1971).

Chouraqui, Frank. "Nietzsche's Science of Love." *Nietzsche-Studien* 44, no. 1 (2015): 267–90. doi:10.1515 /nietzstu-2015-0131.

"Collections with Manuscripts/Mixed Material." Library of Congress. https://www.loc.gov/manuscripts /collections.

D'Aquili, Eugene, and Andrew B. Newberg. *The Mystical Mind: Probing the Biology of Religious Experience*. Minneapolis: Fortress Press, 1999.

"Dave Mustaine Accuses President of Staging Recent Mass Killings." Punknews.org, August 15, 2012. https://www.punknews.org/article/48516/dave-mustaine-accuses-president-of-staging-recent-mass -killings.

District of Columbia et al. v. Heller 07-290 U.S. 2008. http://www.supremecourt.gov/opinions /07pdf/07-290.pdf.

"Editorial: Supervisors Take Curious Approach." *Chico Enterprise-Record*, August 2, 2012. http://www .chicoer.com/general-news/20120802/editorial-supervisors-take-curious-approach.

Emerson, Ralph Waldo. "The American Scholar." In *The Annotated Emerson*, edited by David Mikics, 72–92. Cambridge, MA: Belknap Press of Harvard University Press, 2012.

Forster, E. M. *Aspects of the Novel*. New York: Harvest, 1956.

Foucault, Michel. *Discipline and Punish*. Translated by Alan Sheridan. New York: Vintage, 1995.

Fulghum, Robert. *All I Really Need to Know I Learned in Kindergarten*. New York: Ivy Books, 1988.

"The Hannah Arendt Papers at the Library of Congress." Library of Congress. https://memory.loc.gov /ammem/arendthtml/arendthome.html.

Hartwell, Patrick. "Grammar, Grammars, and the Teaching of Grammar." *College English* 47 (February 1985): 105–27.

"History of the Library." Library of Congress. https://www.loc.gov/about/history-of-the-library.

Hume, David. *Treatise of Human Nature*. New York: Dutton, 1974.

Johnson, George. "Consciousness: The Mind Messing with the Mind." *New York Times*, July 4, 2016. http://www.nytimes.com/2016/07/05/science/what-is-consciousness.html.

Kant, Immanuel. *Foundations of the Metaphysics of Morals*. Translated by Lewis White Beck. Indianapolis: Bobbs-Merrill, 1959.

Krugman, Paul. "Liberals and Wages." *New York Times*, July 17, 2015. http://www.nytimes .com/2015/07/17/opinion/paul-krugman-liberals-and-wages.html.

Kurzweil, Ray. *The Singularity Is Near: When Humans Transcend Biology*. New York: Viking, 2005.

———. "A University for the Coming Singularity." TED, February 2009. Accessed October 29, 2016. http://www.ted.com/talks/ray_kurzweil_announces_singularity_university.

"Members." APS: American Philosophical Society. https://amphilsoc.org/members.

Mill, John Stuart. *Utilitarianism*. Kitchener, ON: Batoche Books, 2001. http://socserv.mcmaster.ca/econ /ugcm/3ll3/mill/utilitarianism.pdf.

Moody, Chris. "Retired Porn Star Jenna Jameson Supports Mitt Romney." Yahoo News, August 3, 2012. https://www.yahoo.com/news/blogs/ticket/retired-porn-star-jenna-jameson-says-she-supports -143703925.html.

Nietzsche, Frederick. "Zarathustra's Prologue." In *Thus Spake Zarathustra*. Translated by Thomas Common. Adelaide, Australia: University of Adelaide. Last modified January 2, 2016. https://ebooks.adelaide .edu.au/n/nietzsche/friedrich/n67a/index.html.

Obama, Barack. "Remarks by the President on the Paris Agreement." The White House, October 5, 2016. https://obamawhitehouse.archives.gov/the-press-office/2016/10/05/remarks-president -paris-agreement.

———. "Weekly Address: Making America Safer for Our Children." The White House, January 1, 2016. https://www.whitehouse.gov/the-press-office/2016/01/01/weekly-address-making-america -safer-our-children.

Pearce, Catherine Owens. *A Scientist of Two Worlds: Louis Agassiz*. Philadelphia: Lippincott, 1958.

"Policy Analyst: The White House." Office of Management and Budget. Accessed February 23, 2017. https://obamawhitehouse.archives.gov/omb/policy_analyst.

Quilter, John. "Letter to the Editor: Taxes and Poor People's Loopholes." *Wall Street Journal*, August 21, 2012. http://www.wsj.com/articles/SB10000872396390444443504577601163646244278.

Roosevelt, Franklin D. "'Four Freedoms Speech': Annual Message to Congress on the State of the Union." Franklin D. Roosevelt Presidential Library and Museum. https://fdrlibrary.org/four-freedoms.

"Rule 37: Brief for an *Amicus Curiae*." *Rules of the Supreme Court of the United States*. Legal Information Institute. Cornell University Law School. Accessed October 30, 2016. https://www.law.cornell.edu /rules/supct/rule_37.

Scheiber, Noam, and Patricia Cohen. "For the Wealthiest, a Private Tax System That Saves Them Billions." *New York Times*, December 29, 2015. http://www.nytimes.com/2015/12/30/business/economy /for-the-wealthiest-private-tax-system-saves-them-billions.html.

Schneider, Susan. "The Problem of AI Consciousness." *Kurzweil Accelerating Intelligence* (blog), March 28, 2016. http://www.kurzweilai.net/the-problem-of-ai-consciousness.

Scott, Gregory M. Review of *Political Islam: Revolution, Radicalism, or Reform?* edited by John L. Esposito *Southeastern Political Review* 26, no. 2 (1998): 512–24.

Stephens, Bret. "Muslims, Mormons and Liberals." *Wall Street Journal*, September 19, 2012, 17.

Tremlin, Todd. *Minds and Gods: The Cognitive Foundations of Religion*. Oxford: Oxford University Press, 2006.

"2017 Eastern Division Meeting: Meeting Program." American Philosophical Association. http://www .apaonline.org/page/2017E_Program.

Virtanen, Michael. "Mark David Chapman, John Lennon's Killer, Denied Parole Again." *Christian Science Monitor*, August 23, 2012. http://www.csmonitor.com/USA/Latest-News-Wires/2012/0823/Mark-David-Chapman-John-Lennon-s-killer-denied-parole-again-video.

The Way of Chuang-Tzu. Translated by Thomas Merton. New York: New Directions Press, 1969.

"Why Visit the National Archives?" National Archives. Last modified September 19, 2016, https://www.archives.gov/locations/why-visit.

Wirz, Matt. "As Corporate-Bond Yields Sink, Risks for Investors Rise." *Wall Street Journal*, August 14, 2012. http://www.wsj.com/articles/SB10000872396390444042704577584792371582220.

INDEX